Regression,
ANOVA, and the
General Linear Model

This book is dedicated with love and affection to my wife, Marla Louise Vik, and my parents, Diane and Robert Vik.

Regression, ANOVA, and the General Linear Model

A Statistics Primer

Peter Vik

Idaho State University

Los Angeles | London | New Delhi
Singapore | Washington DC

Los Angeles | London | New Delhi
Singapore | Washington DC

FOR INFORMATION:

SAGE Publications, Inc.
2455 Teller Road
Thousand Oaks, California 91320
E-mail: order@sagepub.com

SAGE Publications Ltd.
1 Oliver's Yard
55 City Road
London EC1Y 1SP
United Kingdom

SAGE Publications India Pvt. Ltd.
B 1/I 1 Mohan Cooperative Industrial Area
Mathura Road, New Delhi 110 044
India

SAGE Publications Asia-Pacific Pte. Ltd.
3 Church Street
#10-04 Samsung Hub
Singapore 049483

Acquisitions Editor: Vicki Knight
Editorial Assistant: Lyndsi Stephens
Production Editor: Laura Barrett
Copy Editor: QuADS Prepress (P) Ltd.
Typesetter: C&M Digitals (P) Ltd.
Proofreader: Barbara Johnson
Indexer: Virgil Diodato
Cover Designer: Candice Harman
Marketing Manager: Nicole Elliott
Permissions Editor: Adele Hutchinson

Copyright © 2014 by SAGE Publications, Inc.

Printed in the United States of America

Library of Congress Cataloging-in-Publication Data

Vik, Peter.

Regression, ANOVA, and the general linear model: a statistics primer / Peter Vik, Idaho State University.

pages cm
Includes bibliographical references and index.

ISBN 978-1-4129-9735-5 (pbk.)

1. Analysis of variance. 2. Regression analysis. 3. Linear models (Statistics) I. Title.

QA279.V54 2014
519.5–dc23   2012039562

This book is printed on acid-free paper.

SUSTAINABLE FORESTRY INITIATIVE
Certified Sourcing
www.sfiprogram.org
Label applies to the text stock   SFI-00341

13 14 15 16 17 10 9 8 7 6 5 4 3 2 1

Brief Table of Contents

Detailed Table of Contents

Preface

"It would be so simple. Why hasn't someone written a basic, straight-forward book about statistics?"

I was attending the annual meeting of the American Psychological Association in 2003. Some friends and I were dining at a small restaurant on the edge of downtown Toronto.

"Good idea!" Then they challenged me. "So write it."

I'd been complaining that the statistical training our doctoral students received gave them little conceptual understanding and therefore under-prepared them to take their comprehensive exams. Someone needed to write a simple primer that would explain the concepts of statistics. One of the biggest problems was that students tended to learn a bunch of statistical tests without understanding any unifying and underlying concepts (I snidely called this the "cookbook" approach), or they learned the general linear model (GLM) without "generalizing" the approach to standard statistical tests (t test, analysis of variance [ANOVA]). I prefer GLM for its elegance; however, most students did not see a connection between GLM and mainstream statistical tests. Students who learned one approach never learned its relationship to the other approach. It felt like I had to speak two different languages to discuss statistics with students from my own doctoral training program.

Inspired by my friends, I returned to my hotel after dinner, took my laptop to a quiet lounge in the hotel lobby, and over the next several hours proceeded to draft this book. Well, I drafted an early version of it—a very early version! I'm not sure I would even recognize that version today. Nevertheless, I was excited when I called my wife, Marla, the next day and told her of my grand plan to write a book that would teach students statistics from both a traditional test-focused perspective and a general linear approach. And better yet, the book would finally show students that the two approaches were the same (something a senior professor once patronizingly told me I was wrong about). The book would write itself—I expected to have this project wrapped-up within a couple of months.

Nine years passed. What took me so long?

It is only by entire isolation from everything and everyone that one can do any work.

—Gyles Brandreth
Oscar Wilde and a Death of No Importance

What I have learned over the years is that my job gets in the way of my true academic work. Absurd activities that only university administrators can dream up kill academic progress and accomplishment. This book could only be written during school breaks, and typically I had to spend part of that time recalling where I had left off, what I had intended, and just why I had chosen that approach to explain whatever topic I was working on. Additionally, I wanted to use one single data set for demonstrations throughout the book, continually expanding the example to build increasingly complex statistical models to test (I believe this is one of the brilliant conceptual advantages of the GLM). I also wanted to keep the data set very simple so that students could conduct the analyses by hand—an approach that removes statistical analysis from the mysterious computer box and places it in the student's control. I believe working a problem by hand (without getting overwhelmed by arithmetic) helps a student to grasp an analysis. But every time I progressed to a new and more advanced topic, I had to revise the data set to accommodate my new analysis, which had the unfortunate effect of altering the prior demonstrations. I was continually revising the data set and reworking the demonstrations—classic "one step forward and two steps backward."

In addition to stops and starts due to my teaching schedule and repeated analyzing, reworking, and reanalyzing my demonstrations, I harbored pesky doubts that this work would ever get published—an angst familiar to all professors. Each time I resumed writing, I wondered, "Am I wasting my time?" Then, a seemingly innocuous (yet timely) comment by a friend and colleague 2 years ago changed everything. His offhanded remark caused me to realize that it was time to either all-out commit to finish this project or to let it go. And to move forward, I needed to find out if someone would publish it. I reached out to Sage first because I've always found their statistics books easily understandable to a nonstatistician.[1] The evening that I submitted the proposal to Sage, I celebrated with some friends over drinks, never expecting the proposal to get accepted. In fact, I'm pretty

---

1. I am a clinical psychologist who had excellent statistics training from Drs. Judd, McClelland, and Ryan at the University of Colorado.

sure that my friends didn't know why I was celebrating since I preferred to keep it to myself. My good fortune, however, was that Vicki Knight of Sage received the proposal and contacted me with encouraging news—she offered me a book contract.

After the initial proposal was reviewed and feedback provided, one of the most helpful insights offered by a reviewer was to completely reorganize the book. My initial outline presented the traditional test-focused approach separately from the GLM perspective, an approach the reviewer helped me to realize merely replicated the schism that historically existed between the two approaches. The reviewer suggested instead that I write a chapter describing the traditional approach to an analysis (e.g., the *t* test) and follow it with a chapter using GLM to conduct a *t* test. Although this approach was a little more challenging than I initially expected, I have tried to remain faithful to that advice, and I now consider it the backbone and strength of this book. Thank you to that anonymous reviewer![2]

The result of this feedback is the book before you. It begins by introducing the concept of statistical models, model comparison, and the fundamental questions addressed by parametric statistics (Chapter 1). Part I covers the foundations of model comparison and bivariate regression (Chapters 2, 3, and 4). In Part II, I cover correlation, *t* test, and one-way ANOVA (Chapters 5, 6, and 7), followed by Chapter 8 in which I use bivariate regression to conduct each of these standard tests. In Part III, I build on model complexity by introducing multiple regression and interactions (Chapters 9 and 10), two-way ANOVA using both model comparison and traditional approaches (Chapters 11 and 12), one-way ANOVAs with three groups (Chapters 13 and 14), and two-by-three ANOVAs (Chapters 15 and 16). I complete the book by covering analysis of covariance (both traditional and model comparison together in Chapter 17), repeated measures analyses (Chapters 18 and 19), and mixed between and within designs (Chapter 20).

A novelist embarks on writing, motivated no doubt by a desire to pen the Great American novel. In a world resplendent with statistics books, I'm certain that everyone who sets out to write a statistics book believes that she or he will write the perfect book, the *one* that finally makes such a simple concept absolutely clear. So why shouldn't I think any differently than all those who wrote before me? And here it is—my attempt at the Great American statistics book.

---

2. Ironically, after I submitted the first completed draft for review, a different reviewer expressed concern about this approach and suggested I segregate the two approaches into separate sections.

Acknowledgments

The process of writing this book has been aided by several individuals who deserve far more gratitude than merely burying their names on these pages. I must begin by acknowledging those friends with whom I dined so many years ago in Toronto: Drs. Kenneth Grizzle and Tony Cellucci. At a time when I came closest to abandoning this project, Dr. Tom Klein, my friend and colleague in the English Department at Idaho State University (ISU), casually glanced over my shoulder while I sat at a coffee shop scribbling on a chapter. Whatever he saw intrigued him, I guess, and he told me that I needed to publish this book. I agreed on the condition that he would host a release party, complete with a public reading of sections from the book. I have attended many such release parties, typically for friends in the English department, but I've never seen one for a statistics book. The thought of reading aloud sections of a stats book amuses me. Tom has since forgotten that conversation (or so he claims), but it meant a lot to me. I also gratefully acknowledge the owners (Gail and Doc) and baristas of that coffee shop where Tom inspired me, the College Market. That is the place where most of this book was written. Sadly, the College Market closed its doors last week after 20 years of serving friendship, smiles, and lots of caffeine, leaving ISU's best professors and students wandering, decaffeinated, through Pocatello.

I learned statistics from two masters: Charles "Chick" Judd and Gary McClelland. I had already taken graduate and undergraduate courses in statistics, psychometrics, and test theory, completed an empirical master's thesis and published three empirical research articles by the time I started graduate school and enrolled in their graduate statistics course. If you gave me a set of data, I could identify the optimal statistical test to use and interpret the results for you; however, I knew I didn't understand statistics well enough. Then, as a doctoral student, I took statistics classes from Gary and Chick (and Carey Ryan, our teaching assistant, who subsequently coauthored the second edition of their textbook). The model comparison approach that they taught resonated with me immediately. Their approach was simple, yet it provided me with a theoretical foundation that allowed me to advance my statistical knowledge with remarkable ease. Factor analysis, path analysis, structural equation modeling—it all flowed from what Gary and Chick taught. This past spring, both Gary and Chick received teaching awards from the American Psychological Association—honors well deserved—and they taught their final "Chick and Gary show."

I've already mentioned Vicki Knight of SAGE, who took a chance on me. She has been complimentary and encouraging throughout this process. Over the past 2 years, Vicki has been one of the most supportive, enthusiastic, and encouraging individuals I've ever met. She had a seeming instinct as to when my spirits were sluggish, and she would contact me out of the blue with encouraging e-mails. I am also indebted to several students who read early and later versions and offered their perspectives: Jessie Jensen, Jessica Peltan, Catherine Williams, and Nickolas Dasher. One of the most valuable insights offered was to remove the basic statistical topics (e.g., variables, distributions, sampling) to an appendix. As Jessica (now Dr. Peltan) explained to me, anyone reading this book should already know these basics, and placing that information in the body of the book distracted from the book's purpose. I am also indebted to a host of reviewers who previewed the original prospectus and read and critiqued the chapters. My sincerest thanks for the guidance, suggestions, and advice from all of you—those who agreed to reveal their identities were Stephen Armeli, Jeffrey A. Ciesla, John Curtin, Manfred van Dulmen, Michael Granaas, Rafa Kasim, William B. King, Alfred F. Mancuso, and Lela Rankin Williams.

My father, Bob Vik, took an interest in this book. He offered to read and give feedback on the first draft. Dad is a theoretical physicist, a fact that likely influenced his summation of the book—"it reads like a series of lectures." When I shared Dad's impression with my wife, she said, "Well, good! That was your goal!" Thanks Dad, for caring and giving your detailed comments.

Finally, I can't express enough gratitude to my family. My children, Dan, Angie, and Shaina, asked just often enough (but never too often), "How's the book coming?" My wife, Marla, is beyond amazing. First of all, she loves me, which speaks volumes of her patience. Then, she encouraged me along every step and stage of this process. I've no doubt that there were many times when I neglected other pressing matters at home with the excuse that "I've got to work on my book." But Marla always smiled and said, "Good!" Thank you Marla—I love you.

About the Author

Peter Vik was born and raised in San Diego, California. He left the beaches to attend college at the University of California, Davis, and subsequently moved to Boulder, Colorado, where he earned his PhD in clinical psychology. He completed a clinical internship and postdoctoral fellowship with the Department of Psychiatry at the University of California, San Diego. Peter now lives in Pocatello, Idaho, where he is Professor of Psychology and Director of the University Honors Program at Idaho State University. When he is not writing statistics books (which he hopes is most of the time, for a while at least), Peter plays guitar, skis, mountain bikes, and he and his wife take turns holding and staring at their two brand new grandchildren.

1

INTRODUCTION

To weigh the evidence, always incomplete, and correctly intuit the whole, to see the world in a grain of sand, to recognize its beauty, its simplicity, its truth. It's as close as we get to God in this life, and we reside in the glow of such brief flashes of understanding.

—Richard Russo, *Straight Man*[1]

O pen a statistics book and you'll likely encounter one of two approaches to teaching statistics. One approach is a traditional presentation of statistical tests in which the nature of the data (continuous or categorical) determines the appropriate statistic. The statistic is then used to test hypotheses (hypothesis testing approach). The second is a model building approach based on linear regression. Both approaches have merit; however, I believe that learning one in exclusion of the other loses the full and rich detail of what statistical analyses reveal. This statistics primer integrates both perspectives so that students, professionals, and other readers may appreciate the rich simplicity of the most basic statistical analysis.

Statistics is "the collection, organization, and interpretation of numerical data" (*The American Heritage Dictionary of the English Language*, 2000).

---

1. From *Straight Man* by Richard Russo. Published by Chatto & Windus. Reprinted by permission of The Random House Group Limited.

The word derives from the Latin word, *statisticus*, which means "the state of affairs." *Statistics*, then, is a numerical description of the state of things.

Behavioral and social scientists want to describe the "state" of some phenomenon or characteristic, such as drug use, psychiatric distress, or political attitudes. To describe these phenomena, we develop *parametric* statistical models. A *parameter* is a feature or characteristic of a population that can be estimated from data. We "operationally" define that characteristic as a *variable*, measure the variable (i.e., give it a score), collect scores from a group of subjects, and summarize the collected scores using "descriptive" statistics (e.g., central tendency and variation). Common statistical ways to describe or estimate a population characteristic include *central tendencies* (means, medians, and modes), *variation* of scores around the central tendency (standard deviation, variance, and range), and *associations* between two or more characteristics (correlations and regression coefficients). It's by understanding how two or more variables are related that behavioral and social scientists learn about the phenomenon they study. To understand the relationship between two variables, we need to consider three fundamental questions.

◆ FUNDAMENTAL QUESTIONS

Three simple questions characterize the relationship between two variables. Question 1 asks whether the variables are related. If they are related, then a change in one variable corresponds to a change in the other. If the variables are not related, then Questions 2 and 3 are irrelevant. But if they are related, then Questions 2 and 3 are needed to describe the nature of the relationship between the two variables. Question 2 asks the direction of the relationship, and Question 3 asks how strong the relationship is.

Question 1: Are Two Variables Related?

This first question asks whether a variable (Y) is related to another variable (X). Question 1 is answered either yes or no (they are or they are not related). Both the "traditional" hypothesis testing approach[2] and the model building approach use statistical tests (e.g., t tests; analysis of variance;

---

2. "Traditional" is in quotation marks because, ironically, traditionally accepted approaches, historically, have a more recent origin than the general linear model approach advocated in this text. See Cohen, Cohen, West, and Aiken (2003) for a historical review.

regression) to answer this yes–no question.[3] If we decide that the two variables are related, we then *infer* that the population characteristics are related, and we turn to Questions 2 and 3.

Question 2: What Is the Direction of the Relationship Between Two Variables?

If we decide that two variables are related (i.e., as one changes, there is a corresponding change in the other), then we need to know a couple of things about that relationship. Question 2 asks *how* one variable (Y) will change as a second variable (X) changes. As scores on X increase, scores on Y can either increase (a "direct" or "positive" relationship) or decrease (an "inverse" or "negative" relationship). For example, as height (X) increases, weight (Y) increases; or, as age (X) increases, psychomotor speed (Y) decreases.

Question 3: How Strong Is the Relationship Between Two Variables?

So we know that X and Y are related, and we know how they are related (positive or negative). Now we need to know how strong or close to perfect their relationship is. As variable X changes, how accurately can we describe the corresponding change in variable Y? Changes in X (ΔX) may predict changes in Y (ΔY) precisely, fairly precisely, somewhat precisely, with minimal precision, or not at all (although, by definition, if ΔX doesn't predict ΔY, then X and Y aren't related, and we wouldn't even be asking Question 2 or 3!). Put another way, if we use the change in X to predict change in Y, we want to know how much *error* we can expect in our predictions of Y. Understanding error, you'll shortly see, is fundamental to statistical analysis.

Accuracy of prediction is called the *strength* or *magnitude* of the relationship between X and Y. When the relationship is strong between X and Y, then variation or change in X explains a lot of the variation in Y. In a weak relationship, variation of X explains little of the variation of Y. A strong relationship has a large magnitude, whereas a weak relationship has a small magnitude. Strength or magnitude can be described qualitatively using descriptive terms (e.g., weak, moderate, or strong); however, quantitative

---

3. While debates regarding hypothesis testing are beyond the scope of this book, readers should be aware of criticisms regarding hypothesis testing. One is that too often researchers will answer the first question and stop without addressing Questions 2 and 3.

scores describe the relationship with more precision than a qualitative label. Therefore, we will learn numeric statistics to describe the strength of the relationship between two variables. Statistics that describe the strength of the relationship are the regression coefficient (b), correlation coefficient (r), multiple correlation (R), and squared multiple correlation (R^2).

♦ STATISTICAL MODELS

This book introduces the general linear model (GLM) approach to statistical analysis, and contrasts GLM with traditional hypothesis testing approaches. GLM combines one or more independent (predictor) variables into a statistical model that predicts scores on a dependent (outcome) variable.[4]

If we label the outcome or dependent variable "Y," and label the predictor or independent variables "X" (e.g., predictor 1 = X_1, predictor 2 = X_2, predictor 3 = X_3, and so on), we can imagine a statistical model where Y is predicted by several variables (Xs): $\hat{Y}$ = variable X_1 + variable X_2 + variable X_3. A Y without a cap (Y) is a real or measured score, a Y with a cap ($\hat{Y}$) is a score *predicted* by the model, and X_1, X_2, and X_3 are the predictor variables that make up the statistical model.

As alluded to by Question 3, the relationship between each X and Y is unlikely to be perfectly one to one, so we describe the relationship between X and Y using a numeric value or weight, which we'll label β. The relationship between outcome Y and predictor X_1 is β_1, the relationship between Y and variable X_2 is β_2, and the relationship between Y and variable X_3 is β_3. Therefore, a more accurate equation for the model is

$$\hat{Y} = \beta_0 + \beta_1 X_1 + \beta_2 X_2 + \beta_3 X_3.$$

β_0 is a beginning prediction of Y, and that prediction is adjusted by each person's weighted scores on X_1, X_2, and X_3.

Statistical models can vary in complexity. An extremely simple model merely predicts the same score for everyone. For example, an extremely simple model could predict a constant such as zero for everyone ($\hat{Y} = 0$).

---

4. Some researchers are precise about how to label variables. They reserve the terms *dependent* and *independent* only for experimental (perhaps quasi-experimental) research designs because the terms imply a causal relationship (i.e., changes in *X causes Y* to change). I have always preferred the terms *predictor* and *outcome*. I used both here because I want readers to recognize that the terms refer to the same elements of a regression model.

A slightly less simple model could predict the group mean score for every subject $(\hat{Y} = \overline{Y})$. A model becomes a little more interesting and a little more complex by adding a variable (X) to predict the outcome variable (e.g., $\hat{Y} = \beta_0 + \beta_1 X_1$). A model becomes fairly complex by including several predictor variables (e.g., $\hat{Y} = \beta_0 + \beta_1 X_1 + \beta_2 X_2 + \cdots + \beta_i X_i$).

Once we've defined a statistical model, we can use a person's scores on the predictor variables $(X\text{s})$ to predict that person's score on the outcome variable $(\hat{Y})$. If we know the person's real score on Y, we can compare the real score (Y) with the score predicted by the model $(\hat{Y})$ to see how close the model came to predicting that person's actual score. The difference between the actual and the predicted scores $(Y - \hat{Y})$ is the "error." Each subject will have an error score, and we can total the error scores for all subjects to get a sense of how much total error (error for all subjects) exists in our model. The sum (Σ) of these errors $(Y - \hat{Y})$ is written as $\Sigma(Y - \hat{Y})$.

Suppose we had test scores from students in a class, and the average of those scores is 10. An extremely simple model would predict the average score (10) for each student $(\hat{Y} = 10)$. When we compare the prediction of 10 (the mean) with students' real scores, we'd find that we're correct for some students (those who scored 10), too high for some students (those who scored below the mean), and too low for other students (those who scored above the mean).

A model that predicts scores that are fairly close to actual scores will have less error than a model that generates scores that are not so close to actual scores. We have ways to sum the errors of our model's predictions, and we use that error score to inform us as to how well our model predicts the dependent or outcome variable.

MEASURING THE ERROR OF THE MODEL ◆

We've referred to our outcome variable as "Y," and we've alluded to two types of Y: the actual observed score (Y) and the model's predicted score $(\hat{Y})$. A subscript, i, indicates which subject we obtained the scores from. For example, Y_1 would be the actual (observed) score for the first subject, and $\hat{Y}_1$ is the score predicted by the model for the first subject. Y_2 is the observed score for the second subject, and $\hat{Y}_2$ is the score predicted by the model for the second subject. It follows that the difference between what we observed for the second participant (Y_2) and what the model predicted for that person $(\hat{Y}_2)$ is the error of prediction for the second subject $(e_2 = Y_2 - \hat{Y}_2)$.

Some errors will be small, some may be huge. The best way to summarize the error in one single score is to combine all of these individual errors. By convention (and for reasons explained in Chapter 2), we square each individual's error $(Y_i - \hat{Y}_i)^2$ and then add all of the squared errors $\sum(Y_i - \hat{Y}_i)^2$. The result is called the sum of squared errors (SSE). SSE is the basic measure of a model's error.

♦ MODEL COMPARISON

The objective of statistical modeling is to make incremental changes that we think will improve the model, and then to test if the new model produces less error (lower SSE) than the previous model. By incrementally altering a model, it's possible to isolate each predictor variable in the model and test whether including a specific variable improved the model.

As I've already said, one of the simplest models includes no predictor variable at all—it just predicts the mean ($\hat{Y} = \beta_0$, where $\beta_0 = \bar{Y}$). Slightly more complex models add a predictor ($\hat{Y} = \beta_0 + \beta_1 X_1$) and more complex models add several predictors ($\hat{Y} = \beta_0 + \beta_1 X_1 + \beta_2 X_2 + \cdots + \beta_i X_i$). Ideally, we increase complexity incrementally by adding a single predictor at a time. If a new and slightly more complex model predicted Y sufficiently better (has a lower SSE) than the previous less complex model, we conclude that the increased complexity (adding the new predictor X) benefited the model. If the new model didn't reduce the error much, then including the new variable wasn't worth the increased complexity.

♦ SUMMARY

Statistics is the use of data to empirically describe the state of something. We identify a parameter as a characteristic that we want to learn about. We define the characteristic as a measurable variable (labeled "Y"), and we create a statistical model that predicts how people score on that variable. The model is made up of other variables (Xs) that predict the characteristic (outcome variable). The Model *predicts* scores ($\hat{Y}$) that we can compare against actual observed scores (Y). The difference between actual and predicted scores $(Y_i - \hat{Y}_i)$ is the error of prediction.

In this book I'll focus on four statistical tests: (1) the t test, (2) the analysis of variance (ANOVA), (3) correlation, and (4) linear regression. This book was written on a premise that readers have some understanding of basic statistical concepts such as central tendency, variable distributions, statistical assumptions, research design, and hypothesis testing. Therefore, those concepts are not presented in the body of this book. For those who need or desire a review, these topics are addressed in the appendices.

PART I

Foundations of the General Linear Model

2

PREDICTING SCORES

The Mean and the Error of Prediction

Grim, isn't it, what?

Grim, sir?

I mean to say, the difference between things as they look and things as they are.

—P. G. Wodehouse
Very Good, Jeeves![1]

In Chapter 1, I established our goal to build a statistical model that uses one or more independent variables to explain or predict scores on a dependent (outcome) variable. This chapter tells the story of prediction and the errors that come with prediction. A good model should give us a fairly good estimate (prediction) of the person's actual score on the outcome (dependent) variable. This chapter introduces the three components of mode-based data analysis: *data*, *model*, and *error*. We will see how these three elements combine to form a linear equation, Data = Model + Error (Judd, McClelland, & Ryan, 2009). Finally, the chapter introduces a simple model for predicting scores on an outcome variable (data) and demonstrates how to measure the error of the simple model.

---

1. Wodehouse, P. G. (1930). *Very Good, Jeeves!* New York: Doubleday.

◆ THE DATA

The *American Heritage Dictionary of the English Language* (2000) defined data as "values derived from scientific experiments."[2] *Data* can refer to countless variables, scores, and sources of information. In the linear equation Data = Model + Error, the term *Data* refers to scores on a variable that is of key interest to a researcher.

To understand a phenomenon, a behavioral scientist must first *operationally* define it as a measurable variable. She then measures the variable among a sample of research subjects (e.g., people, rats), knowing that individual scores will vary and that she can describe that variation or *distribution* of scores by using basic descriptive statistics. Common descriptive statistics are the mean (M) and standard deviation (S).[3] These scores on her variable are her data, and I'll refer to them as Y. Her research objective is to explain why people score the way they do on variable Y. After measuring her variable Y, her next step is to build a statistical model that explains or predicts scores on Y.

◆ THE MODEL

Prediction is one way to demonstrate understanding of something. A model that predicts a phenomenon well implies that we understand that phenomenon. A researcher's goal is to build a statistical model that predicts data fairly accurately. A good model may evolve incrementally—a researcher begins with a fairly simple model, tests the components of the model (the independent or predictor variables), and keeps the good and jettisons the less useful predictors. The researcher then enhances the resulting model by adding and testing new predictor variables. Building a good model could become a career's obsession.

The journey of prediction using incremental modeling begins with a very simple first model that predicts the mean score of the outcome variable ($\overline{Y}$)

---

2. The *Dictionary* also defines data as the "plural of datum." The writers of the dictionary go on to discuss that popular usage of "data" is no longer restricted to plural. I'm a purist, however. I consider "data" to be plural. It's just classy.

3. Because she does not measure all individuals in the population (she only had a sample of subjects), her descriptive statistics (M & S) are estimations of the populations true mean (mu; μ) and standard deviation (sigma; σ). She, and we, hope they are good estimations—that M and S are pretty close to μ and σ, respectively.

for every subject. An initial model that predicts the mean for every subject serves as the foundation on which subsequent models are based. The single predictive component of the model ($\overline{Y}$) is designated as β_0, and I write the model as a mathematical expression: $Y = \beta_0 + \varepsilon$, where Y are the data (individual scores on Y), β_0 is the model (in this simple model, $\beta_0 = \overline{Y}$), and ε is the error.

Comparing the actual scores on the outcome variable (Y) with the scores that were predicted by the model ($\overline{Y}$ for each subject) reveals how much error exists in this simple model. It is so very unlikely that Y will equal $\overline{Y}$ for every subject that I expect error (i.e., variation in scores). If everybody had the same score, Y would be a most uninteresting variable, and there would be no reason to waste time modeling Y.

So we now know about data (Y) and we have a model (β_0) to predict the data. It's time to compare the score predicted by the model for each subject with the subjects' actual scores. The differences between actual (Y) and predicted ($\overline{Y}$) scores is represented by the third element of the linear equation: *error* (ε).

ERROR OF THE MODEL ◆

Rarely would all of the scores on the dependent variable equal the mean. If they did, the variable would have no variance, and a variable with no variance is just boring.[4] When a model predicts the mean, I expect that some (quite possibly all) of the scores will be different from the mean.

Sometimes I think that statistics is a study of error; we study the error in our model in hopes that we can reduce the error to improve our model. To reduce error, we must be able to measure error. I'll demonstrate how to measure the model's error using the data in Table 2.1. The table provides scores on variable Y for 12 people. The scores range from 2 to 10, and the mean score is 6. A model that predicts that every person scored the mean (6) will have some prediction errors. In fact, in this example, not one person scored the mean so every score is an error. There are three ways to measure the error of the model. I can (1) count the number of incorrect predictions, (2) sum the absolute difference between predicted and actual scores, or (3) sum the squared difference between predicted and actual scores (Judd et al., 2009).

---

4. Okay, so one reviewer corrected this claim, stating that a variable without variance isn't boring—it's a constant. Perhaps so—I think that reviewer is boring.

Table 2.1 Scores on a Variable, *Y*, for 12 Subjects

Person	Y	Ŷ
1	2	6
2	3	6
3	3	6
4	4	6
5	7	6
6	5	6
7	5	6
8	7	6
9	8	6
10	9	6
11	9	6
12	10	6

NOTE: The mean score of *Y* is 6. Therefore, the model, $\hat{Y} = \beta_0$, where $\beta_0 = \bar{Y}$, predicts a score of 6 for every subject.

Counting Errors

A simple approach to measuring error is to count the number of correct predictions. Table 2.2 compares actual scores on *Y* with the predicted score ($\hat{Y} = 6$) for each subject. The final column indicates whether the prediction was correct or incorrect. At the bottom of that column is the total number of incorrect predictions. None of the 12 people actually had a score of 6. An error rate of 100% doesn't make this model look too good, so maybe counting prediction errors isn't such a good way to measure a model's error. After all, some scores were closer to the predictions than others, such as Subjects 5 to 8. Perhaps, we should consider how close the prediction is to the actual observed score when we measure the error.

Sum of the Absolute Errors

The second approach to measuring a model's error takes the arithmetic difference between each predicted and observed score and sums these differences.

Table 2.2   Counting Errors to Measure a Model's Error of Prediction

Person	Y	$\hat{Y}$	Correct
1	2	6	No
2	3	6	No
3	3	6	No
4	4	6	No
5	7	6	No
6	5	6	No
7	5	6	No
8	7	6	No
9	8	6	No
10	9	6	No
11	9	6	No
12	10	6	No
			Total error = 12

Some people scored above the mean and some scored below the mean. By definition, the differences between a mean score and the individual scores will always sum to zero. It just does. While zero error sounds awesome, I know there were errors in our predictions. The problem is that some differences are positive and some differences are negative, and the positives exactly offset the negatives. So simply summing the differences doesn't work. To correct for this arithmetic nuisance, I make all of the scores positive by converting the differences into *absolute values* and summing the absolute differences. Table 2.3 demonstrates this process.

Using this approach, the error of prediction for this simple model is 28. Notice that scores that were closer to the mean contributed less to the total error score than scores that were further from the mean.

Sum of the Squared Errors

Another way to make all of the differences positive is to square the difference between predicted and actual scores. We measure the difference between each subject's actual score (Y_i) and the subject's predicted score ($\hat{Y}_i$), and

Table 2.3 Using Absolute Value of the Difference Between Prediction and Actual Score to Measure a Model's Error of Prediction

Person	Y	$\hat{Y}$	$Y - \hat{Y}$	$|Y - \hat{Y}|$
1	2	6	−4	4
2	3	6	−3	3
3	3	6	−3	3
4	4	6	−2	2
5	7	6	1	1
6	5	6	−1	1
7	5	6	−1	1
8	7	6	1	1
9	8	6	2	2
10	9	6	3	3
11	9	6	3	3
12	10	6	4	4

Total error = 28

then square the differences. We then sum these squared differences (errors) to get a *sum of squared errors*. This approach has an added benefit—it amplifies the error contributed by predictions that are quite different from actual scores, thereby punishing a model for big errors and minimizing the cost of fairly accurate predictions. Notice in Table 2.4 that fairly good predictions (e.g., Subjects 5, 6, 7, and 8) contributed only 1 to the total error, while relatively poor predictors (Subjects 1 and 12) contributed much more error.

Figure 2.1 presents a visual representation of the effect of squaring errors. In the figure, a square is created to illustrate how much error was contributed when the difference was large (Subject 1) and small (Subject 5). Remember that a score of 6 was predicted for every subject. Subject 1 scored 2. Two minus the mean (6) is −4, and −4 squared is 16. In contrast, Subject 5 scored 7, which was fairly close to the predicted score of 6. The difference, 7 minus 6, is 1, and 1 squared is 1. Notice that the square drawn for Subject 1 is 16 times larger than the square drawn for Subject 5.

Table 2.4   Summing Squared Difference Between Predicted and Actual Scores to Measure a Model's Error of Prediction

Person	Y	$\hat{Y}$	$Y - \hat{Y}$	$(Y - \hat{Y})^2$
1	2	6	−4	16
2	3	6	−3	9
3	3	6	−3	9
4	4	6	−2	4
5	7	6	1	1
6	5	6	−1	1
7	5	6	−1	1
8	7	6	1	1
9	8	6	2	4
10	9	6	3	9
11	9	6	3	9
12	10	6	4	16
				Total error = 80

Figure 2.1   Squaring the Errors Amplifies the Contribution of Error for Scores That Are Far From the Mean (Subject 1) and Minimizes the Error for Scores Close to the Mean (Subject 5).

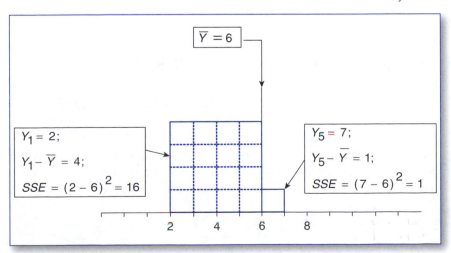

$$\overline{Y} = 6$$

$Y_1 = 2;$

$Y_1 - \overline{Y} = 4;$

$SSE = (2 - 6)^2 = 16$

$Y_5 = 7;$

$Y_5 - \overline{Y} = 1;$

$SSE = (7 - 6)^2 = 1$

We can draw a square depicting the error for each subject. Figure 2.2 shows "error squares" drawn for all 12 of the subjects. The total sum of squared errors is the sum of all of these squares.

Figure 2.2 Squared Errors for Each of the 12 Subjects.

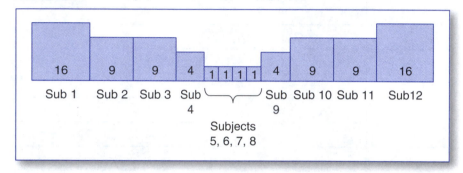

By convention, we'll adopt this method to measure model error. The sum of squared errors (*SSE*) approach to measuring error is expressed by the formula in Equation 2.1:

$$SSE = \Sigma \left(Y_i - \hat{Y}_i \right)^2.$$ (2.1)

Remember that we defined $\hat{Y}$ in the simplest model as equal to the mean. If we substitute the mean ($\bar{Y}$) into Equation 2.1, we get Equation 2.2.

$$SSE = \Sigma \left(Y_i - \bar{Y}_i \right)^2.$$ (2.2)

◆ CONCEPTUAL VERSUS COMPUTATIONAL FORMULA

The formula for *SSE* given in Equation 2.1 captures the *concept* of error by squaring and summing the differences between predicted and actual scores. Although it can be used to calculate the error, it's a bit clumsy, especially when the mean isn't an integer (squaring and summing lots of fractions and decimals can be unpleasant). Fortunately, there is a more convenient formula (Equation 2.3)—a *computational* formula that is easier to use to compute *SSE*.

$\Sigma \left(y_i - \hat{y}_i \right)^2$

$$SSE = \Sigma Y^2 - \frac{(\Sigma Y)^2}{N}.$$ (2.3)

Equation 2.3 does not require subtracting fractions. Instead of calculating a difference for each observed score, I need only square and then sum each score. Table 2.5 demonstrates the convenience of computing *SSE* using the computational formula. I can insert the sum of Y ($\sum Y = 72$) and the sum of Y^2 ($\sum Y^2 = 512$) obtained from Table 2.5 into Equation 2.3 to calculate *SSE*:

$$SSE = 512 - (72^2/12)$$
$$= 512 - (5184/12)$$
$$= 512 - 432$$
$$= 80.$$

computational

Table 2.5 Data Displayed for Computing *SSE* Using Conceptual Formula (Equation 2.3)

Person	Y	Y^2
1	2	4
2	3	9
3	3	9
4	4	16
5	7	49
6	5	25
7	5	25
8	7	49
9	8	64
10	9	81
11	9	81
12	10	100
$\sum =$	72	512

VARIANCE AND STANDARD DEVIATION ◆

This is an ideal opportunity to review two descriptive statistics that are likely already familiar to you. Variance (S^2) and standard deviation (S) describe the variation of scores around a mean. Variance is *SSE* divided by the number of scores minus 1: $SSE \div (N - 1)$. In a rather loose sense, variance is the average squared difference between the observed scores and the mean of those observed scores (see Equation 2.4).

$$S_y^2 = \frac{\Sigma(y_i - \hat{y}_i)^2}{N-1}$$

$$\text{Variance} = S_y^2 = \frac{\Sigma Y^2 - \frac{(\Sigma Y)^2}{N}}{N-1}. \tag{2.4}$$

In our example, we had scores from 12 people and $SSE = 80$, so the *variance* of the data is $80 \div 11 = 7.27$.

Since we squared the differences between Y_i and $\overline{Y}$ to calculate SSE and variance, the metric or scale of these estimates of variation no longer conform to the variable's original scale. Since we squared the variable's scores to make them positive, we take the square root of the variance $\left(\sqrt{S_y^2}\right)$ to return to the variable's original scale. The square root of the variance is called the standard deviation (S), and the formula for S is given in Equation 2.5.

$$S_y = \sqrt{\frac{\Sigma(y_i - \hat{y}_i)^2}{N-1}}$$

$$\text{Standard deviation} = S_y = \sqrt{\frac{\Sigma Y^2 - \frac{(\Sigma Y)^2}{N}}{N-1}}. \tag{2.5}$$

For our data example, $S_y = \sqrt{7.27} = 2.696$.

♦ ANOTHER EXAMPLE

Let's demonstrate the model error with a larger data set. Table 2.6 gives hypothetical depression symptom scores for 24 people.[5] The mean depression score for all 24 people is 13; therefore, the simple model predicts a depression score of 13 for each individual. To compute SSE, I'll subtract the predicted score (the mean) from each observed score, square these differences, and sum them. The resulting SSE is 1,204. Table 2.6 demonstrates this process.

Notice a few things in this example. First, the score predicted for Subject 6 was 13, and this score was fairly close to the actual score for Subject 6, which was 11. Thus, Subject 6 contributed a miniscule amount to the error estimate $(11 - 13 = -2; -2^2 = 4)$. Second, the predicted score of 13 was quite different

---

5. These data are "hypothetical" because I made them up! Please don't take them seriously.

Table 2.6 Estimating Error by Summing the Squared Difference Between Predicted and Actual Scores

Subject	Symptom Score (DV)	Predicted Score	Difference	Difference Squared
1	3	13	−10	100
2	5	13	−8	64
3	6	13	−7	49
4	8	13	−5	25
5	9	13	−4	16
6	11	13	−2	4
7	19	13	6	36
8	15	13	2	4
9	16	13	3	9
10	16	13	3	9
11	19	13	6	36
12	17	13	4	16
13	3	13	−10	100
14	5	13	−8	64
15	4	13	−9	81
16	6	13	−7	49
17	8	13	−5	25
18	10	13	−3	9
19	24	13	11	121
20	24	13	11	121
21	22	13	9	81
22	23	13	10	100
23	19	13	6	36
24	20	13	7	49
				SSE = 1,204

from the actual score of 24 for Subject 19. The 11-point difference between the predicted and actual scores contributed a considerable amount to the error estimate when it was squared ($24 - 13 = 11$; $11^2 = 121$). Thus, squaring the differences penalizes really bad predictions. Third, this example computed *SSE* with the conceptual approach, which is more cumbersome than the computational formula. The computational approach is far simpler (see Table 2.7). Once I have ΣY and ΣY^2, I can very simply obtain *SSE* by inserting ΣY and ΣY^2 into Equation 2.3. Simple—yes?

Table 2.7 Estimating Error Using the Computational Approach

Subject	Symptom Score (Y)	Y^2
1	3	9
2	5	25
3	6	36
4	8	64
5	9	81
6	11	121
7	19	361
8	15	225
9	16	256
10	16	256
11	19	361
12	17	289
13	3	9
14	5	25
15	4	16
16	6	36
17	8	64
18	10	100
19	24	576

Subject	Symptom Score (Y)	Y^2
20	24	576
21	22	484
22	23	529
23	19	361
24	20	400
	312	5,260

Here I need only sum all Ys, then square each Y and sum the Y^2s. No messy fractions!

$$SSE = \sum Y^2 - \frac{(\sum Y)^2}{N}$$

$$= 5260 - \frac{312^2}{24}$$

$$= 5260 - \frac{97344}{24}$$

$$= 5260 - 4056$$

$$= 1204.$$

$\varepsilon \left(y_i - \hat{y}_i \right)^2$

A PREVIEW OF MODEL COMPARISON ◆

The simple model described in this chapter is the standard model against which we'll compare subsequent more complex models. An "augmented" model (Model A) yields a (hopefully) more accurate prediction of our outcome (dependent) variable than the simple (compact) model (Model C) that predicts only the mean. Consider a simple compact Model C where $Y = \beta_0 + \varepsilon$, and an augmented Model A where $Y = \beta_0 + \beta_1 X + \varepsilon$. If the only difference between the two models is the addition of $\beta_1 X_1$, and if the change in *SSE* between Model C and Model A is proportionally large, then we'll conclude that adding $\beta_1 X_1$ improved the model by reducing the initial (total) error we had with the simple Model C. Prior to comparing models, we need to know how to create the augmented Model A. In the next chapter, we'll use bivariate regression to create an augmented (slightly more complex) model that includes a single predictor variable.

◆ SUMMARY

In this chapter, I defined a simple model that predicted the mean score for every observation, and I described the accuracy of the model by summing the squared errors (SSE) between each pair of predicted and observed scores. The error (SSE) of a simple model that predicts the mean for each participant also helped us calculate the variance (S^2) and standard deviation (S) of the dependent variable (Y). S^2 and S describe how scores vary around the mean. This simple model is the foundation on which we will eventually build more complex statistical models. Our goal with increasingly complex models is to reduce the SSE; a better model will reduce the error variance in the outcome variable and, therefore, leave less residual or "unexplained" error (SSE).

3

BIVARIATE REGRESSION

So I think it would be reckless of us to run around trying to tell everybody what we know before we know what we know is.

—Christopher Moore

Fluke: Or I Know Why the Winged Whale Sings[1]

The simple model from Chapter 2 simply predicted the same score (the mean) for everyone. It was not very discerning, and it seemed to have a lot of error. Our model-building goal is to improve prediction and thereby reduce the error. To improve prediction and reduce error, we add a predictor variable (X) to the model. This augmented, slightly enhanced, model is the beginning of a "predictive formula" (Keppel & Zedeck, 2002) that (hopefully) predicts individual outcome variable scores (Y) better than just predicting the mean. That is, we can *predict* a person's score on an outcome (dependent) variable ($\hat{Y}$) based on what we know about that person's score on a predictor (independent) variable (X). If variables X and Y are related to each other, then adding X to our model improves prediction and produces less error (SSE) than the simple model generated.

Since we're now dealing with two models, let's adopt some terminology to keep these models separate. First, we have two models: (1) a simple

---

1. Moore, C. (2003). *Fluke: Or I know why the winged whale sings*. New York: William Morrow & Company. Reprinted with permission.

model from Chapter 2 and (2) an enhanced model (the bivariate regression model). Different writers use different labels for these models; I favor the labels used by Judd et al. (2009) because they make sense, and it's what I learned years ago. So we will refer to the simple model as the *compact* model, and name it Model C. The enhanced model was *augmented* by adding a variable to it, so we'll call it Model A. Neither model is perfect, so both Models A and C will generate error; however, the error produced by Model C is the most error a parametric model can have. Therefore, we'll call the sum of squared errors generated by Model C—the sum of squares total or SST. We'll call the sum of squared errors produced by Model A—SSE_A.

We can partition the sum of squares total error (SST) into two parts: (1) residual error and (2) explained error. The residual error or remaining error is the error from Model A (SSE_A): It's the error we have left over after augmenting the model by adding variable X. Explained error is the difference between the error we started with (SST) and the error we ended up with (SSE_A). It's the amount of error that was reduced by adding variable X. If the predictor variable (X) is related to the outcome variable (Y), then Model A will produce less error than Model C produced (SST > SSE_A). Conversely, if variable X is absolutely not related to Y, then Model A would do no better than Model C at predicting Y and the error for the two models would be almost equal (SST ≈ SSE_A).[2]

Table 3.1 lists the source, name, and label of these different types of error. The total error (SST) is the sum of the explained (or reduced) error (SSR) and the residual or left-over error (SSE_A). Thus, SSR + SSE_A = SST. If we know the total error (error from Model C) and we calculate the error for Model A, then we can determine the explained (reduced) error by subtracting SSE_A from SST: SSR = SST − SSE_A.

Table 3.1   Total Error (SST) Partitioned Into Explained (Reduced) Error (SSR) and Residual Error (SSE_A)

Source	Label	Error
Model C	Total error	SST (SSE_C)
Model A	Residual error	SSE_A
Model A − Model C	Explained error	SSR

---

2. It rarely happens that two variables have a perfect zero correlation. There is always at least some miniscule correlation, even if it is due to measurement error. Even the slightest, and most tiniest, correlation between X and Y can produce a small reduction in error. Consequently, SST is always greater than SSE_A.

With this understanding of the two models, their error, and how error is partitioned, let's launch our voyage into bivariate regression. To begin, we need to understand how to calculate the regression coefficients and measure the model's error.

BIVARIATE REGRESSION ♦

The simple model, Model C, is $Y_i = \beta_0 + \varepsilon_i$, where β_0 is the mean of Y. To improve on this simple model, we *augment* it by adding an independent variable (X) because we believe X is related to Y. That relationship between X and Y is described by a regression coefficient, β_1, which is a numeric value that we can multiply with X ($\beta_1 X$).

Model A predicts a constant (β_0) and then adjusts this initial prediction by adding the product of $\beta_1 X$ to the constant ($\beta_0 + \beta_1 X$). The amount that $\hat{Y}$ changes for each unit of change in X (increase or decrease by 1) is equal to the value of the regression coefficient. If $\beta_1 = .5$, then when X increases by 1 point, Y increases by .5 point. If $\beta_1 = -2$, then when X increases by 1, Y decreases by 2 points. This bivariate regression model is expressed mathematically in Equation 3.1:

$$Y_i = \beta_0 + \beta_1 X_{i1} + \varepsilon_i. \qquad (3.1)$$

The difference between the simple model described in Chapter 2 and the bivariate regression model in Equation 3.1 is the addition of $\beta_1 X$. You may recall from algebra classes that a formula such as described in Equation 3.1 defines a line. The intercept of the regression line (β_0) is the point where the line crosses the y-axis, and β_1 is the slope of the line.

Our hypothesis is that X is related to Y. Our null hypothesis (H_0), therefore, is that X is not related to Y or that scores on X do not predict scores on Y.[3] Look again at Equation 3.1: The only way that the person's score on X has no relationship to the person's score on Y is when β_1 equals zero. If $\beta_1 = 0$, then $\beta_1 X = 0$. No matter what the value of X is, $\beta_1 X$ will always equal zero. Therefore, for the H_0 to be true, the regression coefficient must equal zero ($\beta_1 = 0$).

To consider what effect X may have on our SST, we need to calculate the error of Model A. We'll calculate error the same way we calculated error in Chapter 2—we subtract each subject's score as predicted by Model A ($\hat{Y}_i$) from each subject's actual (observed) score (Y_i). The result is an error score

---

3. See Appendix D for a review of null hypothesis testing.

for each subject $(Y_i - \hat{Y}_i)$. As before, we square those differences $(Y_i - \hat{Y}_i)^2$, and add these squared errors together to get the sum of squared errors $\left(\sum(Y_i - \hat{Y}_i)^2\right)$ for this augmented (bivariate regression) model. We call the sum of squared errors (*SSE*) for this augmented regression model *SSE*_{augmented} or SSE_A. In the next chapter, we'll learn to compare SSE_A with the SST of the simpler "compact" model. Before that we need to learn how to estimate the bivariate regression coefficient, β_1.

◆ THE BIVARIATE REGRESSION COEFFICIENT

To create this model, we need to estimate both β_1 and β_0. In Chapter 2, we used data (scores on Y) to calculate the mean for the simple model. Likewise, we'll use data (this time scores on both Y and X) to estimate our bivariate regression parameters, β_0 and β_1. The real population parameter will be designated with a Greek letter (β); the estimate of the real parameter, which we calculate using our sample data, is designated by the Arabic letter (b). Remember—a true parameter value is a Greek letter (β), and it is an estimate if it is an Arabic letter (b). We actually never know the true population value of parameter β; we only estimate it (b) with our data. First, we'll calculate b_1 (the estimate of β_1). Then, we'll use b_1 to determine b_0 (the estimate of β_0). Equation 3.2 gives the conceptual formula for b_1:

slope

$$b_1 = \frac{\sum(X_i - \bar{X})(Y_i - \bar{Y})}{\sum(X_i - \bar{X})^2}. \qquad (3.2)$$

Look closely at Equation 3.2 and you'll find similarities to the *conceptual* equation we used to compute *SSE* in Chapter 2. And (fortunately, you might say) there again is a *computational* equivalent of Equation 3.2 (Equation 3.3).

$$b_1 = \frac{\sum XY - \dfrac{(\sum X)(\sum Y)}{n}}{\sum X^2 - \dfrac{(\sum X)^2}{n}}. \qquad (3.3)$$

◆ CALCULATE THE REGRESSION COEFFICIENT

To use this computational formula (Equation 3.3) to estimate β_1, we need the sum of X ($\sum X$), sum of Y ($\sum Y$), sum of X^2 ($\sum X^2$), and sum of the cross product of X and Y (ΣXY). To demonstrate how to use the computational equation, look at the small data set in Table 3.2. The table includes the scores on Y, the corresponding scores on X, the squared values of X (X^2), and the cross product of X and Y. Summing these values gives us all of the component parts we need to derive the bivariate regression coefficient using Equation 3.3.

Table 3.2 Sample Data for a Bivariate Regression: X Predicts Y (i.e., Regress Y on X)

Person	Y	X_1	X^2	$X \times Y$
1	2	8	64	16
2	3	9	81	27
3	3	9	81	27
4	4	10	100	40
5	7	6	36	42
6	5	7	49	35
7	5	4	16	20
8	7	5	25	35
9	8	3	9	24
10	9	1	1	9
11	9	2	4	18
12	10	2	4	20
$\Sigma =$	72	66	470	313

Before calculating the regression equations, let's first draw a picture that shows how the two variables are related. In Figure 3.1, the scores on variable X are listed along the horizontal axis, and scores on Y along the vertical axis. In the figure, we've placed a dot for each subject where that subject's X and Y scores intersect. The result is a scatter of dots, with each subject represented by a dot. This graph is called a "scatterplot."

Figure 3.1 Scatterplot Showing the Relationship Between Scores on Variable X and Variable Y.

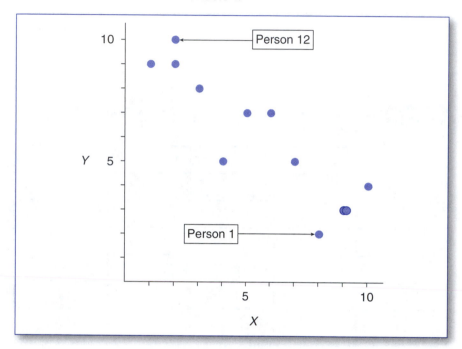

Inserting the sums from Table 3.2 into Equation 3.3 and reducing the formula, we get the estimate (b_1) of the regression coefficient (β_1).

$$b_1 = \frac{\sum XY - \dfrac{(\sum X)(\sum Y)}{n}}{\sum X^2 - \dfrac{(\sum X)^2}{n}}$$

$$b_1 = \frac{313 - \dfrac{(66)(72)}{12}}{470 - \dfrac{(66)^2}{12}} = \frac{313 - 396}{470 - 363} = \frac{-83}{107} = -.776.$$

The estimate of β_1 ($b_1 = -.776$) answers the fundamental Question 2 from Chapter 1: *How* are X and Y related? The answer is that they are inversely (negatively) related. As scores on X increase, scores on Y decrease. More specifically, every time X increases by 1 point, the prediction of Y ($\hat{Y}$) will decrease by .776 point. If X decreases a half point, $\hat{Y}$ will increase by .288.

.288 ?

To complete the regression equation, we need a starting estimate of Y that we can adjust according to scores on X. That starting value is β_0. Another name for the starting value is the "intercept," and it is the predicted value of Y, when $X = 0$. The estimate of the intercept (β_0) is b_0. To calculate b_0, we rearrange the regression model, $\hat{Y} = b_0 + b_1 X$, to solve for b_0 ($b_0 = \hat{Y} - b_1 X$). Then, we substitute the value of b_1 (−.776) into the equation.

$$b_0 = \hat{Y} - (-.776)X. \tag{3.4}$$

If only we knew a value of X and its corresponding prediction of Y that occurs along the regression line, then we could estimate b_0. Fortunately, we do know that any line described by a regression equation will pass through a point defined by the means of X and Y. Because the equation must pass through the means, we can substitute the mean of X and the mean of Y into Equation 3.4 to estimate the intercept. Substituting the mean of X (5.5) and the mean of Y (6) in Equation 3.4, we find that $b_0 = 10.268$.

(y intercept)

$$
\begin{aligned}
b_0 &= \bar{Y} - b_1 \bar{X} \\
&= 6 - (-.776 \times 5.5) \\
&= 6 - (-4.268) \\
&= 10.268.
\end{aligned}
$$

Now we combine the estimates of β_1 ($b_1 = -.776$) and β_0 ($b_0 = 10.268$) to form the bivariate regression equation for these data:

$$Y = 10.268 - .776X + \varepsilon_i.$$

GRAPH THE RELATIONSHIP BETWEEN X AND Y ♦

The bivariate regression equation is the formula for a straight line. We can draw that line on the scatterplot we drew earlier in this chapter (see Figure 3.2).

What's more, we can get a visual sense of the error of this bivariate model by creating squares just as we did in Chapter 2. This time, however, instead of measuring the distance between the actual scores and the mean, we'll measure the distance between the actual scores (the dots) and the regression line. Figure 3.3 shows some of these squares. Notice that the squares are larger when the dots are further from the regression line, and smaller when the dots are close to the regression line.

Figure 3.2 Bivariate Regression Line Superimposed on the Scatterplot of the Relationship Between Variables X and Y.

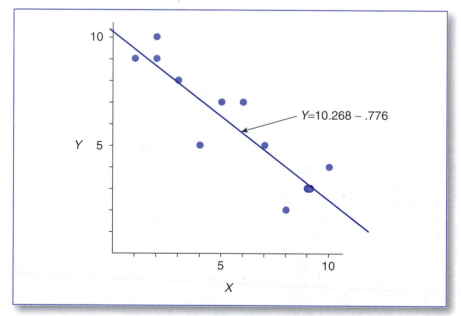

Figure 3.3 Sample Error "Squares" Showing the Squared Difference Between Individual Scores (Dots) and Predicted Scores (Regression Line).

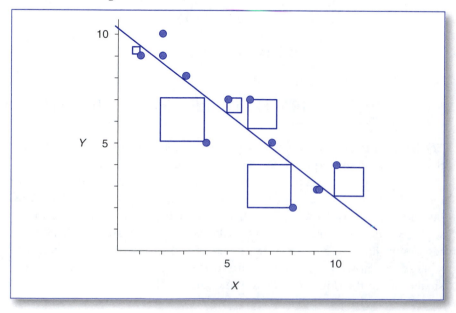

Now that we have the bivariate regression model, which is our Model A, we can compute the error of Model A.

ESTIMATING THE ERROR OF THE MODEL ◆

To estimate the error generated by this augmented model (SSE_A), we need to predict a score on Y for each subject ($\hat{Y}$), find the difference between each subject's predicted ($\hat{Y}$) and actual (observed) scores on Y, square the differences, and add them up. Table 3.3 demonstrates this process. The Y column is the individual scores on Y, the X column is the corresponding individual scores on X. The $\hat{Y}$ column gives the scores on Y predicted by the bivariate regression model. Column 5 gives the difference between predicted and actual Y scores. The final column is the squared differences. If we sum up the squared differences, we find that the error for Model A is 15.617.

Total error (SST) is equal to error explained (SSR) and residual error (SSE_A). Recall that we already computed SSE for the simple compact Model C

Table 3.3   Calculating Error of a Bivariate Regression

Person	Y	X¹	$\hat{Y}$	$(Y - \hat{Y})$	$(Y - \hat{Y})^2$
1	2	8	4.060	−2.060	4.244
2	3	9	3.284	−0.284	0.081
3	3	9	3.284	−0.284	0.081
4	4	10	2.508	1.492	2.226
5	7	6	5.612	1.388	1.927
6	5	7	4.836	0.164	0.027
7	5	4	7.164	−2.164	4.683
8	7	5	6.388	0.612	0.375
9	8	3	7.94	0.06	0.004
10	9	1	9.492	−0.492	0.242
11	9	2	8.716	0.284	0.081
12	10	2	8.716	1.284	1.649
					$SSE_A = 15.617$

in Chapter 2 and found that SSE_C (also called SST) was 80. The difference between total error (SST = 80) and residual error (SSE_A = 15.617) is 64.383. So the error reduced by the model (SSR) is 64.383, leaving a residual of 15.617 error still unexplained. In other words, we partitioned the total error (SSE_C) into explained (reduced) error (SSR) and residual (still remaining) error (SSE_A).

It's difficult to judge if an error reduction of 64.383 is a lot or a little. To help us get a sense of how much error we reduced, we express this reduction in error as a percentage of the total error (SST) that we began with (see Equation 3.5). As you can see in Equation 3.5, Model A explained .805 of the original SST in variable Y.

$$\frac{SST - SSE_A}{SST} = \frac{80 - 15.617}{80} = \frac{64.383}{80} = .805. \tag{3.5}$$

◆ CENTERING THE PREDICTOR VARIABLE: MEAN DEVIATION OF X

For the simple model described in Chapter 2 ($Y = \beta_0 + \varepsilon$), β_0 was a constant equal to the mean of Y $(\overline{Y})$. Since the mean score of Y was 6, $\beta_0 = 6$.

These same Y scores were used for the example in this chapter. Notice, however, that when we calculated the regression equation for Model A, $\beta_0 \neq 6$. The estimate of β_0 ceased to be $\overline{Y}$ and became the predicted value of Y when $X = 0$. Oddly, X never equals zero in this data set, so predicting Y when $X = 0$, isn't very useful. The value of β_0 in this example seems rather meaningless. Furthermore, wouldn't it be sweet if we could set β_0 in Model A to equal $\overline{Y}$ as it did in Model C? Well, we can do that by subtracting a constant from each X value so that the mean of X becomes zero. The constant we subtract is the mean of X, and since we've subtracted the constant from every X, the distribution does not change. Judd et al. (2009) called this process of "centering" a variable around zero the *mean deviation*, and they distinguished it from X by placing a prime after it (X'). In Table 3.4, the mean of X (5.5) is subtracted from each person's score on X to give us X'.

Notice that the sum of X' is zero. This will always be the case when you've centered a variable around zero—the new mean is zero. Now, let's estimate β_1 using the X' values. Table 3.5 gives the sums of Y, X', X'^2, and $X' \times Y$ that we need to calculate β_1.

Table 3.4 Centering (Mean Deviating) X Around Zero

Person	Y	X − 5.5	=	X'
1	2	8 − 5.5	=	2.5
2	3	9 − 5.5	=	3.5
3	3	9 − 5.5	=	3.5
4	4	10 − 5.5	=	4.5
5	7	6 − 5.5	=	0.5
6	5	7 − 5.5	=	1.5
7	5	4 − 5.5	=	−1.5
8	7	5 − 5.5	=	−0.5
9	8	3 − 5.5	=	−2.5
10	9	1 − 5.5	=	−4.5
11	9	2 − 5.5	=	−3.5
12	10	2 − 5.5	=	−3.5
				$\Sigma = 0$

Table 3.5 Recomputing b_1 Using X' Instead of X

Person	Y	X'	X'²	X' × Y
1	2	2.5	6.25	5
2	3	3.5	12.25	10.5
3	3	3.5	12.25	10.5
4	4	4.5	20.25	18
5	7	0.5	0.25	3.5
6	5	1.5	2.25	7.5
7	5	−1.5	2.25	−7.5
8	7	−0.5	0.25	−3.5
9	8	−2.5	6.25	−20
10	9	−4.5	20.25	−40.5
11	9	−3.5	12.25	−31.5
12	10	−3.5	12.25	−35
$\Sigma =$	72	0	107	−83

The values in Table 3.5 can be inserted into the formula for b_1 (see Equation 3.6).

$$b_1 = \frac{\sum XY - \frac{(\sum X)(\sum Y)}{n}}{\sum X^2 - \frac{(\sum X)^2}{n}} = \frac{-83 - \frac{(0)(72)}{12}}{107 - \frac{(0)^2}{12}} = \frac{-83}{107} = -.776. \quad (3.6)$$

The estimate (b_1) of the regression slope (β_1) remained the same $(-.776)$. Centering or mean deviating X around zero did not change b_1. But what did it do to b_0? Let's estimate β_0 and find out (see Equation 3.7). Remember, the mean of X' is zero, so the means we insert for X' and Y are 0 and 6, respectively.

$$b_0 = \hat{Y} - b_1 X \quad \text{or} \quad b_0 = \hat{Y} - (-.776)X \quad \text{or} \quad b_0 = 6 - (-.776) \times 0$$

$$b_0 = 6 - 0 = 6. \quad (3.7)$$

Our estimate of β_0 has changed from 10.268 to 6, which is the mean of Y. So now our regression equation using X' instead of X is as follows:

$$Y = 6 - .776\, X' + \varepsilon.$$

There is elegance to centering X around zero. This new regression equation shows the exact same relationship between Y and X' as we found for Y and X, and if you calculate the error of this regression model, you will get the exact same SSE_A. But now, it can be fun to describe how the model predicts values of Y. To predict someone's score on Y, we begin by predicting the mean score of Y and then we take the person's score on X', multiply it by b_1, and add that value to the mean of Y. Frankly, beginning our prediction of Y with the mean of Y seems far less random than beginning the prediction with 10.268.

We have two models: both predict the mean but one adjusts that prediction based on the person's score on X'. We know that Model A had less error than Model C. But how exactly should we compare these two models? Chapter 4 introduces a 10-step approach to compare the augmented model with the simple compact model.

SUMMARY ◆

We constructed a bivariate regression equation in which one variable (X) was hypothesized as a predictor of the outcome variable (Y). The bivariate regression included an intercept value (β_0), which provided an initial prediction of Y, and a regression coefficient (β_1). The regression coefficient informed us how much our prediction of Y changed for every increase (or decrease) of one point in X. Once we obtained the regression equation, we were able to predict a value of Y ($\hat{Y}$) for each subject. Having a measured value of Y and a predicted value ($\hat{Y}$), we calculated the differences between Y and $\hat{Y}$, squared and summed the differences to obtain a SSE_A for this augmented model. The difference between the simple Model C's error and Model A's error was the amount of error reduced or explained by including $\beta_1 X$ in the model. We also saw that centering the predictor variable created an elegant Model A in which β_0 was the same for both Models A and C.

4

MODEL COMPARISON

The Simplest Model Versus a Regression Model

Every half truth is also a half lie . . .

The only truth worth exploring is the one that leads us closer to the center.

—Katherine Neville

The Magic Circle[1]

The regression equation is the basis of the general linear model (GLM), the model comparison approach, and a range of parametric statistics, from the t test to ANOVA to latent factors and structural equation models. In Chapter 2, we conceptualized GLM as follows:

$$Data = Model + Error.$$

Data are the actual scores, observations, or measurements of the outcome (dependent) variable (Y). The *Model* combines one or more predictor variables (and their corresponding regression coefficients) to predict data scores ($\hat{Y}$). *Error* is the model's accuracy predicting Y. The more accurately the model predicts Y, the better we understand the phenomenon we're interested in. Various labels are used to describe the basic GLM components (data, model, error). Some of these labels are listed in Table 4.1.

---

1. Neville, K. (1999). *The magic circle*. New York: Ballantine Books. Reprinted with permission.

Table 4.1 Corresponding Labels for the Components of the GLM

Data		Model		Error
Outcome	=	Predictor(s)	+	Residual
Y	=	$\beta_0 + \beta_1 X_1$	+	ε
DV	=	IV	+	Error

NOTE: DV = dependent variable; IV = independent variable.

I prefer to consider the model as a predictor of an outcome, where the outcome is the behavioral phenomenon I want to study. If I'm interested in neuropsychological consequences of methamphetamine use, then I'll try to build a model in which meth use predicts neuropsych functioning. That model would look like Equation 4.1.

$$\text{Neuropsych} = \beta_0 + \beta_1 \text{Meth} + \varepsilon. \qquad (4.1)$$

We can measure the error of the model in Equation 4.1, but knowing the error doesn't tell us if methamphetamine use is related to neuropsychological functioning. To answer that question, I need to compare the model with a model that doesn't have methamphetamine as a predictor (see Equation 4.2).

$$\text{Neuropsych} = \beta_0 + \varepsilon. \qquad (4.2)$$

◆ MODEL COMPARISON

Model comparison requires that we have two models that predict the same data. The models also must be "nested," which means that each element of the smaller, "compact" model must be present in the larger augmented model. When a researcher adds a new predictor to the previous model, the previous model is nested within the new model. For example, if we begin with a simple (compact) model that predicts the same score for every participant (Model C), and we enhance (augment) that compact model by adding an independent variable (Model A), then Model C is nested within Model A. Model A is Model C plus something new.

The comparison between Models A and C is conceptualized in the "model comparison box" shown in Table 4.2. What interests us right now is (a) how the models *differ* and (b) the difference in error generated by each model ($SSE_C - SSE_A$). The difference between these models is the addition of a single predictor and its regression coefficient ($\beta_1 X_1$). The difference in error generated by Models A and C is called the *sum of squares reduced*, or *SSR*; it is computed by subtracting SSE_A from SST (SSR = SST − SSE_A). Remember that SST is usually the same as SSE_C. Having added only one single predictor to Model A, we therefore can attribute all reduction in error (SSR) to the addition of that new predictor variable.

Table 4.2 Model Comparison Box—Demonstrating the Concept of Model Comparison

Model A:	$Y = \beta_0 + \beta_1 X_1 + SSE_A$
Model C:	$Y = \beta_0 + SSE_C$
Difference:	$\beta_1 X_1 + SSR$

If Model A is only as good as the Model C, then the error of Model A would exactly equal the error of Model C (SST = SSE_A). If the errors are equal, then SSR (SST − SSE_A) would be zero, and we'd conclude that adding the predictor variable X to create Model A didn't improve prediction of Y. If, on the other hand, Model A generated far less error than Model C, then SSR would be greater than zero. If SSR is large enough (a concept we'll address later), then we can conclude that X did improve prediction of Y.

10 STEPS TO COMPARE MODELS ♦

When we compare two models, we can follow a series of steps. These steps are listed in Table 4.3. We've already seen the model comparison box in Table 4.2. I've found it convenient to compile the information gathered from these 10 comparison steps into this comparison box. As we work through the 10 steps, we'll also add the information to the model comparison box.

Table 4.3 Steps for Comparing Two Models

1. State the compact Model C and an augmented Model A.
2. Identify the null hypothesis (H_0).
3. Count the number of parameters estimated by each model.
4. Calculate the regression equation.
5. Compute the total sum of squares (SSE_C).
6. Compute the sum of squares for Model A (SSE_A).
7. Compute sum of squares reduced (SSR).
8. Compute the proportional reduction in error (PRE or R^2).
9. Complete the summary table.
10. Decide about H_0.

Step 1: State the Compact Model C and an Augmented Model A

Model comparison begins with an initial model. The simplest parametric model predicts the grand mean ($\overline{Y}$) for each subject. In this case, for Model C we estimated a single parameter (β_0).

Model C:	$Y = \beta_0 + \varepsilon$

If we suspect that another variable, X, is related to the phenomenon we're studying (Y), we'll test this hypothesis by adding variable X to the model. The relationship between X and Y is described by a weight, the regression coefficient (β_1). Notice that adding a single predictor variable creates a bivariate regression: $Y = \beta_0 + \beta_1 X_1 + \varepsilon$. And we now have two models to compare.

Model A:	$Y = \beta_0 + \beta_1 X_1 + \varepsilon$
Model C:	$Y = \beta_0 + \varepsilon$

Step 2: Identify the Null Hypothesis (H_0)

The typical working hypothesis is that two variables (X and Y) are related; the null hypothesis (H_0) is that they are not related. A researcher wants to reject H_0.

By rejecting the null hypothesis, the researcher can infer that X and Y *are* related. Now, get this—if the variables are *not un*related, we can "infer" that they *are* related.

Consider the situation when X and Y are not related (H_0 is true). If H_0 is true and X and Y are unrelated, then changes in the value of X will have no effect on the value of Y. For the value of Y to be unaffected by changes in X, the relationship between X and Y must be zero. Since the relationship between X and Y is described by β_1, then H_0 is true when $\beta_1 = 0$. If $\beta_1 = 0$, then $\beta_1 X$ equals zero regardless of the value of X. Therefore, for the null hypothesis to be true, β_1 must equal 0.

We now have defined both models and the H_0.

Model A:	$Y = \beta_0 + \beta_1 X_1 + \varepsilon$
Model C:	$Y = \beta_0 + \varepsilon$
H_0:	$\beta_1 = 0$

Step 3: Count the Number of Parameters Estimated for Each Model

A parameter is any coefficient in a model that was calculated using data. Parameters are indicated with the Greek letter, beta (β). Counting the parameters in a model is as simple as counting the βs in the model. In this example, Model A had two parameters (β_0 and β_1), so we'll say the Model A parameters (noted as "PA") is equal to 2. Model C estimated a single parameter (β_0), so PC = 1.

Model A:	$Y = \beta_0 + \beta_1 X_1 + \varepsilon$	PA = 2
Model C:	$Y = \beta_0 + \varepsilon$	PC = 1
H_0:	$\beta_1 = 0$	

Step 4: Calculate the Regression Equation

Next we define the models by calculating the regression coefficients. For a bivariate regression model, we estimate those coefficients (β_0 and β_1) just as we did in Chapter 3.

Step 5: Compute the Total Sum of Squares (SSE_C or SST)

The SST is always the SSE for the simple Model C that predicts the mean score for each subject. The SST is computed just as it was computed in Chapter 2: Predict the mean score for each subject (i.e., $\beta_1 = \overline{Y}$), subtract the mean from each subject's actual score on $Y(Y_i - \overline{Y})$, square the difference $(Y_i - \overline{Y})^2$, and sum these squared differences $\left(\Sigma\left[Y_i - \overline{Y}\right]^2\right)$. The result is the SSE for Model C, or SST.

Model A:	$Y = \beta_0 + \beta_1 X_1 + \varepsilon$	PA = 2	
Model C:	$Y = \beta_0 + \varepsilon$	PC = 1	$SSE_C = \Sigma(Y_i - \overline{Y})^2$
H_0:	$\beta_1 = 0$		

Step 6: Compute the Sum of Squares for Model A (SSE_A)

The SSE for Model A is computed just as the error for the bivariate regression was computed in Chapter 3. Use Model A to predict a score for each subject $(\hat{Y}_i)$, find the difference between each actual and predicted score $\left(Y_i - \hat{Y}_i\right)$, square these differences $\left(Y_i - \hat{Y}_i\right)^2$, and sum them $\left(\Sigma\left[Y_i - \hat{Y}_i\right]^2\right)$.

Model A:	$Y = \beta_0 + \beta_1 X_1 + \varepsilon$	PA = 2	$SSE_A = \Sigma\left(Y_i - \hat{Y}_i\right)^2$
Model C:	$Y = \beta_0 + \varepsilon$	PC = 1	$SST = \Sigma\left(Y_i - \overline{Y}_i\right)^2$
H_0:	$\beta_1 = 0$		

Step 7: Compute Sum of Squares Reduced (SSR)

Once we know the error for each model, we can subtract SSE_A from SST to get the SSR. SSR tells us how much error was reduced by adding X to augment the model. If X is not related to Y, then there should be little to no difference in error generated by Models A and C, and SSR will be close to zero. On the other hand, if X is related to Y, then Model A should generate better predictions of Y than were generated by Model C, and SSR will be larger than zero. SSR will never be negative.

Model A:	$Y = \beta_0 + \beta_1 X_1 + \varepsilon$	PA = 2	$SSE_A = \sum\left(Y_i - \hat{Y}_i\right)^2$
Model C:	$Y = \beta_0 + \varepsilon$	PC = 1	$SST = \sum\left(Y_i - \bar{Y}_i\right)^2$
H_0:	$\beta_1 = 0$		$SSR = SST - SSE_A$

Step 8: Compute the Proportional Reduction in Error (PRE or R^2)

The value of SSR by itself conveys little information about the amount of error reduced by adding X relative to the total error we began with. In other words, the relative reduction in error between Model A and Model C will help us gauge how much adding X improved our prediction of Y. For example, an SSR of 15 is not much if SST = 1,000; it only reduced the error 1.5%. But, an SSR of 15 is a lot if SST = 20. In that case, X would have explained 75% of the error!

To address this issue, Judd and McClelland (1989) recommended calculating a *proportional* error reduction score. The "Proportional Reduction in Error" (PRE; Judd et al., 2009) is the ratio of reduced error (SSR) to initial total error (SST). Most researchers and statisticians might refer to PRE as the "variance explained" or R^2. PRE or R^2 is computed by dividing SSR by SST.

Model A:	$Y = \beta_0 + \beta_1 X_1 + \varepsilon$	PA = 2	$SSE_A = \sum\left(Y_i - \hat{Y}_i\right)^2$
Model C:	$Y = \beta_0 + \varepsilon$	PC = 1	$SST = \sum\left(Y_i - \bar{Y}_i\right)^2$
			$SSR = SST - SSE_A$
H_0:	$\beta_1 = 0$		$R^2 \ (PRE) = SSR \div SST$

Step 9: Complete the Summary Table

We've generated a lot of scores by this point, and we need a way to organize these scores so that they can help us make a decision about H_0. To manage this information, we use a summary table (Table 4.4). The summary table organizes information obtained in Steps 1 to 8 in a manner that allows us to calculate several pieces of information we'll need to finish our model comparison. These pieces of information include the *degrees of freedom* (*df*), mean square errors, and (ultimately) the *F ratio*. It's the *F* ratio that helps us answer the first key question about the relationship between the two variables: Are X and Y related?

The degrees of freedom (*df*) are based on the sample size (*N*) and the number of parameters in each model (PA and PC). The total *df* is the number of subjects minus 1 (*N* − 1). The *df* for the model comparison (top line of Table 4.4) is the difference in parameters between Models A and C (PA − PC). The residual *df* is the difference between total *df* and model comparison *df*.

The mean square (*MS*) is determined by dividing each *SSE* by its corresponding *df*. Finally, *F* is calculated by dividing *MS* for the model comparison by *MS* residual.

Step 10: Decide About H_0

Data collected in a research study are used to *estimate* the true relationship between X and Y. We'll never really know the true value of β_1, but if in reality β_1 truly does equal 0, the estimate (b_1) will probably (most often) be close to zero. Random influences, however, will likely make b_1 not exactly zero. On rare occasions, b_1 might even be quite different from zero even though β_1 is really zero. A researcher ultimately has to decide if (a) her estimate of β_1 (b_1) is sufficiently different from zero to infer that β_1 probably does not equal zero, or (b) b_1 is too close to zero to conclude that $\beta_1 \neq 0$. If the researcher decides that b_1 is different from zero, she rejects H_0. If she decides that b_1 is not different enough from zero, she fails to reject H_0.

To determine if X is related to Y (i.e., $\beta_0 \neq 0$), the researcher uses the information in the summary table to conduct an analysis of variance (ANOVA). The ANOVA generates an *F* ratio (Column 5 of Table 4.4). If two variables (X and Y) are *not* related, then *F* should hover around 1. If X and Y are truly not related, there is still a small chance (a low probability) that any given ANOVA will by fluke produce a large *F* ratio anyway. So when an ANOVA

Table 4.4 Summary Table

Source	SS	df	MS	F	R^2
Model comparison	SSR	PA − PC	$MS_{model} =$ SSR ÷ (PA − PC)	$MS_{model} \div MS_{residual}$	SSR ÷ SST
Residual	SSE_A	N − PA	$MS_{residual} =$ SSA ÷ (N − PA)		
Total	SST	N − PC			

NOTE: SSR is the reduction in error ($SSE_C - SSE_A$), SSE_C is the error of Model C, and SSE_A is the error of Model A.

produces an F ratio much larger than 1.0, the researcher needs to consider the probability (p) that she would get an F ratio that size if X and Y truly are not related. If the probability of getting an F ratio of a certain size is small,[2] then the researcher concludes that the F ratio is too large to believe the null hypothesis. Rather than assume that a large F is one of those rare times (fewer than 5 occurrences out of 100 or $p \leq .05$) when X and Y are not related ($\beta_1 = 0$) but F was large, it's simpler and far safer to reject H_0 and conclude that X and Y *are* related ($\beta_0 \neq 0$).

When we reject a H_0, we either make a correct decision (correctly reject a false H_0) or an error (rejected a true H_0). Rejecting a true H_0 is called a *Type I error*. We never know if we've made a Type I error, but we can know the probability that our decision to reject H_0 was a Type I error. The probability of making a Type I error is called α, and it is the same as the probability of getting an F ratio much larger than 1. By convention, we typically reject H_0 if $\alpha \leq .05$ and we fail to reject H_0 when $\alpha > .05$. How we determine the probability will be described in a later chapter.

MODEL COMPARISON EXAMPLE ◆

For now, let's explore these 10 steps using the small set of scores we used to demonstrate bivariate regression in Chapter 3. Table 4.5 gives these 12 pairs of scores.

Table 4.5 Pairs of Scores Used for Demonstrating Model Comparison

Person	Y	X
1	2	8
2	3	9
3	3	9
4	4	10
5	7	6
6	5	7

(Continued)

2. Conventionally, a small probability is considered as less than .05 or occurring fewer than 5 times out of 100.

Table 4.5 (Continued)

Person	Y	X
7	5	4
8	7	5
9	8	3
10	9	1
11	9	2
12	10	2

Step 1: Define the Initial, Compact Model C and an Augmented Model A

The compact model (Model C) predicts the mean of the dependent variable for every subject. The mean score on variable Y is 6, so Model C is $Y = 6 + error$. We augment Model C by adding a predictor variable, X. Thus, Model A will be $Y = \beta_0 + \beta_1 X_1 + \varepsilon$. This information is shown in the model comparison box below.

Model A:	$Y = \beta_0 + \beta_1 X_1 + \varepsilon$	PA =	$SSE_A =$
Model C:	$Y = 6 + \varepsilon$	PC =	$SSE_C =$
H_0:			R^2 (PRE) =

Step 2: Identify the Null Hypothesis (H_0)

The null hypothesis (H_0), that X and Y are *not* related, is true only when $\beta_1 = 0$. Therefore, H_0 is that $\beta_1 = 0$.

Model A:	$Y = \beta_0 + \beta_1 X_1 + \varepsilon$	PA =	$SSE_A =$
Model C:	$Y = 6 + \varepsilon$	PC =	SST =
H_0:	$\beta_1 = 0$		R^2 (PRE) =

Step 3: Count the Number of Parameters Estimated in Each Model

We estimated a single parameter for Model C (the mean of the scores on Y), so the parameters of Model C (PC) equal 1. Since we'll estimate two parameters for Model A (β_0 and β_1), PA equals 2.

Model A:	$Y = \beta_0 + \beta_1 X_1 + \varepsilon$	PA = 2	SSE_A =
Model C:	$Y = 6 + \varepsilon$	PC = 1	SST =
H_0:	$\beta_1 = 0$		R^2 (PRE) =

Step 4: Calculate the Regression Equation

The bivariate regression, Model A, was already estimated in Chapter 3 using these data. That equation was $\hat{Y} = 10.268 - .776X$, and it's been added to the model comparison box below.

Model A:	$Y = 10.268 - .776\ X_1 + \varepsilon$	PA = 2	SSE_A =
Model C:	$Y = 6 + \varepsilon$	PC = 1	SST =
H_0:	$\beta_1 = 0$		R^2 (PRE) =

Step 5: Compute the Total Sum of Squares (SST or SSE_C)

Model C predicted a score of 6 for every subject. Differences between actual and predicted scores ($Y - \overline{Y}_1$ or $Y - 6$) are squared and summed. In Chapter 2, we computed SST, and it was 80.

Model A:	$Y = 10.268 - .776\ X_1 + \varepsilon$	PA = 2	SSE_A =
Model C:	$Y = 6 + \varepsilon$	PC = 1	SST = 80
H_0:	$\beta_1 = 0$		R^2 (PRE) =

Step 6: Compute the Sum of Squares for Model A (SSE_A)

Error for Model A is calculated by using the regression model to generate a predicted score on Y. The predicted score ($\hat{Y}$) is subtracted from the actual value (Y), the difference squared, and the squared differences summed. In Chapter 3, we computed the SSE_A, which was 15.617.

Model A:	$Y = 10.268 - .776\, X_1 + \varepsilon$	PA = 2	$SSE_A = 15.617$
Model C:	$Y = 6 + \varepsilon$	PC = 1	SST = 80
H_0:	$\beta_1 = 0$		R^2 (PRE) =

Step 7: Compute Sum of Squares Reduced (SSR)

The difference in error between Model C and Model A ($SST - SSE_A$) is $80 - 15.617$, or 64.383.

Model A:	$Y = 10.268 - .776\, X_1 + \varepsilon$	PA = 2	$SSE_A = 15.617$
Model C:	$Y = 6 + \varepsilon$	PC = 1	SST = 80
			SSR = 64.383
H_0:	$\beta_1 = 0$		R^2 (PRE) =

Step 8: Compute the Proportional Reduction in Error (PRE or R^2)

Dividing SSR (64.383) by SST (80), we get an R^2 of .805. An R^2 of .805 tells us that adding $\beta_1 X_1$ to the model reduced or explained 80.5% of the error in Model C.

Model A:	$Y = 10.268 - .776\, X_1 + \varepsilon$	PA = 2	$SSE_A = 15.617$
Model C:	$Y = 6 + \varepsilon$	PC = 1	SST = 80
			SSR = 64.383
H_0:	$\beta_1 = 0$		R^2 (PRE) = .805

The first eight model comparison steps are listed in Table 4.6.

Step 9: Complete the Summary Table

We now have all of the components we need to complete the summary table (Table 4.7). Total SS (SST) is 80, residual SSE (SSE_A) is 15.617, and SSR is 64.383.

Table 4.6   Results of the first 8 steps comparing Models A and C

Step	
1	State the compact Model C and an augmented Model A.
	Model C: $\hat{Y} = \beta_0$
	Model A: $\hat{y} = \beta_0 + \beta_1 X_1$
2	Identify the null hypothesis (H_0)
	H_0: $\beta_1 = 0$
3	Count the number of parameters estimated by each model
	PA = 2
	PC = 1
4	Calculate the regression equation
	Model C: $\hat{Y} = 6$
	Model A: $\hat{Y} = 10.268 - .776X_1$
5	Compute total sum of squares (SSE_C)
	$SSE_C = 80$
6	Compute sum of squares for Model A (SSE_A)
	$SSE_A = 15.617$
7	Compute sum of squares reduced (SSR)
	SSR = 64.383
8	Compute the proportional reduction in error (PRE or R^2)
	PRE = R^2 = .805

Total *df* ($N - $ PC) is $12 - 1$ or 11. Residual *df* ($N - $ PA) is $12 - 2$ or 10. Therefore, 1 *df* was used for this analysis (entered on the Model Comparison line). By dividing the error explained (or reduced) by Model A (SSR) by the number of *df* for the model (1), we get MS_{model} (which is 64.383). Dividing the residual error (SSE_A) by the residual number of *df* (10) gives $MS_{residual}$ (1.562). The *F* ratio is calculated by dividing MS_{model} by $MS_{residual}$:
$F = 64.383 \div 1.562 = 41.218$.

Table 4.7 Summary Table

Source	SS	df	MS	F	R^2
Model comparison	64.383	1	64.383	41.218	.805
Residual	15.617	10	1.562		
Total	80	11			

NOTE: SSR is the reduction in error ($SST - SSE_A$), SST is the error of Model C, and SSE_A is the error of Model A.

Step 10: Decide About H_0

This F ratio (41.22) clearly does not equal 1.0. We next need to determine the probability that we could get an F of 41.22 if X and Y truly are not related. The probability of getting an F of 41.22 will depend on how many df we used (in this example, we used 1 because PA − PC = 1) and the number of residual df we have (in this example, residual df is 10). An $F \geq 41.22$, with 1 and 10 df, would happen fewer than 1 time out of a thousand if H_0 is true. In other words, if X and Y really are not related to each other, and we repeated this study 1,000 times, we might get an $F \geq 41.22$ once. That's pretty rare; certainly less than .05. If we reject H_0 (and we'd be silly not to), the probability that we would make a Type I error (i.e., rejected a true H_0) is miniscule (less than one out of 1,000). Certainly it's safest to reject H_0.

The beauty of this analysis is that it answered all three fundamental statistical questions from Chapter 1. The unusually large F led us to reject H_0 and infer that X and Y are related (Question 1). The negative regression coefficient (−.776) indicated that X and Y have an inverse (negative) relationship: As X gets larger, Y gets smaller (Question 2). Finally, R^2 revealed the strength or magnitude of the relationship between X and Y (Question 3). The R^2 of .805 means that by adding X to create Model A, we reduced 80% of the error produced by just predicting the mean score of Y for every subject (Model C).

◆ SUMMARY

In this chapter, we identified and compared two regression models that differed by the addition of a single predictor variable X. When the error associated with the augmented (more complex) model (Model A) is sufficiently less than the error associated with the compact (simpler) model (Model C), we can conclude that the addition of the new predictor in Model A improved prediction of the outcome variable (Y). We used the results of the statistical analysis to compute a single statistic, the F ratio, that we used to infer the relationship between X and Y. When F is unusually large (probability, p, less than 5 times out of 100 or $p \le .05$), we reject the H_0 that X and Y are unrelated. Consequently, we infer that X is related to Y. Had the error of Model A not been sufficiently less than the error of Model C, we would have obtained a much smaller F and concluded that adding the new predictor (X) did not improve our prediction of Y.

PART II

Fundamental Statistical Tests

5

CORRELATION

Traditional and Regression Approaches

Science is organized knowledge. Wisdom is organized life.

—Immanuel Kant

In Chapter 1, I identified three fundamental questions that a statistical analysis should answer. Question 1 asked whether or not two variables are related to each other. If two variables are related, then we want to know the direction of the relationship: As one variable increases, does the second variable increase or decrease (Question 2)? We also want to know the strength or magnitude of the relationship between the two variables (Question 3). Questions 2 and 3 are somewhat inseparable—they reveal the *magnitude* and *direction* of the relationship between the variables.

MAGNITUDE

The strength or magnitude of a relationship between two variables can span from nonexistent to weak to very strong or nearly perfect. A perfect relationship exists when a change in one variable corresponds precisely and consistently to a change in the second variable. Perfect relationships are rare and frankly not interesting. If a relationship exists but it is not a perfect relationship, then we want to know how close to (or far from) perfect the relationship is. A correlation coefficient is a statistic that describes the degree to which an association between two variables departs from the perfect. The correlation coefficient reveals to us the magnitude of association between the two variables. Values of the correlation coefficient (designated by a lowercase r) range from −1 to +1. If a perfect relationship exists, then r is either −1 or +1. As the relationship departs from the perfect, r approaches 0. A correlation coefficient equal to 0 indicates that there is absolutely no relationship between the two variables. The variables are as different as yin and yang, Pinky and the Brain, or chocolate chocolate-chip ice cream (yum!) and pungent, overcooked broccoli (yuk!).

◆ DIRECTION

The correlation coefficient also describes the direction of a relationship between two variables. A *positive correlation* ($r > 0$) indicates that as scores on one variable increase, scores on the other variable also increase. A *negative correlation* ($r < 0$) indicates an *inverse* relationship: As scores on one variable increase, scores on the other variable decrease.

The correlation coefficient informs us whether two variables are related (i.e., whether r is reliably different from 0), how strong the relationship is (i.e., how different r is from 0), and the direction of the relationship (i.e., whether r is positive or negative). A correlation coefficient, therefore, answers the three questions from Chapter 1. Although correlations can be conceptualized and calculated in many ways, I'll review the most common computational approach: the Pearson product moment correlation coefficient. Unless otherwise specified, the term *correlation* usually refers to the Pearson correlation (Warner, 2008). Before computing a correlation, though, let's first visualize what a correlation looks like.

◆ PICTURE THE CORRELATION

Let's return to the data we used in Chapters 3 and 4 to compute a bivariate regression and compare models. These data are given again in Table 5.1. We have 12 participants, and each person has a score on variable X and a score on variable Y.

We graph these data along two axes (horizontal and vertical) and, by convention, place variable X along the horizontal axis and variable Y along the vertical axis (see Figure 5.1). We place a dot on the graph for each person at the point where his or her X score intersects with his or her Y score. For example, Person 1 had a score of 8 on variable X and 2 on variable Y. We move out 8 points on the horizontal (X) axis and up 2 points along the vertical

Table 5.1 Pairs of Scores Used for Demonstrating a Model Comparison

Person	Y	X
1	2	8
2	3	9
3	3	9
4	4	10
5	7	6
6	5	7
7	5	4
8	7	5
9	8	3
10	9	1
11	9	2
12	10	2

(*Y*) axis, and we put a dot at that spot to represent Person 1. Once we've plotted the *X* and *Y* scores for each person in our sample, we have created a *scatterplot* of the relationship between the scores on *X* and the scores on *Y*.

The scatterplot gives us our first hunch about the relationship between variables *X* and *Y*. Look for two things in the graph: (1) do the scores cluster to resemble a line, or do they form a big circular glob, and (2) if they approach a line, in what direction does the line slope? Looking at Figure 5.1, the dots generally form a line, and the line slopes downward as you move from left to right along the *x*-axis (horizontal axis). When the dots in a scatterplot approximate a line or, perhaps, a cigar shape, it gives us our first hunch that there is a relationship between the two variables. When the cigar formed by the dots slopes downward as you move from left to right across the *x*-axis, it suggests that the relationship between *X* and *Y* is negative: As the scores on *X* get larger, the scores on *Y* get smaller. If the cigar slopes upward, then as *X* increases, *Y* increases, and their relationship is positive.

Figure 5.2 presents four basic ways in which two variables might relate to each other. In the upper left quadrant, we see that the cluster of dots resembles a cigar shape, and the cigar slopes upward as we move along the *x*-axis. When we see a scatterplot such as this, we suspect that the two variables have

Figure 5.1 Scatterplot Graph of Variables X (Horizontal Axis) and Y (Vertical Axis).

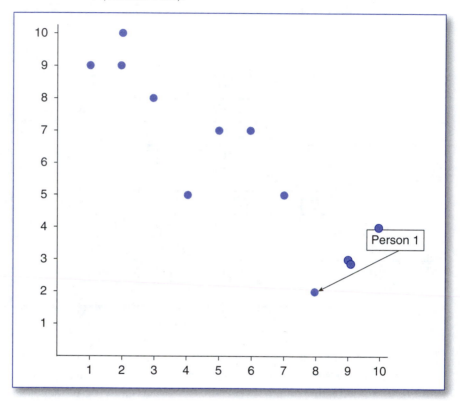

a positive relationship. The upper right quadrant reflects a negative relationship where the dots cluster to form a cigar shape that slopes downward as we move right along the x-axis. Notice the similarity between this plot and the scatterplot in Figure 5.1.

In the lower left quadrant of Figure 5.2, the dots don't form a line at all. In fact, they look like they form a ball or a big zero. When two variables are not related, the dots don't cluster other than to look like a big scatter, as if you've dropped a vase and the shards of broken crystal have spewn across the floor in all directions. Finally, the dots in the lower right quadrant form a curved line. This type of scatter plot suggests that the two variables might be related but the direction of the relationship (positive or negative) is different at lower versus higher levels of X. In this "curvilinear" scatterplot, it looks like the scores on Y increase as the scores on X increase at lower values of X, but the scores on Y appear to decrease as the scores on X increase at higher values of X. The scores on Y appear unrelated to values in the middle ranges of X.

Figure 5.2   Basic Ways in Which Variables *X* and *Y* Might Be Related.

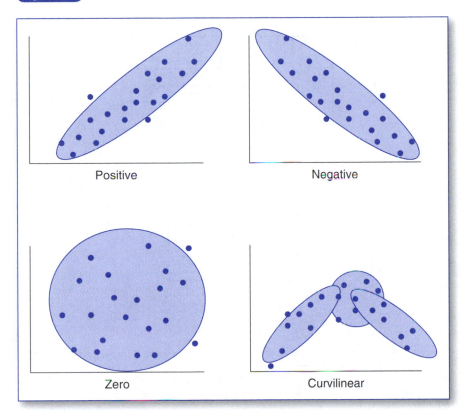

CALCULATE THE CORRELATION   ◆

The scatterplot provides a visual sense of how two variables are related. It's the correlation coefficient, however, that confirms the impression given by the scatterplot. To compute a correlation, we need to know two things: (a) the total or combined error of variables *X* and *Y* and (b) the common error shared by both variables.

Look at Figure 5.3, and imagine that the error of variable *X* is represented by Box *A* and the error of variable *Y* is represented by Box *C*. Variables *X* and *Y* "share" or overlap on some of their error. In the second panel in Figure 5.3, Boxes *A* and *C* overlap, and area *B* (with the crossed hash marks) represents the error shared between variables *X* and *Y*. The correlation coefficient is the ratio of the shared error (area *B*) to the combined areas. To calculate the correlation, we need to first find the total or combined error and then calculate the shared or common error.

Figure 5.3 Demonstration of Total and Shared Error.

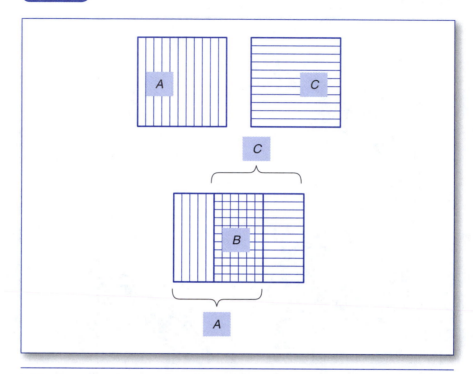

NOTE: Square A is the error of variable X, and square C is the error of variable Y. The two errors overlap at the crossed hash marks (B). B is the shared error variance; A + C − B is the total error variance.

Total or Combined Variance

The variance of two variables (*X* and *Y*) can be combined to provide a measure of how much total variance exists among the two variables. Total variance (or combined variance) is the square root of the product of the sum of squared errors (*SSE*) of *X* and the *SSE* of *Y* (Kenny, 1987) (see Equation 5.1 below).

$$\text{Combined variance} = \sqrt{SSE_X \times SSE_Y}. \tag{5.1}$$

In Chapter 2, we learned a conceptual formula to compute *SSE*. We insert the conceptual formulas for SSE_X and SSE_Y into Equation 5.1 to create an equation that will give us the combined variance:

$$\text{Combined variance} = \sqrt{\sum(X - \bar{X})^2 \times \sum(Y - \bar{Y})^2}. \tag{5.2}$$

Although Equation 5.2 can be used to calculate the combined variance of two variables, it's somewhat clumsy. Recall that in Chapter 2 we identified a convenient computational formula that calculated *SSE* much more easily than the conceptual formula. By replacing the conceptual formula with the computational formula, we get a more manageable formula for combined variance:

$$\text{Combined variance} = \sqrt{\left[\sum X^2 - \frac{(\sum X)^2}{N}\right]\left[\sum Y^2 - \frac{(\sum Y)^2}{N}\right]}. \qquad (5.3)$$

Equation 5.3 will become the denominator of the formula for the correlation coefficient.

Common or Shared Variance

A portion of the combined error can be shared by the two variables. Shared variance refers to how much the two variables tend to move or vary together. This common or shared error variance is called the *covariance* of *X* and *Y* (Kahane, 2001). We calculate the shared error in a way that is similar to calculating the *SSE* of a single variable. We still find the difference between each score and its mean, but in this case we do it for the two variables (*X* and *Y*) simultaneously. This time, however, instead of squaring the difference between a score and its corresponding mean, we multiply each person's difference on one variable $(X - \bar{X})$ with the difference on the other variable $(Y - \bar{Y})$. We calculate this product of the differences, $(X - \bar{X})(Y - \bar{Y})$, for each subject. Once we have a product of the differences for each subject, we sum them. Kenny (1987) called this the "sum of cross products" (p. 111). Notice that this conceptual formula for the sum of cross products (Equation 5.4) resembles the conceptual formula for *SSE* (Equation 5.2).

$$\text{Sum of cross products} = \sum (X - \bar{X})(Y - \bar{Y}). \qquad (5.4)$$

Fortunately, as with variance, we can use a more efficient computational formula to calculate the covariance between two variables:

$$\text{Sum of cross products} = \sum XY - \frac{(\sum Y)(\sum X)}{N}. \qquad (5.5)$$

Pearson Correlation Coefficient

The correlation coefficient is obtained by dividing the sum of cross products (Equation 5.5) by the combined variance (Equation 5.3). The complete formula for a correlation coefficient is given in Equation 5.6:

$$r = \frac{\sum XY - \frac{(\sum Y)(\sum X)}{N}}{\sqrt{\left[\sum X^2 - \frac{(\sum X)^2}{N}\right]\left[\sum Y^2 - \frac{(\sum Y)^2}{N}\right]}} \qquad (5.6)$$

Adding the shared and unshared variance together gives us the combined variance; the shared variance is a portion of the combined variance. The correlation coefficient tells us what proportion of the combined variance is shared, so the value of r can never be larger than +1 or smaller than −1. It can, however, equal 0.

♦ DEMONSTRATION

To demonstrate how to calculate a correlation coefficient, we'll again use the data from our examples in Chapters 3 and 4 (see Table 5.1). To complete Equation 5.6, we'll need the following pieces of information: the sum of all Y scores ($\sum Y$), the sum of all X scores ($\sum X$), the sum of all squared Y scores ($\sum Y^2$), the sum of all squared X scores ($\sum X^2$), and the sum of the $X \times Y$ products ($\sum XY$). Table 5.2 is laid out to give us all the information we need to compute the correlation coefficient.

By substituting the pieces of information from Table 5.2 into Equation 5.6, we get

$$(1) \quad r = \frac{313 - \frac{(66)(72)}{12}}{\sqrt{\left(470 - \frac{(66)^2}{12}\right)\left(512 - \frac{(72)^2}{12}\right)}}.$$

And now, reduce to solve this equation for r:

$$(2) \quad r = \frac{313 - 396}{\sqrt{(470 - 363)(512 - 432)}} = \frac{-83}{\sqrt{(107)(80)}} = \frac{-83}{\sqrt{8560}} = \frac{-83}{92.52} = -.897.$$

Table 5.2 Variables X and Y, X^2 and Y^2, and the Cross Product of X and Y $(X \times Y)$

Person	Y	Y^2	X	X^2	$X \times Y$
1	2	4	8	64	16
2	3	9	9	81	27
3	3	9	9	81	27
4	4	16	10	100	40
5	7	49	6	36	42
6	5	25	7	49	35
7	5	25	4	16	20
8	7	49	5	25	35
9	8	64	3	9	24
10	9	81	1	1	9
11	9	81	2	4	18
12	10	100	2	4	20
Σ	72	512	66	470	313

The resulting correlation coefficient (−.897) tells us that the relationship between X and Y is not perfect (i.e., $r \neq +1$ or -1), but it also is not equal to 0. We suspect that the relationship is large because it is close to −1 and far from 0, and we know that the relationship is negative (i.e., as scores on X increase, scores on Y decrease). The fact that r is quite different from 0 leads us to suspect that X and Y are related or correlated. This simple correlation has answered all three of the questions identified in Chapter 1: (1) Are X and Y related? (2) How strong is their relationship? (2) What direction is their relationship?

NULL HYPOTHESIS AND CORRELATION ◆

A correlation of −.897 is pretty close to −1, so we might easily concluded that X and Y are related. But what if we had obtained an r of −.15? Would we still feel confident concluding that X and Y are correlated? What if r was −.05? At what point would we consider r to be too close to 0 for us to conclude that a true relationship exists between X and Y? To answer that question, we need to determine the *statistical significance* of r. As with bivariate regression, we begin with a null hypothesis (H_0).

The null hypothesis for a correlation is that no association exists between the two constructs and therefore the correlation is 0 (H_0: $r = 0$). If there is no real association between X and Y (H_0 is true), then we expect the calculated r to equal or be close to 0. A calculated r may not exactly equal 0 even though H_0 is true. Still, if H_0 is true, we expect that most of the time the r that we calculate will be very small, if not 0. When r is close to 0, we typically decide not to reject H_0, and if r is sufficiently different from 0, we decide to reject H_0.

On occasion, rotten luck might curse us with an unusually large r even though H_0 is true. When we decide to reject H_0 because the calculated r is large, we recognize and acknowledge the possibility that this might be one of those unusual circumstances when H_0 is true and r should be 0, but we obtained a large calculated r anyway. Therefore, when we report r, we also report the probability of getting that value of r if H_0 is really true.

If we obtain an r that has a low probability of occurring if H_0 is true, then we decide that the odds are in our favor to reject H_0, and we hope we are making a correct decision and not a Type I error.[1] By convention, we define a low probability as a 5% or lower chance, or $p \le .05$.[2]

If we obtain an r that has a high probability of occurring when H_0 is true, then the odds are in our favor if we do not reject H_0, and we hope we are making a correct decision and not a *Type II error*. A Type II error occurs when H_0 is false and should be rejected, but we decide not to.

Calculating the probability of an r of a certain size isn't something we can do easily. The probability of obtaining a certain r depends on the size of the sample. With small samples, random errors have a greater impact on the calculation of r. Thus, an unusually large r occurs more often with small samples than with larger samples. Fortunately, computer programs that calculate the correlation coefficient will automatically give you the probability of that correlation coefficient occurring if the null hypothesis is true.

If you've computed a correlation coefficient by hand, you can estimate the probability of that coefficient by using a table of probabilities. To use such a table, you need to calculate the *degrees of freedom (df)* for this correlation test.

"Degrees of freedom," which we first dealt with in Chapter 3, is a devilish thing to explain. You may recall from Chapter 3 that *df* was related to the number of subjects you had and the number of parameters you calculated. Look again at the conceptual formula for the numerator (Equation 5.3) and denominator (Equation 5.4) of the correlation. Observe that we computed two parameters (the mean of X and the mean of Y). Subtracting these two

---

1. Recall from Chapter 4 that a Type I error occurs when we reject a true H_0.

2. "$p < .05$" is the notation for "probability less than or equal to 5%.

parameters from the total sample size (N), we get our df: $N - 2 = 12 - 2 = 10$. As you work through this book, you'll acquire an "implicit" understanding of df. With patience, as we get into the general linear model, eventually the concept of df will begin to make sense to you.

Well armed with our knowledge that df is 10 and r is .897, I can venture into a correlation table that will tell me the smallest value of r needed to reject H_0 with a probability less than or equal to 5% ($p \le .05$) of making a Type I error. Whether determined by a computer statistics program or a correlation table, the probability of obtaining $r = .897$ with $df = 10$ if H_0 is true is smaller than 1 in 1,000. With such a low probability ($p \le .001$), we should reject H_0. Since H_0 predicted that X and Y are not related, by rejecting H_0, we can infer that X and Y are related.

CORRELATION COEFFICIENT AND VARIANCE EXPLAINED ◆

We have a correlation ($r = -.897$) that describes the strength of the relationship between variables X and Y. In Chapter 4, the bivariate regression also gave us a statistic (proportional reduction in error [PRE] or R^2) that described the relationship between X and Y ($R^2 = .805$). In fact, if we take the square root of R^2, we have the correlation: $\sqrt{R^2} = r$, $\sqrt{.805} = .897$. So the regression analysis also gave us r—we needed only to take the square root of the variance explained to get the correlation coefficient. We know the sign of r (the direction of the relationship) from the sign of the regression coefficient. If b_1 is negative, then r too is negative. If b_1 is positive, then r is positive.

SUMMARY ◆

The correlation coefficient addresses all three research questions: (1) Are the variables related (i.e., is H_0 true or false?) (2) How strong is their relationship? (3) What is the direction of their relationship?

Correlation is an index of how much two variables vary or change together. Scores on a variable vary, and scores on two different variables will covary to some extent (the shared variance) and vary independently of each other to some extent (the unshared variance). A correlation coefficient is the ratio of the shared variance (covariance) to the total (shared plus unshared) variance. The coefficient ranges from a perfect relationship between the two variables (either $r = -1$ or $r = +1$) to absolutely no relationship between the variables ($r = 0$).

6

THE TRADITIONAL *t* TEST

Concepts and Demonstration

Weary the path that does not challenge.

Doubt is an incentive to truth and patient inquiry leadeth the way.

—Hosea Ballou

The correlation tested the relationship between two continuous variables, and as we've seen, the bivariate regression likewise described the relationship between two continuous variables. The bivariate regression also can give us the correlation between the variables by taking the square root of R^2. Regression variables often are continuous, which raises the question of how to test a relationship between two variables when one is not continuous (i.e., a categorical or group variable). This chapter introduces one way to test a relationship between one continuous and one categorical variable.

Experimental and quasi-experimental research designs investigate whether a categorical independent variable (X) is related to a continuous dependent variable (Y). In both experimental and quasi-experimental designs, the dependent variable (DV) is continuous but the independent variable (IV) is categorical. The simplest categorical variable is dichotomous—it has only two possible scores. Both possible scores on X represent or identify a group, category, or level. Even though a dichotomous variable consists of two groups, the "scores" still vary between which group a participant is in. The experimentalist uses statistics to decide if scores on a DV depend on or are related to which group a subject is in. Thus, we're still asking if the two variables (the DV or Y and the IV or X) are related.

In a study with a dichotomous IV, asking if scores on the DV (variable Y) change as scores on the IV (variable X) change is the same as asking if scores on Y are different, on average, among members of Group 1 than among members of Group 2. Therefore, an obvious statistical approach is to compare directly the mean score on Y for Group 1 with the mean score on Y for Group 2.

◆ COMPARING GROUP MEANS

To compare the mean scores from two groups, we routinely use the t test. The t test helps us decide if the mean score for Group 1 is different from the mean score for Group 2. If the mean score on variable Y is different for Group 1 than for Group 2, then we conclude that differences in variable X (group assignment or membership) are related to scores on variable Y, and therefore variables X and Y are related. If the t test leads us to conclude that mean scores for the two groups are different, then we conclude that how someone scores on variable Y depends on which group (or level) of the IV that person came from.

When comparing two groups, the *null hypothesis* is that the mean score on the DV for Group 1 $(\bar{Y}_1)$ is not different from the mean score on the DV for Group 2 $(\bar{Y}_2)$. Put another way, the null hypothesis is that $\bar{Y}_1$ and $\bar{Y}_2$ are equal $(H_0 : \bar{Y}_1 = \bar{Y}_2)$. The alternative or working hypothesis is that the mean value on the DV for Group 1 is different from the mean value of the DV for Group 2 $(H_A : \bar{Y}_1 \neq \bar{Y}_2)$.

In an ideal world, we would just look at the two mean scores to see if they are identical. If identical, then we would conclude that group membership does not affect scores on the DV (we wouldn't reject H_0). If $\bar{Y}_1$ and $\bar{Y}_2$ were not identical, we would infer that group membership was somehow related to someone's score on the DV (we'd reject H_0). Remember, though, that statistics based on samples only estimate real-world parameters. A sample mean is subject to error—there is a "band" of error surrounding a mean calculated from a sample. Thus, two different sample mean scores may not necessarily represent a true difference in the population means if those error bands overlap considerably. To conduct a t test, we must go beyond merely comparing the group means and consider also the error around each sample mean.

To illustrate the t-test concept, consider the four extreme scenarios depicted in Figure 6.1. In one scenario, two group means can be very close together with a wide range of scores around each mean (see Figure 6.1, Panel a). In this case, the difference between the means appears small relative to the large score variation in each group. In such a case, we'd likely fail to reject the H_0 because it doesn't really look like the means are all that much different, given the amount of score variation.

In the second scenario, the difference between two group means might be very large, and the variance around the means very narrow (Figure 6.1, Panel b). In this case, the difference in means relative to the variance in scores makes it look like scores on *Y* are very different for the two groups. This time, we'd likely reject H_0 and conclude that the group someone belongs to will influence that person's score on *Y*.

Figure 6.1 Sample Relationships Between the Numerator and the Denominator of the t Score.

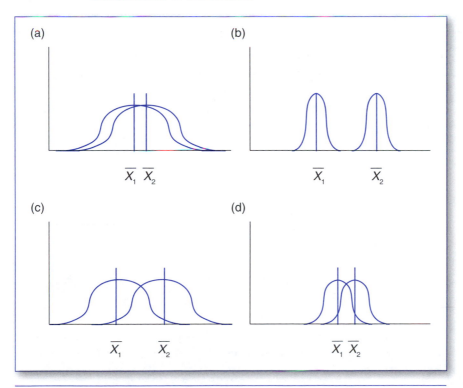

NOTES: (a) Means might be close together with considerable variation around the means. (b) Means might be far apart with little variation around the means. (c) Means might be far apart and have considerable variation around them. Finally, (d) means might be close together with small variation around them.

Scenarios a and b are fairly unambiguous. The next two scenarios, however, generate equivocal conclusions. The two means can appear quite different, yet large score dispersion around the means makes it unclear whether the means are really different (Figure 6.1, Panel c). Finally, scores surrounding two means might form narrow distributions, but the means themselves might not differ greatly (Figure 6.1, Panel d). The small difference in means relative to the little bit of variance in scores makes it difficult again to conclude whether the means were really all that different.

Fortunately, the *t* test guides our decision about whether the group means are different by taking into consideration the size of the difference in mean scores relative to the amount of variation in scores around the means. Like the correlation, the *t*-test equation is a ratio. In the *t* test, the difference between means (the numerator) is divided by the pooled variance of scores (the denominator).

◆ *t*-TEST FORMULA

The formula for the *t* test (Equation 6.1) is simple in concept. The numerator of *t* directly compares the two group means by subtracting one from the other $(\bar{Y}_1 - \bar{Y}_2)$. The denominator of *t* adjusts the difference in means by dividing the mean difference by the pooled variance in the scores from each group (S^2_{pooled}).

$$t = \frac{\bar{Y}_1 - \bar{Y}_2}{S^2_{pooled}}. \tag{6.1}$$

The pooled variance (S^2_{pooled}) is a combination of the variance of Group 1 (S^2_1) and the variance of Group 2 (S^2_2). These variances are pooled using the formula in Equation 6.2.

$$S^2_{pooled} = \sqrt{\frac{(N_1 - 1)S^2_1 + (N_2 - 1)S^2_2}{N_1 + N_2 - 2}\left(\frac{1}{N_1} + \frac{1}{N_2}\right)}. \tag{6.2}$$

By inserting the formula for S^2_{pooled} (Equation 6.2) into Equation 6.1, we have the formula to compute the *t* test (Equation 6.3). We need only fill in the values to solve for *t*.

$$t = \frac{\bar{Y}_1 - \bar{Y}_2}{\sqrt{\frac{(N_1 - 1)S^2_1 + (N_2 - 1)S^2_2}{N_1 + N_2 - 2}\left(\frac{1}{N_1} + \frac{1}{N_2}\right)}}. \tag{6.3}$$

Let's look closely at this *t*-test formula with regard to our examples in Figure 6.1. In Panel a of Figure 6.1, the means are close together, so the numerator of *t* $(\bar{Y}_1 - \bar{Y}_2)$ will be small. The scores vary widely around these means, so the pooled variance (denominator of *t*) will be large. A small numerator and a large denominator produce a small *t*. Therefore, when group means are not different, *t* should be small. In Panel b, $\bar{Y}_1 - \bar{Y}_2$ is large, so the numerator of *t* is large, and the pooled variance (denominator of *t*) is small. A large numerator and a small denominator result in a large *t*. So if group means are different, *t* should be large (either in a positive or a negative direction). Panels c and d are more equivocal: A large mean difference in the numerator is offset by a large pooled variance in the denominator in Panel c, and a small mean difference is divided by a small pooled variance in Panel d.

Let's consider what the value of *t* should be if the null hypothesis (H_0) is true. H_0 asserts that $\bar{Y}_1$ and $\bar{Y}_2$ are equal. As the difference between $\bar{Y}_1$ and $\bar{Y}_2$ becomes smaller, the value of *t* approaches zero. When $\bar{Y}_1$ is exactly equal to $\bar{Y}_2$ (as the null hypothesis asserts), then the numerator of *t* is zero, and therefore *t* must equal zero. Thus, when the null hypothesis is true, $\bar{Y}_1 = \bar{Y}_2$, the true *t*-test value should equal zero.

Because $\bar{Y}_1$ and $\bar{Y}_2$ are estimates of the true group means, the estimates may not be identical even though the true population means are equal (H_0 is true). As differences between $\bar{Y}_1$ and $\bar{Y}_2$ increase, the value of *t* will no longer equal zero—*t* becomes increasingly different from zero, either in a positive (if $\bar{Y}_1 > \bar{Y}_2$) or a negative (if $\bar{Y}_1 < \bar{Y}_2$) direction.

If H_0 is true, we should expect our estimated *t* test to be zero or very close to zero. As a *t* test gets farther from zero, our confidence that the true *t*-test value is zero begins to fade. As with a correlation, we can find the probability of getting a certain value of *t* when H_0 is true (i.e., when the *t* test *should* equal zero).

USING *t* TO DECIDE ABOUT H_0 ♦

If a small *t* test (close to zero) implies that the two group means probably are not different, then an unusually large *t* test (i.e., one that is quite different from zero, either in a positive or a negative direction) implies that the means are different and H_0 is false. But how much different from zero does *t* need to be for us to decide that the group means are different and H_0 is false? That decision is based on the *probability* of getting that *t* value if in reality H_0 is true. If the probability is low that we would get our value of *t* when H_0 is really true, then we suspect H_0 is not true, and we reject it.

The *t* Distribution

Imagine that we could repeat the same study many many thousands of times and obtain a *t* value for each study. Imagine too that H_0 is true: $\overline{Y}_1 = \overline{Y}_2$. We could graph those thousands of *t* values: Across the horizontal axis are the *t*-test values, and up the vertical axis is the frequency of occurrence of each *t* value. When H_0 is true, then the true value of *t* is zero, and we'd expect most of our estimates of *t* to be zero or fairly close to zero. The distribution of our thousands of estimates of *t* values would resemble a normal (symmetrical) curve with the central tendency at zero (the true value of *t* when H_0 is true). Most *t* values will be close to zero and few *t* values farther away from zero. Figure 6.2 shows how *t*-test scores are distributed when H_0 is true. Even though most *t*-test scores equal or are close to zero, there are those rare and pesky occurrences when we obtain a *t* value that is an unusually different from zero (those that fall in the striped sections under the curve) even though H_0 is really true.

Although the probability is small that we'd get an unusually large *t* when the null hypothesis is true, *it is not impossible!* So when a researcher decides to reject H_0 because of an unusually large *t*, there is a small, but not impossible, chance that H_0 is true. When a researcher rejects a true H_0, we call it a Type I error.

Figure 6.2 Distribution of *t* Test Scores.

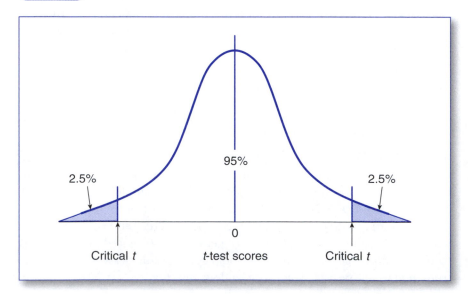

95%

2.5%

2.5%

0

Critical *t*

t-test scores

Critical *t*

We define an unusually large *t* test based on the *probability* of obtaining that *t* value when the null hypothesis is true. As with regression, the conventional definition of *unusual* is a *t*-test value that would only occur 5 or fewer times out of 100 (probability "*p*" ≤ .05) when the null hypothesis is true. Look at Figure 6.2. Ninety-five percent of the *t*-test scores either equal zero or fall close to zero, but 2.5% are quite a bit larger than zero (shaded area to the right of 0) and 2.5% are quite a bit lower than zero (shaded area to the left of 0). The "critical value of *t*" is that point at which a *t* value becomes unusually larger or smaller than zero. Since we want to limit our chances of being wrong (Type I error) to only 5 times out of 100, and because we can make a Type I error due to an unusually large or unusually small *t* test, we split our 5 errors equally to the high and low ends of the *t* distribution. Therefore, we define the critical *t*-test scores as the values of *t* that indicate the highest 2.5% and the lowest 2.5% of *t*-test scores. This is called a "two-tailed" *t* test because we've accounted for extreme (unusual) scores in both tails of the *t* distribution.

The shape of a *t* distribution, and the corresponding 95% critical *t* cutoff points, depends on how many observations (subjects) were used in each separate study. When studies have a small number of observations, the *t* distribution is wider than when studies have large number of observations. Figure 6.3 shows three different *t* distributions. The widest distribution (dotted line) is a distribution for which we had a small sample (few subjects) in the study. The narrowest distribution (solid line) is a distribution that had a lot of subjects. Notice how the critical *t* value moves farther from zero as

Figure 6.3   Three Different t-Test Distributions Based on the Number of Subjects Included in Each Sample Used to Compute the t Test.

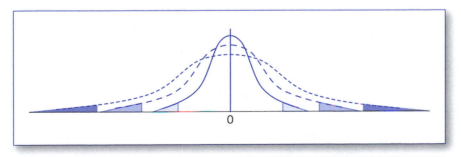

NOTE: When few subjects are used, the *t* distribution is wide (dotted line). When many subjects are used to compute the *t* test, the distribution is narrow (solid line). Note that the critical values of *t* are farther from zero when fewer subjects are used in the study.

fewer subjects are included in a study. This means that with fewer subjects, a researcher needs a larger t-test score to be able to reject H_0.

There are innumerable possible distributions of t. Not only is the shape altered by the number of subjects, but the critical (cutoff) value moves depending on what probability of a Type I error you are willing to make. As already noted, the conventional probability for a Type I error is <.05 (the probability of a Type I error is called alpha, α). If making a Type I error is especially risky and you want to minimize this risk, you can select a more conservative probability (α) than .05, such as $p < .01$. In this case, critical t values would be farther from zero, and you would need a larger t to reject H_0 than if you kept the α at .05. Conversely, suppose there is a situation in which making a Type I error isn't such a big deal, but you'd really hate to miss a real relationship between your IV and DV (i.e., you don't want to fail to reject a false H_0). In such a case, you could select a larger α, say $p < .10$. These critical t values will be closer to center. Figure 6.4 demonstrates the relative position of a critical t value based on Type I error probabilities of $\alpha = .01$, $\alpha = .05$, and $\alpha = .10$.

We determine the t distribution that determines our critical t value based on (a) the *degrees of freedom* (*df*; which is based on the number of

Figure 6.4 Critical t Cutoff Points for Different Probabilities of a Type I Error.

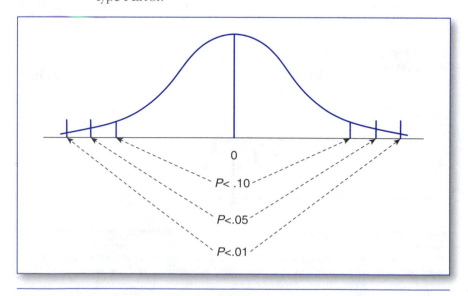

NOTE: Notice that critical t increases as probability of rejecting a true H_0 reduces.

subjects included in a study) and (b) the α (probability of Type I error) we select. We add the number of subjects in Group 1 (n_1) to the number of subjects in Group 2 (n_2) and subtract 2 to get the *df* for a *t* test ($df = n_1 + n_2 - 2$). Knowing our *df* and α, we can use a table of *t* probabilities to find out critical values for *t*.

Table 6.1 gives an example of a *t* table for an α probability $p \leq .05$. To use this table, locate the number of *df* ($df = N - 2$) used in your study and find the associated critical *t* value. Notice that there are two critical *t* values for each *df*: a "one-tailed" and a "two-tailed" critical *t*. Recall that the *t* distribution was a symmetrical normal curve (Figure 6.2) and that unusual *t* values were located on both extremes (tails). The sign of the *t* test (positive or negative) is based on which group mean was subtracted from the other. If the

Table 6.1 Table of Critical *t* Values for α Probability, $p \leq .05$

df	One-Tailed	Two-Tailed	df	One-Tailed	Two-Tailed
1	6.31	12.71	18	1.73	2.09
2	2.92	4.30	19	1.73	2.10
3	2.35	3.18	20	1.73	2.09
4	2.13	2.78	21	1.72	2.08
5	2.02	2.57	22	1.72	2.07
6	1.94	2.45	23	1.71	2.07
7	1.90	2.37	24	1.71	2.06
8	1.86	2.31	25	1.71	2.06
9	1.83	2.26	26	1.71	2.06
10	1.81	2.23	27	1.71	2.05
11	1.80	2.20	28	1.70	2.05
12	1.78	2.18	29	1.70	2.05
13	1.77	2.16	30	1.69	2.04
14	1.76	2.15	40	1.68	2.02
15	1.75	2.13	60	1.67	2.00
16	1.75	2.12	120	1.66	1.98
17	1.74	2.11	∞	1.65	1.96

smaller mean was subtracted from the larger mean, our t would be positive; however, if the larger mean was subtracted from the smaller mean, our t would be negative. Most of the time, we don't specify (hypothesize) a specific difference between the means—we reject the null hypothesis regardless as to which mean is larger and which is smaller. If we don't specify which mean is larger, then we consider a nonzero t unusually different from zero regardless as to whether it is positive or negative. In that case, the conventional 5% tolerance for a Type I error is split equally on either side (tail) of the t distribution. Therefore, most of the time we'll use the critical t value from the two-tailed column.

On occasion, we might specifically predict that one group (e.g., Group 1) will have a larger mean score than the other group (Group 2). In that case, we would only reject our null hypothesis when it reveals that Group 1 > Group 2. Because we're still willing to tolerate a 5% chance of incorrectly rejecting a true H_0, but we won't reject H_0 based on a t value at one end (tail) of the curve (i.e., if Group 1 < Group 2), we instead move all 5% of our "tolerable" errors to the end of the curve that reflects Group 1 > Group 2. Therefore, when we limit our rejection of H_0 to one direction, we can select a critical t cutoff using a one-tailed t test.

Once we know the critical t based on our df and α, we compare it with the t we actually obtained from our study. For example, if we had 30 subjects in a study, we would have 28 df (30 − 2). If we used the standard two-tailed t test, our critical t would be 2.05. If our obtained t exceeded the critical t of 2.05, then we would conclude that our obtained t is unusually large for H_0 to be true. And so we reject H_0.

◆ DEMONSTRATION

In Chapter 2, we used a sample of 24 depression scores to demonstrate how to measure variability or sum of squared errors (SSE). Let's say that half of the data were collected from subjects diagnosed with depression (Depressed) and half were from subjects with no psychiatric diagnosis (No Dx). We can use a t test to compare the scores according to *Diagnosis* to see if depressed subjects, on average, scored differently than No Dx subjects. These data are presented in Table 6.2. The question we'll test is whether Depressed subjects scored differently on this depression measure than No Dx subjects scored.

The null hypothesis (H_0) is that the mean depression score for Depressed subjects is equal to the mean depression score for No Dx ($H_0 : \overline{Y}_{\text{Depressed}} = \overline{Y}_{\text{NoDx}}$). According to Table 6.2, the mean depression score is 6.5 for the No Dx subjects and 19.5 for the Depressed subjects. Obviously,

Table 6.2   Depression Scores

Subject	Symptom Score (Y)	Diagnosis Group (IV)	Y²
1	3	No Dx	9
2	5	No Dx	25
3	6	No Dx	36
4	8	No Dx	64
5	9	No Dx	81
6	11	No Dx	121
7	19	Depressed	361
8	15	Depressed	225
9	16	Depressed	256
10	16	Depressed	256
11	19	Depressed	361
12	17	Depressed	289
13	3	No Dx	9
14	5	No Dx	25
15	4	No Dx	16
16	6	No Dx	36
17	8	No Dx	64
18	10	No Dx	100
19	24	Depressed	576
20	24	Depressed	576
21	22	Depressed	484
22	23	Depressed	529
23	19	Depressed	361
24	20	Depressed	400
Σ	312		5,260
	Mean	ΣY	ΣY²
Entire Sample	13	312	5,260
Depression Group	19.5	234	4,674
No Dx Group	6.5	78	586

these sample means are not equal. But is their difference of 13 points enough for us to conclude that the true means for people with Depression versus those without psychiatric diagnosis are different so that we can reject H_0 as false?

To calculate the t test, we need the mean score and variance for both groups. Since we already know the mean scores, we only need to calculate the variances. Equation 6.4 gives the computational formula for calculating variance that we learned in Chapter 2:

$$S^2 = \frac{\sum Y^2 - \frac{(\sum Y)^2}{N}}{N-1}. \tag{6.4}$$

We need to calculate variance separately for each group (Depressed and No Dx). To calculate each variance ($S^2_{\text{Depressed}}$ and S^2_{NoDx}), we need the sum of Y ($\sum Y$) separately for Depressed and No Dx subjects, and the sum of Y-squared ($\sum Y^2$) for each group. The sum of depression scores ($\sum Y$) for Depressed subjects is 234, the sum of squared depression scores for Depressed subjects ($\sum Y^2$) is 4,674, and $N = 12$. Plugging these values into Equation 6.4 gives us a variance in depression scores of 10.091 for the Depression group. Following the same steps, we get a variance in depression scores of 7.182 for the No Dx group.

Now that we know the group means, the group variances, and the number of subjects in each group, we can insert these values into the t-test equation (Equation 6.3) to compute t (see below).

$$t = \frac{\bar{Y}_1 - \bar{Y}_2}{\sqrt{\frac{(N_1-1)S_1^2 + (N_2-1)S_2^2}{N_1+N_2-2}\left(\frac{1}{N_1}+\frac{1}{N_2}\right)}}.$$

$$t = \frac{19.5-6.5}{\sqrt{\frac{(12-1)7.182+(12-1)10.091}{12+12-2}\left(\frac{1}{12}+\frac{1}{12}\right)}} = \frac{-13}{\sqrt{\frac{(11)7.182+(11)10.091}{22}\left(\frac{2}{12}\right)}}.$$

$$t = \frac{-13}{\sqrt{\frac{79.002+111.001}{22}\left(\frac{2}{12}\right)}} = \frac{-13}{\sqrt{\frac{190.003}{22}\left(\frac{2}{12}\right)}} = \frac{-13}{\sqrt{8.6365\left(\frac{2}{12}\right)}} = \frac{-13}{\sqrt{1.4393}}.$$

$$t = \frac{-13}{1.1997} = -10.836.$$

The value of t is −10.836. The valence of t (positive or negative) simply reflects whether we subtracted the Depressed group mean from the No Dx group mean or vice versa. Had we subtracted the No Dx group mean from the Depressed group mean, our t would have been +10.836. The point is that our obtained t is not zero. The important question is whether −10.836 is far enough from zero to conclude that real t is not zero and therefore that we should reject H_0.

To check whether t is unusually different from zero requires that we find the critical t value in Table 6.1 to see if the obtained t exceeds the critical value of t. Because we didn't specify that the Depressed group should score higher or lower than the No Dx group, we use the two-tailed column in Table 6.1. The critical t based on 22 df ($N − 2 = 24 − 2 = 22$) is 2.07. For an obtained t to be unusually different from zero with 22 df, the obtained t would have to be larger than 2.07 or smaller than −2.07. Obviously, our obtained t (−10.836) meets this criterion, so we reject H_0.

An alternative to using the t table to find a critical value is to find the exact probability of obtaining measured certain t if H_0 is true. Finding the exact probability would be a real hassle, except that statistical programs routinely give us that probability. With 22 df, the exact probability of t equaling ±10.836 when H_0 is true is less than 1 in 1,000. In other words, if H_0 is true and we were to do this same study 1,000 times, we'd get a t of ±10.836 or larger no more than once (maybe not even once). By the convention of tolerating a Type I error probability of ≤.05, a t that has a probability of ≤.001 suggests that the observed t of −10.836 is pretty unusual. This t is sufficiently different from zero that we decide to reject H_0.

By rejecting H_0, we hope that we've made a correct decision; however, it is possible we made an error and H_0 is really true. What we know for certain is that we haven't made a Type II error—the only way to make a Type II error is to not reject H_0. Since we did reject H_0, we can't possibly have made a Type II error.

SUMMARY ◆

The t test allows us to test if two variables are related. The IV (X) has two levels, and the DV (Y) is continuous. We compare the mean score on Y for one group or level of the IV with the mean score on Y for the second group of the IV. Based on the differences between means $(\overline{Y}_1 − \overline{Y}_2)$, adjusted by the pooled variances, we can calculate a t test. The t test helps us decide whether the sampled mean difference observed between two groups is real or if the difference is spurious (i.e., due to various sources of error).

The t test helps us decide whether or not to reject H_0. If H_0 is true, t should equal or be close to zero. Therefore, if t is unusually different from zero, we reject H_0. If t is not so different from zero, we fail to reject H_0.

The t test isn't the only way to compare group means, and it has significant limitations. Namely, t can only test the relationship between a DV and a single IV. Not only that, but the categorical IV can only have two categories (groups or levels). Fortunately, there are two statistical tests that compare groups and have more flexibility than t. The next chapter introduces one of these tests: the analysis of variance.

7

ONE-WAY ANOVA

Traditional Approach

I'm not sure what we've got here Charlie, but if we've got what I think we've got, we've got something.

—Prof. Ned Brainard

The Absent-Minded Professor[1]

As with the *t* test, researchers use analysis of variance (ANOVA) to test if two variables, *X* and *Y*, are related. Also, as with a *t* test, ANOVA is used when the dependent variable is continuous and the independent variable is nominal (categorical). Unlike the *t* test, ANOVA can be used with a vast array of applications. ANOVA does everything a *t* test can do and more. The *t* test is only used with a single IV (independent variable), yet in real life, multiple factors or variables may predict an outcome. ANOVA can simultaneously test the relationship between a DV (dependent variable) and multiple IVs. Often, too, an IV has more than two levels or groups. A *t* test compares only two groups; ANOVA, however, can test an IV that has two, three, or more groups. For example, a researcher could use ANOVA to compare simultaneously four different treatment conditions, such as (1) cognitive–behavioral, (2) motivational–enhancement, (3) acceptance–commitment, and (4) attention–placebo conditions. ANOVA also tests interactions between

---

1. © Walt Disney Co.

multiple IVs.[2] With ANOVA, then, the world of research blossoms into far more interesting research questions and complex designs.

◆ ANOVA Concepts

These advantages of ANOVA will be further introduced and described in subsequent chapters. For now, we'll look at ANOVA as an alternative to the *t* test when comparing just two groups. The purpose of this chapter is to convey a cursory and conceptual overview of ANOVA using the same data and simple design we tested with *t* in Chapter 6.

Scores on a variable must vary. As the name implies, ANOVA *analyzes* the *variance* of scores on a variable. When the analysis is complete, we will have separated (partitioned) the total variance of a DV (*Y*) into two parts: (1) the variance we can *explain* by knowing a person's score on the IV (i.e., which group the person is in) and (2) the variance in *Y* that we have not explained or predicted.

ANOVA generates a statistic, the *F ratio*, which conveys to a researcher the proportion of variability in *Y* that is *explained* by *X* (the IV or predictor) relative to the proportion of variability in *Y* that was not explained by *X*. If *X* and *Y* are related, then a large proportion of *Y*'s variance will be *explained* relative to the unexplained variance. Explained variance contributes to the numerator of the *F* ratio; therefore, a large portion of explained variance will produce a large *F* ratio. If *X* and *Y* are not related, then *X* explains little variance in *Y* and the *F* ratio is small (close to 1.0).

To conduct an ANOVA, we first need to calculate the total variance of the DV—called the sum of squares total and abbreviate it SST. I'll then partition SST into the *explained* and *residual* (or unexplained) variance. In Chapter 4, we used the *SSE* of the outcome variable (*Y*) as the *total SSE*. ANOVA will also use the *SSE* of *Y* as the SST. SST is calculated as it was in Chapters 2 and 4: the sum of squared differences (errors) between each score and the mean of *Y* $(\text{SST} = \Sigma(Y_i - \overline{Y})^2)$.

◆ BEGIN WITH SST

Let's return to the Depression scores first used to demonstrate computation of *SSE* in Chapter 2 and then used to demonstrate a *t* test in Chapter 6. When

---

2. Interactions are great, but not relevant to the present chapter. I'll describe interactions in Chapter 11 when we consider models with multiple IVs.

we computed the SST for depression scores in Chapter 2, we subtracted each score from the mean of all of the scores on Y. ANOVA generates several mean scores: two or more group means (the mean of Y for only the subjects within each of the groups) and a grand mean, which is the mean of Y for the entire sample regardless of group membership. Since the independent (X) variable "Diagnostic Status" has two groups (No Dx and Depressed), we'll have two group means (mean of Y for Depressed subjects and mean of Y for No Dx subjects) and one grand mean (mean of Y for all 24 subjects). We use the grand mean (designated $\overline{Y}_{grand}$) to compute SST. The depression data has a total of 24 subjects, and the average depression score for all 24 subjects ($\overline{Y}_{grand}$) is 13. In Chapter 2, we subtracted $\overline{Y}_{grand}$ from each individual subject's score, squared each difference, and summed all of the squared differences. This process gave an SST of 1,204. These data are presented again in Table 7.1, along with the process of subtracting the mean from each score, squaring the difference, and summing the squared differences. Once we have SST, we need to partition it into error *explained* by the IV and the error variance not explained, called the *residual error*.

Table 7.1 Depression Scores (Y) and the Independent (X) Variable "Diagnostic Status" (No Dx vs. Depressed) for Each Participant

Subject	Symptom Score (Y)	Diagnosis (No Dx = −1, Depressed = 1)	$Y - Y_{grand}$	$(Y - Y_{grand})^2$
1	3	−1	−10	100
2	5	−1	8	64
3	6	−1	−7	49
4	8	−1	−5	25
5	9	−1	−4	16
6	11	−1	−2	4
7	19	1	6	36
8	15	1	2	4
9	16	1	3	9
10	16	1	3	9
11	19	1	6	36

(Continued)

Table 7.1 (Continued)

Subject	Symptom Score (Y)	Diagnosis (No Dx = −1, Depressed = 1)	$Y - Y_{grand}$	$(Y - Y_{grand})^2$
12	17	1	4	16
13	3	−1	−10	100
14	5	−1	−8	64
15	4	−1	−9	81
16	6	−1	−7	49
17	8	−1	−5	25
18	10	−1	−3	9
19	24	1	11	121
20	24	1	11	121
21	22	1	9	81
22	23	1	10	100
23	19	1	6	36
24	20	1	7	49
	Symptom means		SST =	1204
	Grand mean =	13		
	No Dx mean =	6.5		
	Depressed mean =	19.5		

◆ COMPUTE EXPLAINED *SS*

A curious mystery of statistical analyses is the many aliases that a given term might have. Here is such an example. In many ANOVA designs, the explained *SSE* is also called the *between SSE* because the *F* ratio compares the variances *between* two or more groups. Explained or between SS is also called SSB. Similar, in a way, to the *t* test, but only loosely, I'll calculate a ratio where the variation *between* groups is divided by the pooled *within* variation that includes all of the subjects regardless of group membership. To be consistent with ANOVA language and notation, I'll use the SSB label for the explained variance. To determine SSB, we need to sum all of the scores *within* a group (i.e., the sum of Depression scores for everyone in the No Dx group and the sum of Depression scores for everyone in the Depressed group (given in Table 7.1).

SSB is determined using Equation 7.1. The equation has two parts. The first part is determined by getting the sum of scores for each group, squaring that sum, and dividing by the number of subjects in that group. Essentially, this is an average of the squared sum for the group. We have to compute this average of the squared sum separately for each group in the study. Since we have two groups in this demonstration (Depressed and No Dx), we'll compute this value twice (see Equation 7.2).

$$\text{SSB} = \Sigma \left[\frac{\left(\Sigma Y_{\text{group}}\right)^2}{N_{\text{group}}} \right] - \frac{\left(\Sigma Y\right)^2}{N_{\text{total}}}. \tag{7.1}$$

In the second part of Equation 7.1, we take the sum of scores for the entire sample, square that value, and divide by the total number of subjects. I'll call this second value the *correction term*.

$$\text{SSB} = \left[\frac{\left(\Sigma Y_{\text{NoDx}}\right)^2}{N_{\text{NoDx}}} \right] + \left[\frac{\left(\Sigma Y_{\text{depressed}}\right)^2}{N_{\text{depressed}}} \right] - \frac{\left(\Sigma Y\right)^2}{N_{\text{total}}}. \tag{7.2}$$

Table 7.2 presents the Depression scores for subjects with no diagnosis on the left and subjects with depression on the right. The table also provides a sum of the scores for each group. This information will allow me to complete Equation 7.2. I'll need the average of the squared sum for the No Dx group, the average of the squared sum for the Depressed group, and the correction term.

Let's begin with the average squared sum for the No Dx group. According to Table 7.2, the sum of the scores for subjects with no diagnosis is 78. We square that sum ($78^2 = 6084$) and divide that number by 12 (the *N* of the No Dx group) to get the average of the squared sum for No Dx (507). Next, to get the average of the squared sum for the Depressed group, we take the sum of scores for the Depressed group (234), square that value ($234^2 = 54,756$), and divide by the number of subjects in the Depressed group (12) to get an average of the squared sum (4563). We add these two average squared sums together to get the first part of Equation 7.1 ($507 + 4563 = 5070$).

Table 7.2 Depression Scores (Y) Organized by Those With (Depressed) or Without (No Dx) Depression

Subject	No Dx (Depression Score (Y))	Subject	Depressed (Depression Score (Y))
1	3	7	19
2	5	8	15
3	6	9	16
4	8	10	16
5	9	11	19
6	11	12	17
13	3	19	24
14	5	20	24
15	4	21	22
16	6	22	23
17	8	23	19
18	10	24	20
Σ	78	Σ	234

To get the second part (correction term) of Equation 7.1, we sum all 24 scores (312), square that value ($312^2 = 97,344$), and divide by the total N ($97,344 \div 24$) to get the correction term (4056). Now, that we have the first part of Equation 7.1 (5070) and the correction term (4056), we subtract the correction term from the first part to get the SSB ($5,070 - 4,056$), which is 1,014.

◆ COMPUTE RESIDUAL *SSE*

Once we know SST and SSB, we can solve for the unexplained or residual *SSE*. As with SSB, $SSE_{residual}$ is often called by a different name in ANOVA: *SSE within*, or SSW. Again, to be consistent with ANOVA, I'll call the residual error SSW. Recall that SST = SSB + SSW. Subtracting SSB from SST gives us SSW: SST − SSB = SSW. In this example, SSW = 1204 − 1014 = 190.

Of course, computing SSW by subtracting SSB from SST is too easy. I want you to know how to compute SSW using your data. Besides, calculating SSW separately allows you to check your work. If your calculated SSW doesn't match SST − SSB, then you know there is a mistake somewhere. And of course, there is a formula to calculate SSW (Equation 7.3). It is a little more cumbersome than most equations, but it works, and you can use it to check your work.

$$\text{SSW} = \Sigma Y^2 - \Sigma \left[\frac{\left(\Sigma Y_{\text{group}} \right)^2}{N_{\text{group}}} \right]. \tag{7.3}$$

Equation 7.3 also has two parts. The first part is simply the sum of Y^2 for the entire sample. The second part is the sum of the average of the squared sums for each group. The second part should look familiar—it's the same as the first part of Equation 7.1 above. In Table 7.3, we squared each Depression score and summed those squared values to get the ΣY^2, which is 5,260 (see Table 7.3). This value will be the first part of Equation 7.3. We already know the second part of the equation (we calculated it when getting SSB). The second part is 5,070. When we subtract the first part of Equation 7.3 (5,260) from the second part (5,070), we get an SSW of 190. Fortunately, this value matches the SSW we got when we subtracted SSB from SST.

Table 7.3 Computation of ΣY^2

Subject	(Depression Score (Y))	Y^2
No Dx		
1	3	9
2	5	25
3	6	36
4	8	64
5	9	81
6	11	121
13	3	9
14	5	25
15	4	16

(Continued)

Table 7.3 (Continued)

Subject	(Depression Score (Y))	Y²
16	6	36
17	8	64
18	10	100
Depressed		
7	19	361
8	15	225
9	16	256
10	16	256
11	19	361
12	17	289
19	24	576
20	24	576
21	22	484
22	23	529
23	19	361
24	20	400
	Σ =	5260

◆ ANOVA SUMMARY TABLE

To keep track of the different components of an ANOVA, it is helpful to put them in a summary table. This is the same summary table that we used in Chapter 4 to compare the regression models. Table 7.4 presents the ANOVA summary table and reviews how to complete it. Column 1 of this table (*Source*) outlines how SST was partitioned. In this example, it was partitioned into two sources: (1) SS explained by the IV "Diagnostic Status" (SSB) and (2) SS not explained by the IV (SSW). Column 2 will give the actual values for SST, SSB, and SSW.

Before computing *F*, we first need to adjust each *SS* by the "degrees of freedom" (*df*). The equations printed under the *df* column (Column 3) in Table 7.4 tell how to compute *df*. Total *df* is the total number of subjects in the study (*N*) minus 1. Since we have 24 subjects, total *df* is 24 − 1 or 23.

Table 7.4 Format for the Summary Table

1	2	3	4	5
Source	SS ÷	df =	MS	F
Sex	SSB	K – 1	SSB/df	MS_B/MS_W
Residual	SSW	N – 1 – (k – 1)	SSW/df	
Total	SST	N – 1		

The *df* associated with the IV is the number of IV groups (indicated by the letter *k*) minus 1. In this example, *k* = 2 since the IV (Diagnosis) had two levels (Depressed and No Dx). Since *k* = 2, *df* for Diagnosis is 2 – 1 or 1. Residual *df* is the difference between total *df* and the *df* associated with the IV: residual *df* = 23 – 1 or 22.

To complete this ANOVA example, I'll enter the values for SSB, SSW, and the degrees of freedom into the ANOVA summary table (Table 7.5). The mean square (*MS*) for each source (Column 4) is found by dividing the *SS* for that source (Column 2) by the *df* corresponding to that source (Column 3): *SS* ÷ *df* = *MS*. With the *MS* for each source, I'm a heartbeat from determining the *F* ratio, which is computed by dividing the *MS explained* (MSB) by the residual *MS* (MSW). Dividing SSB (1,014) by 1 *df* gives me a MSB of 1,014 for Diagnosis groups. Dividing SSW (190) by 22 *df* gives me a MSW of 8.636. Dividing MSB by MSW gives the *F* value of 117.415.

After conducting the ANOVA, we can also graph the means to get a visual sense of how the groups differed on the dependent variable. Figure 7.1 presents a bar graph with the independent variable groups along the horizontal axis and Depression (DV) scores along the vertical axis. The columns reflect the average score on the DV (depression score) separately for each group.

Table 7.5 Summary Table to Compute F Ratio Testing the Relationship Between Sex (IV) and Depression (DV)

Source	SS	df	MS	F
Diagnostic group	1,014	*1*	1,–14	117.415
Residual	190	22	8.636	
Total	1,204	23		

Figure 7.1 Bar Graph Comparing Average Depression Scores for Each Diagnostic Group.

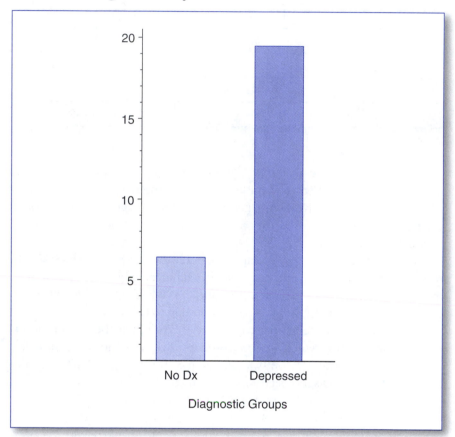

When reporting an F ratio, the standard practice is to (a) provide (in parentheses) the degrees of freedom attributed to the IV and the residual df, (b) state the value of the F ratio, and then (c) report the probability of obtaining an F ratio of that size *if the null hypothesis is true*. Therefore, this example is presented as, $F(1, 22) = 117.415$, $p < .001$. As with the t test, there are two ways to find the probability of obtaining a certain F when H_0 is true. The easiest way, of course, is to let a statistical program generate the exact p value for our F ratio.

The alternative "old-fashioned" approach to determine the p value is to refer to an F table, such as Table 7.6. Using this table requires that we know the number of df used to calculate MSB (df between) and the df used to calculate MSW (df within). This example used 1 df for MSB and 22 df for MSW. Finally, we need to decide what minimum probability (p) of making a Type I

Table 7.6   Sample of a Table of Critical *F* values

df Within	df Between							
	1		2		3		4	
	$p \leq .05$	$P \leq .01$	$p \leq .05$	$p \leq .01$	$p \leq .05$	$p \leq .01$	$p \leq .05$	$p \leq .01$
1	161	4,052	200	4,999	216	5,403	225	5625
2	18.51	98.49	19.00	99.00	19.16	99.17	19.25	99.25
3	10.13	34.12	9.55	30.82	9.28	29.46	9.12	28.71
4	7.71	21.20	6.94	18.00	6.59	16.69	6.39	15.98
5	6.61	16.26	5.79	13.27	5.41	12.06	5.19	11.39
6	5.99	13.74	5.14	10.92	4.76	9.78	4.53	9.15
7	5.59	12.25	4.74	9.55	4.35	8.45	4.12	7.85
8	5.32	11.26	4.46	8.65	4.07	7.59	3.84	7.01
9	5.12	10.56	4.26	8.02	3.86	6.99	3.63	6.42
10	4.97	10.04	4.10	7.56	3.71	6.55	3.48	5.99
11	4.84	9.65	3.98	7.20	3.59	6.22	3.36	5.67
12	4.75	9.33	3.89	6.93	3.49	5.95	3.26	5.41
13	4.67	9.07	3.81	6.70	3.41	5.74	3.18	5.20
14	4.60	8.86	3.74	6.51	3.34	5.56	3.11	5.03
15	4.54	8.68	3.68	6.36	3.29	5.42	3.06	4.89
16	4.49	8.53	3.63	6.23	3.24	5.29	3.01	4.77
17	4.45	8.40	3.59	6.11	3.20	5.18	2.97	4.67
18	4.41	8.28	3.56	6.01	3.16	5.09	2.93	4.58
19	4.38	8.18	3.52	5.93	3.13	5.01	2.90	4.50
20	4.35	8.10	3.49	5.85	3.10	4.94	2.87	4.43
21	4.33	8.02	3.47	5.78	3.07	4.87	2.84	4.37
22	4.30	7.94	3.44	5.72	3.05	4.82	2.82	4.31
23	4.28	7.88	3.42	5.66	3.03	4.76	2.80	4.26
24	4.26	7.82	3.40	5.61	3.01	4.72	2.78	4.22
25	4.24	7.77	3.39	5.57	2.99	4.68	2.76	4.18

error (α) we will accept (i.e., the probability of rejecting a true H_0). As before, the conventional probability accepted for a Type I error is $\alpha = .05$.

With 1 *df* between, 22 *df* within, and $\alpha = .05$, we look to Table 7.6 to find the critical *F*. Critical *F* is the smallest *F* value that allows us to reject H_0. The probability of getting an *F* larger than Critical *F* when H_0 is true is less than .05 ($p < .05$). The first column of Table 7.5 gives the within *df*. The next column gives critical *F* values when *df* between is 1 and α probability is $\leq .05$. We scan down Column 1 until we reach the row for 22 *df* within. The critical *F* value at that point for *df* between (1) and $\alpha = .05$ is 4.30.

My obtained *F* of 117.415 is much larger than the critical *F* of 4.30; the chances of getting an *F* of 117.415 (with 1 and 22 *df*) if H_0 is true is far smaller than .05. Although the table doesn't tell the exact probability, we do know that *p* is $< .05$ and that meets my criterion for *F* being unusually large for H_0 to be true. Therefore, my best choice is to reject H_0.

I've now tested the relationship between an IV (Diagnosis) and a DV (Depression scores) two ways: with a *t* test and an ANOVA (*F*). Both tests led us to the same conclusion—to reject H_0. Here's one final cool thing about *t* test and ANOVA. The *t* obtained in Chapter 6 was −10.836, and the *F* obtained in this chapter was 117.415. If we square the *t* value from Chapter 6 (-10.836^2), we get the *F* we obtained in this chapter (117.415). This is because $t^2 = F$. How excellent! So the *t* test and ANOVA not only led us to the same conclusion (fail to reject H_0) but they also in fact gave us the exact same answer.

◆ SUMMARY

ANOVA produces an *F* ratio, and as we did with the *t* test, the *F* ratio guides our decision whether or not to reject the null hypothesis. To understand ANOVA and *F*, we first must recognize that the DV is a continuous variable, and therefore the scores on the DV should vary. We measure the variance in the DV to get the total sum of squared errors (SST), and then partition it into variance explained by the IV (SSB) and variance that is left over (SSW or residual error). ANOVA is a ratio, of sorts, of explained to unexplained variance, after adjusting those variances by *df*. Finally, it turns out that the *F* we obtained from ANOVA is equal to t^2.

I've now demonstrated two seemingly different ways to test the relationship between an IV and DV and found that both give us the exact same answer. There is a third way to test the relationship between a categorical IV and a continuous DV. We can use the bivariate regression model comparison approach. Chapter 8 will introduce this approach to compare group means, once again using the same depression data.

8

t TEST, ANOVA, AND THE BIVARIATE REGRESSION APPROACH

The Road to Paradise is plain,
And holds scarce one,
Not that it is not firm
But we presume
A Dimpled Road
Is more preferred

—Emily Dickinson

We come now to a point where the two paths to statistics can split along seemingly divergent courses: (1) the traditional approaches (*t* test and analysis of variance, ANOVA) for group comparisons and (2) the regression model. For some, the paths are separate but parallel. For me, the paths intertwine and cross frequently. They vary in directness, ease, and clarity, but they rely on each other and ultimately lead to the same destination. I do not consider regression and traditional approaches as two distinct statistical paths—I regard them as the same. Chapters 6 and 7 introduced the traditional approaches for group comparison. In this chapter, I will describe and demonstrate bivariate regression as a method to compare group means.

♦ TEST TWO GROUPS USING MODEL COMPARISON

It's possible, in fact simpler, to use the model comparison approach from Chapter 4 to perform the very same analyses we conducted with the t test and ANOVA. We'll again follow the same 10 model comparison steps to compare groups. To demonstrate the use of regression to compare groups, once again we'll use the Depression scores as DV (Y) and subject Diagnosis as the IV (X). These data are presented in Table 8.1.

Table 8.1 Depression Scores, Diagnosis, and the Elements Needed to Estimate b_1 (ΣY, ΣX, ΣX^2, and ΣXY)

Subject	Symptom Score (Y)	Diagnosis (X) (No Dx = −1, Dx = 1)	X^2	$X \times Y$
1	3	−1	1	−3
2	5	−1	1	−5
3	6	−1	1	−6
4	8	−1	1	−8
5	9	−1	1	−9
6	11	−1	1	−11
7	19	1	1	19
8	15	1	1	15
9	16	1	1	16
10	16	1	1	16
11	19	1	1	19
12	17	1	1	17
13	3	−1	1	−3
14	5	−1	1	−5
15	4	−1	1	−4
16	6	−1	1	−6
17	8	−1	1	−8
18	10	−1	1	−10
19	24	1	1	24

Subject	Symptom Score (Y)	Diagnosis (X) (No Dx = –1, Dx = 1)	X²	X × Y
20	24	1	1	24
21	22	1	1	22
22	23	1	1	23
23	19	1	1	19
24	20	1	1	20
Σ	312	0	24	156
	Symptom means			
	Grand mean =	13		
	No Dx =	6.5		
	Psych Dx =	19.5		

Step 1: State the Compact Model C and an Augmented Model A

The simplest model (Model C) predicts the grand mean $(\bar{Y}_{grand})$ for Depression scores. Recall that $\bar{Y}_{grand}$ for these data is 13, so

$$\text{Model C: Depression} = \beta_0 + \varepsilon_i, \quad \text{where } \beta_0 = 13.$$

The research question (do Depressed subjects have different depression scores from those with no diagnosis) is the same as asking if adding Diagnosis as a predictor variable (X) to the model will predict Depression scores better than Model C, which predicted the grand mean for every subject. To create this augmented model (Model A), we'll create a bivariate regression model with Diagnosis as the predictor variable (X) and Depression scores as the outcome variable (Y). That bivariate regression model would look like this:

$$\text{Model A: Depression} = \beta_0 + \beta_1 \times \text{Diagnosis} + \varepsilon_i.$$

Step 2: Identify the Null Hypothesis

The null hypothesis (H_0) for this study is that the mean Depression score for the No Dx group is not different from the mean Depression score for the Depressed group. In a model comparison, the H_0 means that adding Diagnosis to the model does not reliably improve prediction of Depression. For Diagnosis to have no effect on Depression, β_1 must equal 0. Thus, H_0 is $\beta_1 = 0$.

Step 3: Count the Number of Parameters Estimated in Each Model

Model C estimated 1 parameter (β_0), so PC is 1. Model A estimated 2 parameters (β_0 and β_1), so PA is 2.

Step 4: Calculate the Regression Equation

To create the bivariate regression equation, we first compute b_1. To compute b_1, we need the sum of Depression scores (ΣY), the sum of the values of the Diagnosis variable (ΣX), the sum of the squared Diagnosis values (ΣX^2), and the sum of the cross products between Depression and Diagnosis (ΣXY). These sums are given in Table 8.1. We can add the Depression scores to get ΣY, but we then face a dilemma: How do we arithmetically sum concepts of Depressed and No Dx together to get ΣX? And while we're at it, how do we multiply Depression scores by Diagnosis values to get ΣXY? And just what is a squared Diagnosis, and how do we add these values to get ΣX^2? Diagnosis (Depressed and No Dx) is a categorical concept without any true numerical values.

To resolve these questions, we can assign a numerical value to subjects in the No Dx group and a different value to represent subjects in the Depressed group. We can choose any numbers we like; however, we're better off if we keep these "codes" fairly simple, such as small integers. In fact, I will deliberately select -1 for the No Dx group and $+1$ for the Depressed group. This is a special type of code called a "contrast code." A contrast code is very much like the mean deviation used for the predictor (independent variable, IV) in Chapter 3. If you use contrast codes and if you have the same number of subjects in both groups, the "scores" (codes) on X will sum to 0. In this example, I have 12 No Dx subjects with codes of -1 ($-1 \times 12 = -12$) and 12 Depressed subjects coded $+1$ ($1 \times 12 = 12$). These scores will sum to 0 ($-12 + 12 = 0$).

Armed with our contrast codes, we can now proceed to calculate b_1. Plugging the values from Table 8.1 into the formula for b_1 (Equation 8.1), we obtain $b_1 = 6.5$ as an estimate of β_1.

$$b_1 = \frac{\Sigma XY - \dfrac{(\Sigma X)(\Sigma Y)}{n}}{\Sigma X^2 - \dfrac{(\Sigma X)^2}{n}}, \tag{8.1}$$

$$b_1 = \frac{156 - \dfrac{0 \times 312}{24}}{24 - \dfrac{0^2}{24}} = \frac{156}{24} = 6.5.$$

Having b_1, the next step is to find the value of b_0. Recall that a regression line always passes through a point defined by the means of X and Y. Thus, $\overline{Y} = b_0 + b_1 \overline{X}$ or $b_0 = \overline{Y} - b_1 \overline{X}$. Substituting the mean Depression score (13) and the mean Diagnosis score (0) into this equation gives $b_0 = 13 - (6.5 \times 0) = 13$.

Knowing both b_1 and b_0, we have the bivariate regression equation for Model A:

Model A: Depression = 13 + 6.5(Diagnosis) + ε_i.

Let's take a moment to study Model A. Because N was equal in both groups and Diagnosis was contrast coded (−1 for No Dx and +1 for Depressed), Model A has some impressive features. First, notice that b_0 equals the Grand mean for all 24 subjects (13). That's no accident—having equal N and using contrast codes made that happen. That's why I chose contrast codes.

Second, if we insert the code for No Dx (−1) into Model A, the model predicts the same score for all subjects with no diagnosis (13 − 6.5 = 6.5). What's more, the score predicted for all the No Dx subjects (6.5) is equal to the *group* mean for the No Dx group. It's not surprising, then, that when we insert the score assigned to the Depressed subjects (+1), the model predicts a Depression score of 19.5, which happens to be the group mean for subjects with a depression diagnosis. Because the sample sizes were equal in each group and we contrast coded Diagnosis, our intercept is the Grand mean $(\overline{Y}_{grand})$. The intercept provides an initial prediction of depressive symptoms, and the score on the predictor variable (Diagnosis) adjusts the intercept (Grand mean) to equal the means for each group. Not all models are this sweet (after all, we're not often so lucky to have equal Ns in each group), so we need to savor it when we can.

Step 5: Compute the Total Sum of Squares

The total sum of squares (SST) is always the sum of squares from the simplest model (Model C). To get SST, we'll predict 13 for every subject, find the difference between the actual Depression score and the Depression score predicted for each subject (13), square the difference, and then sum these squared differences. The result, which is shown in Table 8.2, gives us an SST of 1,204. Notice that the SST for the bivariate regression is identical to the SST found with ANOVA in Chapter 7—as it should be.

Table 8.2 Difference Between Actual Depression (Y) and Predicted Depression ($\overline{Y}_{grand}$) Scores for Each Subject

Subject	Symptom Score (Y)	Predicted Y	$Y - \hat{Y}$	$(Y - \hat{Y})^2$
1	3	13	−10	100
2	5	13	−8	64
3	6	13	−7	49
4	8	13	−5	25
5	9	13	−4	16
6	11	13	−2	4
7	19	13	6	36
8	15	13	2	4
9	16	13	3	9
10	16	13	3	9
11	19	13	6	36
12	17	13	4	16
13	3	13	−10	100
14	5	13	−8	64
15	4	13	−9	81
16	6	13	−7	49
17	8	13	−5	25
18	10	13	−3	9
19	24	13	11	121
20	24	13	11	121
21	22	13	9	81
22	23	13	10	100
23	19	13	6	36
24	20	13	7	49
Σ	312	312	0	1,204

Step 6: Compute the Sum of Squared Errors for Model A

The sum of squared errors for Model A (SSE_A) is computed just as the error for the bivariate regression was computed in Chapter 3 (see Table 8.3). We find the difference between each observed (Y) and predicted ($\hat{Y}$) score, square the difference, and then sum these squared differences to get the *SSE* for Model A. The SSE_A is 190, and it is the amount of error we still have after using Diagnosis to account for some of the variance in Depression scores (i.e., our "residual" error, $SSE_{residual}$). Notice again that SSE_A is identical to the residual error or SSW (*SSE* "within") obtained for the ANOVA in Chapter 7—again . . . as it should be.

Table 8.3 Difference Between Actual and Predicted Depression Scores for Each Subject

Subject	Symptom Score (Y)	Predicted Y	$Y - \hat{Y}$	$(Y - \hat{Y})^2$
1	3	6.5	−4	12
2	5	6.5	−2	2
3	6	6.5	−1	0
4	8	6.5	2	2
5	9	6.5	3	6
6	11	6.5	5	20
7	19	19.5	−1	0
8	15	19.5	−5	20
9	16	19.5	−4	12
10	16	19.5	−4	12
11	19	19.5	−1	0
12	17	19.5	−3	6
13	3	6.5	−4	12
14	5	6.5	−2	2
15	4	6.5	−3	6
16	6	6.5	−1	0
17	8	6.5	2	2
18	10	6.5	4	12
19	24	19.5	5	20
20	24	19.5	5	20
21	22	19.5	3	6
22	23	19.5	4	12
23	19	19.5	−1	0
24	20	19.5	1	0
Σ	312	312	0	190

Step 7: Compute the Sum of Squares Reduced

Once we know the error for Model C (1,204) and Model A (190), we compute the reduction in sum of squares (SSR) by subtracting SSE_A from SST. The difference (1,204 – 190) is 1,014. Notice that SSR is the same as the explained error or SSB (SSE "between") obtained for the ANOVA in Chapter 7—as it . . . well, you get the point.

Step 8: Compute the Proportional Reduction in Error

SSR by itself conveys little absolute information about the relative reduction in error between Model A and Model C. It's more useful to compute the proportion of the total error (SST) that was reduced by adding Diagnosis to the model. We compute this proportional reduction in error (PRE or R^2) by dividing SSR by SST. In this example, $R^2 = 1014 \div 1204 = .842$.

Table 8.4 summarizes the findings from these first eight steps.

Table 8.4 First Eight Steps Comparing Models With and Without Diagnosis Groups as a Predictor

Step 1	State the compact Model C and an augmented Model A	
	Model C:	$\hat{Y} = \beta_0$
	Model A:	$\hat{Y} = \beta_0 + \beta_1 X_1$
Step 2	Identify the null hypothesis (H_0)	
	H_0:	$\beta_1 = \beta_2 = 0$
Step 3	Count the number of parameters estimated by each model	
	PA = 2	
	PC = 1	
Step 4	Calculate the regression equation	
	Model C:	$\hat{Y} = \beta_0,$
	Model A:	$\hat{Y}$
Step 5	Compute total sum of squares (SSE_C)	
	$SSE_C = 1,204$	
Step 6	Compute the sum of squares for Model A (SSE_A)	
	$SSE_A = 190$	

Step 7	Compute the sum of squares reduced (SSR)
	SSR = 1,014
Step 8	Compute the proportional reduction in error (PRE or R^2)
	PRE = R^2 = .842

We can take all of the information gathered thus far and enter it into a model comparison box (Table 8.5). This box helps us organize the information so that we can fill out the summary table.

Table 8.5 Model Comparison Information for Completing the Summary Table

Model C:	$Y = 13 + e$	PC = 1	SST = 1204
Model A:	$Y = 13 + 6.5(\text{Diagnosis}) + \varepsilon$	PA = 2	$SSE_A = 190$
H_0	$\beta_1 = 0$	R^2 (PRE) = .842	SSR = 1014

Step 9: Complete the Summary Table

The information needed to complete the summary table is available from the model comparison box (Table 8.5). This information is put into the summary table (Table 8.6).

Table 8.6 Completed Summary Table for This Example

Source	SS	df	MS	F	R^2
Sex	1,014	1	1,014	117.415	.842
Residual	190	22	8.636		
Total	1,204	23			

Step 10: Decide About H_0

The summary table gave an *F* value of 117.415. As we saw in Chapter 7, the probability (*p*) of getting an *F* of 117.415 if H_0 is true is miniscule (*p* < .001), or less than 1 time out of 1,000. It is certainly smaller than the conventional $p < .05$; so, as with the t test in Chapter 6 and the ANOVA in Chapter 7, we again decide to reject H_0 in this example.

◆ COMPARE THE RESULTS OF t TEST, ANOVA, AND BIVARIATE REGRESSION

The completed regression summary table generated an F of 117.415 with 1 and 22 degrees of freedom. In fact, this summary table for the bivariate regression is identical to the ANOVA summary table in Chapter 7. The F value from this bivariate regression is identical to the F found with the ANOVA in Chapter 7. Both of the Fs generated by these examples are equal to the squared t value (t^2) obtained for these data in Chapter 6.

The regression model comparison results were identical results to the results of the traditional t and ANOVA tests. This observation is critical to the objective of this book—which is to show that model comparison gives identical results to those obtained by the traditional statistical approaches.

◆ SUMMARY

Whether using a t test, ANOVA, or bivariate regression, we arrive at identical conclusions. The t test allowed us to test if two variables are related. One variable (the IV) is dichotomous and composed of two groups; we compare the mean score on the dependent variable (DV) from one group (or level) of the IV with the mean DV score for the second group of the IV. The t gives a sense as to whether a difference between two (estimated) means implies a real population difference. The t test helped me decide whether or not to reject H_0. The ANOVA also allowed me to compare the two means. As we'll see in subsequent chapters, ANOVA does far more than t by allowing us to test more than one IV, and the IVs need not be limited to only two groups.

Now we've tested whether two group means are statistically different by using the model comparison approach. Using a special case of bivariate regression (special because the predictor variable, Diagnosis, was dichotomous), we partitioned SST into SSR (which is the same thing as SSB) and $SSE_{residual}$ (which is the same thing as SSW). We used the regression model comparison to generate an F, and as I did in Chapter 7, we used F to guide our decision about H_0. The regression model comparison approach can be used to conduct a t test and ANOVA. Having used regression to replicate an ANOVA, we're ready to explore more complex analyses, both with regression and with ANOVA.

PART III

Adding Complexity

9

MODEL COMPARISON II

Multiple Regression

How far the unknown transcends the what we know.

—Henry Wadsworth Longfellow

Nature

We've used a variety of statistical methods (*t* test, ANOVA, and correlation) to test the relationship between two variables, and we've found that we can use a linear regression model comparison approach to conduct all of these analyses. In all cases, we used a single variable to predict an outcome. But behavior is not explained by a single variable— predicting behavior is infinitely complex. So too the potential complexity of a statistical model (although not infinite) is far greater than using a single variable to predict an outcome. In this chapter, I'll demonstrate how to build and test a more interesting regression model.

Previously, we compared a bivariate regression model (Model A) that used a single variable to predict an outcome with a simple compact model (Model C) that predicted the grand mean for every subject. In multiple regression, we'll further augment Model A by adding a second predictor to the regression model. Table 9.1 presents a model comparison box that demonstrates the concept of comparing Model C (the simple compact model) with the newly augmented multiple regression model that now uses two variables (X_1 and X_2) to predict the outcome (Y).

Table 9.1 Comparison of a Model A That Has Two Predictors With a Simple Model C

Model A:	$Y = \beta_0 + \beta_1 X_1 + \beta_2 X_2 + SSE_A$	SSE_A	$PA = 3$
Model C:	$Y = \beta_0 + SSE_C$	SSE_C	$PC = 1$
Difference:	$\beta_1 X_1 + \beta_2 X_2$	SSR	SSR

The model comparison in Table 9.1 tests whether a model with two predictors (X_1 and X_2) is better than a model that just predicts the mean ($\overline{Y}$) for every person. The null hypothesis for this *omnibus* model is that β_1 and β_2 both equal zero (H_0: $\beta_1 = \beta_2 = 0$). If the null hypothesis is true, then neither X_1 nor X_2 are related to Y.

The models are analyzed in the same way as when Model A had a single predictor. We estimate the parameters of Model A (β_0, β_1, and β_2) and Model C (β_0), calculate the error for Model A (SSE_A), the error for Model C (SST), and complete the model comparison. When the comparison is completed, we will have an F value to help us answer Question 1 (Is Y related to X_1 and X_2). We will also know the proportional reduction in error (PRE or R^2), which tells us the strength of the relationship between Y and the predictors (Question 2). The regression coefficients (β_1 and β_2) will tell us the direction of the relationship between Y and X_1 and between Y and X_2 (Question 3).

◆ CONDUCTING THE OMNIBUS TEST

Our augmented Model A ($Y = \beta_0 + \beta_1 X_1 + \beta_1 X_2 + \varepsilon$) is also called the "omnibus model." Comparing Model A against the simple Model C ($Y = \beta_0$, where $\beta_0 = \overline{Y}$) is called the "omnibus test." The omnibus test evaluates all predictors (X_1 and X_2) at once against the simple model with no predictor variables.

The data used in Chapters 3 and 4 to demonstrate testing a relationship between two variables, Y and X_1, are presented again in Table 9.2 along with scores on a third variable, X_2, for these 12 subjects. In this chapter, we'll include both predictors X_1 and X_2 simultaneously in the omnibus model to predict Y.

The first eight steps to compare the omnibus model (Model A) with the simple model (Model C) are listed in Table 9.3, along with the results of each step. First we define the models (Step 1) and then articulate the null hypotheses (Step 2). As presented in Table 9.1, Model A is $Y = \beta_0 + \beta_1 X_1 + \beta_1 X_2 + \varepsilon$

Table 9.2   Scores for 12 Subjects on Three Variables (Y, X_1, and X_2)

Person	Y	X_1	X_2
1	2	8	1
2	3	9	2
3	3	9	2
4	4	10	3
5	7	6	8
6	5	7	9
7	5	4	9
8	7	5	10
9	8	3	5
10	9	1	6
11	9	2	7
12	10	2	7

and Model C is $Y = \beta_0$ (where β_0 is the Grand mean). Because there are two predictors in Model A, we have two null hypotheses: $\beta_1 = 0$ and $\beta_2 = 0$. Since the omnibus test tests the entire model at once, we can also state the nulls as $H_0: \beta_1 = \beta_2 = 0$.

In Step 3 we count the number of parameters estimated. The simple model still estimated a single parameter (β_0), so PC = 1. This time, however, the omnibus Model A estimated three parameters (β_0, β_1, and β_2), so PA = 3. The difference in parameters estimated (PA – PC) is 3 – 1 or 2.

Next, we use the data to estimate the regression equation for the omnibus Model A (Step 4). With bivariate regression, we easily calculated the regression coefficients (b_0 and b_1) by hand. We're not so lucky with multiple regression—or maybe we're very lucky, depending on your perspective. Although we could compute the equation by hand, the formula consumes pages and would probably take an entire semester to calculate by hand (although admittedly I have only seen this equation once, during graduate school, and I have never tried to calculate a multiple regression by hand, let alone timed myself doing so). I recommend using a computer to do the work. After mere seconds, we get the regression equation for

Table 9.3 First Eight Model Comparison Steps

Step 1	State the compact Model C and an augmented Model A
	Model C: $\hat{Y} = \beta_0$
	Model A: $\hat{Y} = \beta_0 + \beta_1 X_1 + \beta_2 X_2$
Step 2	Identify the null hypothesis (H_0)
	H_0: $\beta_1 = \beta_2 = 0$
Step 3	Count the number of parameters estimated by each model
	PA = 3
	PC = 1
Step 4	Calculate the regression equation
	Model C: $\hat{Y} = 6$
	Model A: $\hat{Y} = 9.201 - 0.708 X_1 + 0.121 X_2$
Step 5	Compute sum of squares error for Model C (SSE_C)
	$SSE_C = 80$
Step 6	Compute sum of squares error for Model A (SSE_A)
	$SSE_A = 14.547$
Step 7	Compute sum of squares reduced (SSR)
	SSR = 65.453
Step 8	Compute the proportional reduction in error (PRE or R^2)
	PRE = R^2 = .818

the omnibus model. Based on the data in Table 9.2, the multiple regression is as follows:

$$\hat{Y} = 9.201 - 0.708 X_1 + 0.121 X_2.$$

The simple Model C still predicts the mean for each person, as it did in Chapter 4. The mean of Y is 6, so the equation for Model C is $\hat{Y} = 6$.

Once we have estimated the models, we calculate the sum of squares error for Model C (SST[1]; Step 5) and for the omnibus Model A (SSE_A; Step 6).

---

1. When the Model C we use is the simplest model having no predictor variables, the sum of squared errors of Model C (SSE_C) is the same as the total sum of squares (SST). In this case, I'll refer to the total error as SST.

Model C has not changed since Chapter 3, so SST is still 80. Model A has obviously changed. To find the error for the omnibus Model A, we use the Model A regression equation to predict a score for each subject $(\hat{Y})$, subtract each person's predicted score from her or his actual score $(Y - \hat{Y})$, square the difference $(Y - \hat{Y})^2$, and sum the squared differences. For example, Subject 1 scored 8 on X_1 and 1 on X_2. Plugging these values into Model A, we predict a score on Y of 3.658 for Subject 1 $((9.201 - 0.708(8) + 0.121(1))$. The difference between the real score (2) and the predicted score (3.658) for Subject 1 is −1.658. When we square this difference, we get 2.749. Thus, Subject 1 contributed 2.749 to the SST.

We follow these steps to compute the squared differences for every subject and sum them to get SSE_A. The real and predicted scores, and the squared differences between them, are presented for all 12 subjects in Table 9.4. Summing the squared differences, we find that the error for the omnibus model (SSE_A) is 14.547.

For Step 7, the sum of squares reduced (SSR) is found by subtracting SSE_A (14.547) from SST (80), which gives an SSR of 65.453. To compute the

Table 9.4 Using the Scores Predicted for Y Using Model A to Compute the SSE_A

Person	Y	$\hat{Y}$	$(Y - \hat{Y})^2$
1	2	3.658	2.749
2	3	3.071	0.005
3	3	3.071	0.005
4	4	2.484	2.298
5	7	5.921	1.164
6	5	5.334	0.112
7	5	7.458	6.042
8	7	6.871	0.017
9	8	7.682	0.101
10	9	9.219	0.048
11	9	8.632	0.135
12	10	8.632	1.871
	$SSE_A =$		14.547

proportional reduction in error (PRE; Step 8), divide the reduction in error (SSR = 65.453) by the total error (SST = 80). The result (65.453 ÷ 80) is a PRE of .818. PRE (R^2) tells us the percentage of the initial error (SST) that was explained or reduced by the addition of variables X_1 and X_2. Together these two variables explained 81.8% of SST.

The information gathered from Steps 1 through 8 is organized in the model comparison box (Table 9.5), and we'll use this information to complete Step 9, the formal summary table (see Table 9.6). Table 9.6 gives us an F value of 20.247. By most standards, 20.247 is a very large F ratio. In fact, the probability of getting an F of 20.247 or better, were H_0 true, is so small (probability less than .001) that we'd be way too daring if we didn't reject H_0. Having an omnibus (combined) effect in which X_1 and X_2 predict Y, we therefore conclude that X_1 and X_2 *together* are related to Y. We report the ANOVA as "$F(2, 9) = 20.247, p < .001, R^2 = .818$." The probability that we made a Type I error (rejected a true H_0) is very small ($p < .001$). The chance that we made a Type II error (failed to reject a true H_0) is nonexistent. We didn't fail to reject H_0, so there is no possibility that we *incorrectly* failed to reject H_0.

Table 9.5 Model Comparison Box Displaying the Information Necessary to Complete the Summary Table

Model C:	$Y = 6 + \varepsilon$	PC = 1	SST = 80
Model A:	$Y = 9.201 - 0.708X_1 + 0.121X_2 + \varepsilon$	PA = 3	$SSE_A = 14.547$
Difference:			SSR = 65.453
H_0:	$\beta_1 = \beta_2 = 0$		R^2 (PRE) = .818

Table 9.6 Summary Table Comparing the Omnibus Model A and the Simple Model C

Source	b	SS	df	MS	F	P	R^2
Model A		65.453	2	32.726	20.247	.000	.818
Residual (SSE_A)		14.547	9	1.616			
Total		80	11				

ISOLATING THE EFFECTS OF X_1 AND X_2 ♦

We've decided that Model A is better than Model C. But there is still one complication. We know that the null hypothesis is false, but we don't know why. It could be that both β_1 and β_2 do not equal zero. Alternatively, it could be that β_1 equals zero, but β_2 does not. Or it could be that β_2 equals zero, but β_1 does not. Whenever we conduct a model comparison in which the degrees of freedom (*df*) used (PA – PC) is greater than 1, we are confronted with this conundrum, and until we resolve it, we can't definitively answer our statistical questions (Is there a relationship between Y and X_1 and/or X_2? If so, what is the strength and direction of those relationships?).

To figure out if either (or both) of our parameters (β_1 or β_2) does not equal zero, we need to isolate the individual (unique) relationship between Y and each predictor (X_1 and X_2). Fortunately, we can test the unique effects of each predictor by comparing the omnibus Model A with a modified Model C. First, let's modify Model C to isolate the relationship between X_2 and Y (i.e., to test whether Y and X_2 are related).

Testing the Relationship Between X_2 and Y

Our omnibus Model A has two predictors (X_1 and X_2). In Chapter 4, we tested a bivariate regression that included one of those predictors (X_1). We can use the bivariate regression from Chapter 4 ($\hat{Y} = \beta_0 + \beta_1 X_1$) as a modified Model C (let's call it Model C_1), and compare it against the omnibus Model A ($\hat{Y} = \beta_0 + \beta_1 X_1 + \beta_2 X_2$). The difference between models A and C_1 is the addition of $\beta_2 X_2$ to Model A (see the Table 9.7). Comparing the error of Model A (SSE_A) with the error of Model C_1 (SSE_{C1}) helps us infer whether or not including $\beta_2 X_2$ improved the prediction of Y. By the way, notice that the difference in parameters estimated for Models A and C_1 (PA – PC) is 1 (3 – 2 = 1). This will be a 1 *df* test, and 1 *df* tests help us resolve (in part) our conundrum.

Table 9.7 Comparison of the Modified Model C (Bivariate Regression) and the Augmented Model A (Multiple Regression)

Model C_1:	$Y = \beta_0 + \beta_1 X_1 + SSE_{C1}$	$PC_1 = 2$
Model A:	$Y = \beta_0 + \beta_1 X_1 + \beta_2 X_2 + SSE_A$	$PA = 3$
Difference:	$\beta_2 X_2 + SSE_{C-A}$	1

The results of the first eight model comparison steps are presented in Table 9.8, and the findings organized in Table 9.9. Notice that PRE or R^2 is .069. This PRE or R^2 indicates that adding X_2 to the model reduced or explained 6.9% of the error variance in Y that wasn't explained by the bivariate regression (Model C_1). Of course, to determine if the reduction in error is statistically significant, we need to complete the ANOVA summary table (Table 9.10).

Adding the model comparison information from Table 9.9 to Table 9.10, we obtain an F test specific to variable X_2. The new information, specific to X_2, is italicized in Table 9.10. Dividing the SSR attributed to X_2 (1.07) by the

Table 9.8 First Eight Steps of Comparing Model A and the Modified Model C_1

Step 1	State the compact Model C and an augmented Model A
	Model C_1: $\hat{Y} = \beta_0 + \beta_1 X_1 +$
	Model A: $\hat{Y} = \beta_0 + \beta_1 X_1 + \beta_2 X_2$
Step 2	Identify the null hypothesis (H_0)
	H_0: $\beta_2 = 0$
Step 3	Count the number of parameters estimated by each model
	PA = 3
	$PC_1 = 2$
Step 4	Calculate the regression equation
	Model C_1: $\hat{Y} = 10.266 - 0.776 X_1$
	Model A: $\hat{Y} = 9.201 - 0.708 X_1 + 0.121 X_2$
Step 5	Compute total sum of squares (SSE_C)
	$SSE_{C1} = 15.617$
Step 6	Compute sum of squares for Model A (SSE_A)
	$SSE_A = 14.547$
Step 7	Compute sum of squares reduced (SSR)
	SSR = 1.07
Step 8	Compute the proportional reduction in error (PRE or R^2)
	PRE = R^2 = 0.069

Table 9.9 Comparison of Models A and C_1, Using the Data From Table 9.3, to Isolate the Effects of Adding $\beta_2 X_2$

Model C_1:	$Y = 10.266 - 0.776X_1 + SSE_{C2}$	$PC_1 = 2$	$SSE_{C1} = 15.617$
Model A:	$Y = 9.201 - 0.708X_1 + 0.121X_2 + SSE_A$	$PA = 3$	$SSE_A = 14.547$
Difference:	$0.121X_2 + SSR$	1	$SSR = 1.07$
H_0:	$\beta_2 = 0$	Partial R^2 (PRE) = 0.069	Semipartial R^2 (PRE) = 0.013

Table 9.10 ANOVA Summary Table With the Isolated Effect of X_2

Source	b	SS	df	MS	F	p	R^2 (sr^2)
Model A		65.453	2	32.726	20.247	0.000	0.818
X_2	0.121	1.07	1	1.07	0.662	0.437	0.013
Residual (SSE_A)		14.547	9	1.616			
Total		80	11				

single *df* used by adding X_2 to the model gives an *MS* of 1.07 for X_2. Dividing the *MS* of X_2 (1.07) by the *MSE* (1.616) gives an *F* value of 0.662. That is not a very impressive *F*. In fact, the probability of getting an *F* of 0.662 (with 1, 9 *df*) is .437. Since that probability isn't so hot (it definitely isn't <.05), we do *not* reject H_0 (properly put, we've "failed to reject H_0"). Because we failed to reject H_0, there is no chance we made a Type I error (we can only make a Type I error when we actually reject H_0); however, we might have made a Type II error. A Type II error happens when we fail to reject a H_0 that really is false. As a result of this analysis, we infer that X_2 and Y are not related.

Testing the Relationship Between X_1 and Y

Having isolated the effects of adding X_2 to the model predicting Y, the same steps are used to isolate the effects of including X_1 in the model. Table 9.11 presents the conceptual comparison of the omnibus Model A with a modified Model C that isolates the effects of adding X_1.

This new comparison model (call it Model C_2) includes X_2, but not X_1, as a predictor of Y. The difference between Model A ($\hat{Y} = \beta_0 + \beta_1 X_1 + \beta_2 X_2$) and Model C_2 ($\hat{Y} = \beta_0 + \beta_2 X_2$) is the inclusion of $\beta_1 X_1$ in Model A. If β_1 is different

Table 9.11 Comparison of Model A and the Modified Model C (C_2) That Includes $\beta_2 X_2$ as a Predictor of Y

Model C_2:	$Y = \beta_0 + \beta_2 X_2 + SSE_{C2}$	$PC_2 = 2$	$SSE_{C2} =$
Model A:	$Y = \beta_0 + \beta_1 X_1 + \beta_2 X_2 + SSE_A$	$PA = 3$	$SSE_A =$
Difference:	$\beta_1 X_1 + SSE_{C-A}$	1	$SSR =$
H_0:	$\beta_1 = 0$	R^2 (PRE) =	

from zero, then X_1 is related to Y; if β_1 is not different from zero, then X_1 would be unrelated to Y. I won't go through all 10 steps again—by now you should have a good understanding of the comparison process. The results of the first eight steps are presented in Table 9.12, and the findings are organized in Table 9.13.

Table 9.12 Comparison of Models A and C_2 to Isolate the Effects of Adding $\beta_1 X_1$ to the Model

Step 1	State the compact Model C and an augmented Model A
	Model C_1: $\hat{Y} = \beta_0 + \beta_2 X_2$
	Model A: $\hat{Y} = \beta_0 + \beta_1 X_1 + \beta_2 X_2$
Step 2	Identify the null hypothesis (H_0)
	$H_0: \beta_1 = 0$
Step 3	Count the number of parameters estimated by each model
	$PA = 3$
	$PC_1 = 2$
Step 4	Calculate the regression equation
	Model C_1: $\hat{Y} = 3.024 + 0.518 X_2$
	Model A: $\hat{Y} = 9.201 - 0.708 X_1 + 0.121 X_2$
Step 5	Compute total sum of squares (SSE_C)
	$SSE_{C2} = 51.529$
Step 6	Compute sum of squares for Model A (SSE_A)
	$SSE_A = 14.547$
Step 7	Compute sum of squares reduced (SSR)
	$SSR = 36.982$
Step 8	Compute the proportional reduction in error (PRE or R^2)
	$PRE = R^2 = 0.462$

Table 9.13 Comparison of Models A and C_2 to Isolate the Effects of Adding $\beta_1 X_1$ to the Model

Model C_2:	$Y = 3.024 + 0.518X_2 + SSE_{C2}$	$PC_2 = 2$	$SSE_{C2} = 51.529$
Model A:	$Y = 9.201 - 0.708X_1 + 0.121X_2 + SSE_A$	$PA = 3$	$SSE_A = 14.547$
Difference:	$\beta_1 X_1 + SSR$	1	$SSR = 36.982$
H_0:	$\beta_1 = 0$	R^2 (PRE) = 0.462	

The error of this modified Model C_2 (SSE_{C2}) is 51.529. Subtracting the error of the omnibus Model A ($SSE_A = 14.547$) from SSE_{C2} gives an SSR of 36.982. Dividing SSR by SSE_{C2} gives a PRE of 0.462. Therefore, adding X_1 to the model that already had X_2 explained an additional 46.2% of the variance of Y. That's a whopping big percentage, and in all likelihood, it is statistically significant. But, to be proper, we must complete the ANOVA summary table (Table 9.14). The difference in the number of parameters for Model A ($PA = 3$) and Model C_2 ($PC_2 = 2$) is 1, so we used 1 df. Dividing the SSR for X_1 by the single df gives us an MS of 36.982 for X_1. Dividing the MS for X_1 (36.982) by the MSE (1.616), we get an F value of 22.885. That's a big F value, and the probability of $F(1, 9) = 22.885$ (if H_0 is true) is less than 1 in 1,000 ($p < .001$). So we're going to figure that H_0 is probably *not* true. We reject H_0 and infer that X_1 and Y are related. Having rejected H_0, what type of error (I or II) might we have made?

Table 9.14 Summary Table Comparing the Omnibus Model A and the Simple Model C

Source	b	SS	df	MS	F	p	R^2 (sr^2)
Model A		65.453	2	32.726	20.247	0.000	0.818
b_0	9.201						
X_1	−0.708	36.982	1	36.982	22.885	0.001	
X_2	0.121	1.07	1	1.07	0.662	0.437	
Residual (SSE_A)		14.547	9	1.616			
Total		80	11				

◆ SUMMARY

In our quest to ask a more sophisticated research question, this chapter has covered a lot of material. By adding an additional predictor (X_2) to our bivariate regression model, we were able to compare an omnibus Model A that included two predictors (X_1 and X_2) against our simple Model C that included no predictor variables. While the difference was impressive, it didn't tell us if we needed both predictors in Model A. So we isolated the effects of each predictor by comparing Model A against a couple of modified Model Cs (Model C_1 and Model C_2). By isolating these individual effects, we were able to decide that X_1, but not X_2, was related to Y.

Thus begins our introduction to multiple regression. In fact, the multiple regression models can become even more complex. You can continue to add additional predictors until you run out of *df*. Of course, you'll also need to isolate the effects of every predictor you add. Suppose you had four predictors in your omnibus (overall) model $(\hat{Y} = \beta_0 + \beta_1 X_1 + \beta_2 X_2 + \beta_3 X_3 + \beta_4 X_4)$. You would need four modified Model Cs to isolate the effects of adding each predictor. For example, the modified Model C that would test the effects of adding X_4 to the model is $\hat{Y} = \beta_0 + \beta_1 X_1 + \beta_2 X_2 + \beta_3 X_3$.

Now that we've tested the effects of having two predictor variables in our regression model, there is one more feature of this two-predictor multiple regression that we need to consider—the *interaction* between variables X_1 and X_2. In the next chapter, I'll define an interaction and consider whether the relationship between one predictor and the outcome variable (Y) depends on the second predictor variable.

10

MULTIPLE REGRESSION

When Predictors Interact

The universe is a strange and wondrous place. The truth is quite odd enough to need no help from pseudoscientific charlatans.

—Richard Dawkins

When we added a second predictor variable in Chapter 9, we isolated and tested the unique effects of each predictor. And we were pleased by the potential to enhance the prediction and understanding of our outcome variable.

It probably won't surprise you to learn that we can advance this multiple regression another step. We've tested the direct relationship between an outcome (Y) and two predictor variables (X_1 and X_2). But what if the relationship between Y and one of the predictors (e.g., X_1) depended on the person's score on the other predictor (X_2)? The actual relationship between Y and X_1 might change or fluctuate according to how a person scored on X_2. It's possible! Perhaps Y and X_1 have a positive relationship when the value of X_2 is low, but a negative relationship when the value of X_2 is high. We call this an *interaction*. Not only can we test for it, but often it presents some of our most interesting research findings.

To test for an interaction, we multiply X_1 and X_2. This gives us a third predictor variable, X_3, where $X_3 = X_1 \times X_2$. In this chapter, we'll learn how to add X_3 to our multiple regression model, isolate its effect as a predictor of Y, and (if it's statistically significant) interpret its impact on the prediction of Y.

◆ MEAN DEVIATION REVISITED

Before we multiply X_1 and X_2, we need to set their means equal to zero. The importance of this simple step will become apparent later when we interpret the interaction. In Chapter 3, we learned to mean deviate a predictor variable so that its mean value became zero by subtracting the mean score from the raw score $(X - \bar{X})$. We called the deviated variable "X prime" and wrote it as X'. We can mean deviate both predictors in a multiple regression equation:

$$X_1' = X_1 - \bar{X}_1 \text{ and } X_2' = X_2 - \bar{X}_2.$$

◆ THE INTERACTION TERM: A CROSS PRODUCT OF THE PREDICTORS

Once we've mean deviated X_1 and X_2, we get the interaction term by multiplying the two deviated variables together: $X_3' = X_1' \times X_2'$. We then add the interaction term to our regression to get a new augmented Model A:

$$\hat{Y} = \beta_0 + \beta_1 X_1' + \beta_2 X_2' + \beta_3 X_3'.$$

With the interaction term added to our model, we next need to test the effects of including that term. We test this just as we did with multiple regression in Chapter 9—we define a modified Model C (let's call this one Model C_3) and isolate the effects of including the interaction term in the model. If there is an interaction effect, then the regression coefficient for X_3' (β_3) should not equal zero. It follows, then, that the null hypothesis (i.e., that there is no interaction effect) is $\beta_3 = 0$. The model comparison that tests the interaction is presented in Table 10.1.

To demonstrate the interaction let's add the interaction term to the multiple regression tested in Chapter 9 using the small ($N = 12$) data set.

Table 10.1 Conceptual Model Comparison for Testing the Interaction Term

Model A: $Y = b_0 + b_1C_1 + b_2C_2 + b_3C_1 \times C_2 +$	SSE_A	PA = 4
Model C: $Y = b_0 + b_1C_1 + b_2C_2 +$	SSE_C	PC = 3
Difference $b_3C_1 \times C_2$	SSR	PA-PC = 1

Recall from Chapter 9 that Model A had two predictors (X_1 and X_2), and we isolated the "Main Effects" of each predictor by comparing the omnibus Model A against the two modified compact models. We'll use the same model comparison steps to test the impact of the interaction term on our prediction of Y. First, however, we need to mean deviate the two predictors (X_1 and X_2) and then multiply them to get X_3. Table 10.2 demonstrates this step. The third and fourth columns of Table 10.2 show the original values of X_1 and X_2 respectively. The fifth column (X_1') has the mean-deviated values of X_1: They were obtained by subtracting the mean of X_1 (5.5) from each X_1 score ($X_1 - 5.5$). Likewise, the scores for X_2' in the sixth column were formed by subtracting the mean of X_2 (5.75) from each subject's score on X_2 ($X_2' = X_2 - 5.75$). The last column is the cross product, and it was found by multiplying each X_1' score with its corresponding X_2' score.

With the mean-deviated predictors for X_1' and X_2' and their cross product (X_3'), we can now compare Models C_3 and A (see Table 10.1) to test the effect of adding X_3 to the model. The first eight comparison steps are presented in Table 10.3.

Table 10.2 Mean Deviation and Cross Product of X_1 and X_2 to Create X_3

1	2	3	4	5	6	7
Person	Y	X_1	X_2	X_1'	X_2'	X_3'
1	2	8	1	2.5	−4.75	−11.875
2	3	9	2	3.5	−3.75	−13.125
3	3	9	2	3.5	−3.75	−13.125
4	4	10	3	4.5	−2.75	−12.375
5	7	6	8	0.5	2.25	1.125
6	5	7	9	1.5	3.25	4.875
7	5	4	9	−1.5	3.25	−4.875
8	7	5	10	−0.5	4.25	−2.125
9	8	3	5	−2.5	−0.75	1.875
10	9	1	6	−4.5	0.25	−1.125
11	9	2	7	−3.5	1.25	−4.375
12	10	2	7	−3.5	1.25	−4.375
Means		5.5	5.75	0	0	

Table 10.3 First Eight Model Comparison Steps to Test X_3

Step 1	State the compact Model C and an augmented Model A	
	Model C_3:	$\hat{Y} = \beta_0 + \beta_1 X_1 + \beta_2 X_2$
	Model A:	$\hat{Y} = \beta_0 + \beta_1 X_1 + \beta_2 X_2 + \beta_3 X_3$
Step 2	Identify the null hypothesis (H_0)	
	H_0:	$\beta_2 = 0$
Step 3	Count the number of parameters estimated by each model	
	PA = 4	
	$PC_3 = 3$	
Step 4	Calculate the regression equation	
	Model C_3:	$\hat{Y} = 6 - 0.708X_1 + 0.121X_2$
	Model A:	$\hat{Y} = 6.232 - 0.686X_1 + 0.059X_2 + 0.047X_3$
Step 5	Compute total sum of squares (SSE_C)	
	$SSE_{C3} = 14.547$	
Step 6	Compute sum of squares for Model A (SSE_A)	
	$SSE_A = 14.214$	
Step 7	Compute sum of squares reduced (SSR)	
	SSR = 0.333	
Step 8	Compute the proportional reduction in error (PRE or R^2)	
	PRE = R^2 = .004	

Step 1: State the models. Model C_3 is $\hat{Y} = \beta_0 + \beta_1 X_1 + \beta_2 X_2$; Model A is $\hat{Y} = \beta_0 + \beta_1 X_1 + \beta_2 X_2 + \beta_3 X_3$.

Step 2: State the null hypothesis. H_0: $\beta_3 = 0$.

Step 3: Computed the degrees of freedom. PA (4) − PC (3) is 1, so testing this interaction used 1 *df.*

Step 4: Use the data to estimate the models. The regression equation for Model C_3 is the same as our Model A in Chapter 9: $\hat{Y} = 6 - 0.708X'_1 + 0.121X'_2$; the equation for Model A is $\hat{Y} = 6.232 - 0.686X'_1 + 0.059X'_2 + 0.047X'_3$.

Step 5: Calculate the error of the compact model. Our compact model (Model C_3) is identical to the augmented model we tested in Chapter 9. Recall that the error of that model was 14.547, and it will be the same error this time as well. Therefore, $SSE_{C3} = 14.547$.

Step 6: Determine the error of the new augmented model.

By now you should be familiar with calculating *SSE* of Model A; however, I'll demonstrate it again for review and practice. The process to get SSE_A involves predicting an outcome score $(\hat{Y})$ for each subject, finding the difference between predicted and actual outcome scores $(Y - \hat{Y})$, squaring the difference $(Y - \hat{Y})^2$, and summing the squared differences $\left[\sum (Y - \hat{Y})^2 \right]$ (see Table 10.4). The resulting SSE_A is 14.214.

Table 10.4 Computation of SSE_A

Person	Y	$\hat{Y}$	$Y - \hat{Y}$	$(Y - \hat{Y})^2$
1	2	3.679	−1.679	2.818
2	3	2.993	0.007	0.000
3	3	2.993	0.007	0.000
4	4	2.401	1.599	2.556
5	7	6.075	0.925	0.856
6	5	5.624	−0.624	0.389
7	5	7.224	−2.224	4.945
8	7	6.726	0.274	0.075
9	8	7.991	0.009	0.000
10	9	9.281	−0.281	0.079
11	9	8.501	0.499	0.249
12	10	8.501	1.499	2.247
			$SSE_A =$	14.214

In Step 7, we obtained the SSR by subtracting SSE_A (14.214) from SSE_{C3} (14.547), which is 0.333. In Step 8, we found R^2 or PRE by dividing SSR by SST. Our R^2 is 0.333 ÷ 80, which is 0.004. The findings from Steps 1 to 8 are organized and presented in the summary box (Table 10.5).

Table 10.5 Information Necessary to Complete Table 10.6

Model C_3:	$Y = 6 - 0.708X_1 + 0.121X_2 + \varepsilon$	PC = 3	$SSC_3 = 14.547$
Model A:	$Y = 6.232 - 0.686X_1 + 0.059X_2 + .047X_3 + \varepsilon$	PA = 3	$SSE_A = 14.214$
Difference:			SSR = 0.333
H_0:	$\beta_3 = 0$		R^2 (PRE) = 0.004

Adding X_3 to the model explained very little additional error variance of Y (0.4%). Of course, we haven't determined if that's a statistically significant reduction in error, but less than 1% is not too promising. Even so, we'll finish Step 9 by completing the ANOVA summary table (see Table 10.6). The summary table generates the F, and we'll consider the probability of getting that F when we decide if adding the interaction term ($\beta_3 X_3$) improved our prediction (Step 10). An F of 0.187 based on 1 and 8 dfs will occur 676 times out of 1,000 when H_0 is true. With those odds, it's wise not to reject H_0.

Table 10.6 Summary Table With the Test of β_3 Added

Source	b	SS	df	MS	F	P	R^2 (sr^2)
Model A		65.786	3	32.726	20.247	0.000	0.818
b_0	6.232						
X_1	−0.686	31.302	1	31.302	17.615	0.003	0.391
X_2	0.059	0.135	1	0.135	0.076	0.789	0.002
X_3	0.047	0.333	1	0.333	0.187	0.676	0.004
Residual (SSE_A)		14.214	8	1.777			
Total		80	11				

♦ INTERPRETING THE INTERACTION

Although the interaction was not statistically significant, let's take a moment to consider how we would interpret an interaction if it were significant (after all, we're bound to get a statistically significant interaction one of these days). Remember that our goal with these analyses is to describe the relationship between one predictor and the outcome variables. Let's begin by describing the relationship between Y and X_1. According to the regression equation, the basic relationship between Y and X_1 is β_1, and we estimated β_1 as b_1 or -0.686. This regression coefficient tells us that for every increase of 1 point in X_1, the predicted value of Y decreases 0.686.

$$\hat{Y} = [\beta_0 + \beta_2 X_2'] + [\beta_1 X_1' + \beta_3 X_3'].\tag{10.1}$$

Now consider the entire regression equation (Equation 10.1). Notice that I've taken the liberty of slightly rearranging and clustering some of the terms. I've created one cluster in particular that will help us interpret the interaction $[\beta_1 X_1' + \beta_3 X_3']$. Since X_3' is the product of X_1' times X_2', we can substitute that product for X_3' into the equation (see Equation 10.2).

$$\hat{Y} = [\beta_0 + \beta_2 X_2'] + [\beta_1 X_1' + \beta_3 X_1' \times X_2'].\tag{10.2}$$

Next, since both elements in this cluster include an X_1' term $[\beta_1 X_1' + \beta_3 X_1' \times X_2']$, we can factor X_1' out of the cluster to get Equation 10.3.

$$\hat{Y} = [\beta_0 + \beta_2 X_2'] + [\beta_1 + \beta_3 X_2'] X_1'.\tag{10.3}$$

Look at the clustered term in front of X_1' (i.e., $[\beta_1 + \beta_3 X_2']$). This cluster is a sophisticated description of the relationship between X_1' and Y (so long as $\beta_3 \neq 0$). It tells us that the relationship between X_1' and Y begins at -0.686, and it is then adjusted by the value of b_3 as X_2' changes.

The relationship between Y and X_1' is β_1 when the value of X_2' is zero. Remember also that we mean deviated X_2', so zero is the average value of X_2'. Therefore, the relationship between X_1' and Y is β_1 at the average value of X_2' (i.e., $X_2' = 0$).

$$\hat{Y} = [6.232 + 0.059 X_2'] + [-0.686 + 0.047 X_2'] X_1'.\tag{10.4}$$

I replaced the βs with the estimated regression coefficients in Equation 10.4. If our interaction term had been statistically different from zero, then we would interpret the interaction in the following way. At the average level of X_2' (zero), the relationship between Y and X_1' is -0.686. When X_2' increases by 1 point, the relationship between Y and X_1' changes 0.047 and becomes −0.639. If X_2' increases another point, the relationship between Y and X_1' changes another 0.047 (it becomes −0.592). In other words, the relationship between Y and X_1' approaches zero as X_2' increases in value.

In contrast, as scores on X_2' drop below its mean, the relationship between Y and X_1' becomes stronger. When X_2' drops one point below its mean, the relationship between Y and X_1' changes from −0.686 to −0.733. If X_2' drops another point below its mean, the relationship strengthens again, changing from −0.733 to −0.780. To summarize this interaction, the relationship between Y and X_1' approaches zero (no relationship) as X_2' increases in value, and the relationship becomes stronger as X_2' decreases in value.

◆ INTERACTION WITHOUT MEAN DEVIATION

At the beginning of this chapter, I emphasized the importance of mean deviating or centering our predictors around zero. Mean deviating allowed us to interpret the coefficient for X_1' (β_1) as the relationship between Y and X_1' *at the average level of* X_2'. Had we not mean deviated these predictors, we would have ended up with a different regression equation (see Equation 10.5). And I'll run into some difficulty interpreting the interaction when we cluster the regression components.

$$\hat{Y} = 11.15 - 0.955X_1 - 0.199X_2 + 0.047X_3. \tag{10.5}$$

Specifically, the cluster that describes the relationship between Y and X_1' [$\beta_1 + \beta_3 X_2$] now tells me that the relationship is β_1 when X_2 is zero, and the relationship decreases β_3 as X_2 decreases below zero. The problem is that X_2 never actually equals zero, and it never drops below zero. Hence, β_1 is an estimate of the relationship between Y and X_1 at an unrealistic value of X_2; hence, is β_1 is rather meaningless.

The problem with β_1 is further evident if we consider the results of our example had we not mean deviated X_1 and X_2. Equation 10.6 compares the mean deviated and non–mean deviated equations. Notice that the regression coefficients for X_1' and X_2' are completely different from the coefficients for X_1 and X_2. Not only are they different, but were we to conduct the statistical analysis, we'd find that the results are different as well. Specifically, while we found a main effect for X_1', when we didn't mean deviate the variables, we no longer had a main effect for X_1.

Mean deviated: $\hat{Y} = 6.232 - 0.686X_1' + 0.059X_2' + 0.047X_3'.$ (10.6)

Non–mean deviated: $\hat{Y} = 11.15 - 0.955X_1 - 0.199X_2 + 0.047X_3.$

◆ SUMMARY

We have notched up the complexity and sophistication of our regression model in this chapter by multiplying two predictors together to get an interaction term. The null hypothesis is that the regression coefficient for the interaction term is equal to zero. By isolating the effects of adding just that interaction to the model, we tested to see if the interaction improved the prediction of Y. Although in this example we failed to reject H_0 (i.e., it looks like the interaction didn't improve the prediction of Y), we learned how to interpret an interaction in a multiple regression model. The interaction term essentially revealed how the relationship between X_1 and Y changed as the score on X_2 changed.

11

TWO-WAY ANOVA

Traditional Approach

Statistics are to baseball what a flaky crust is to Mom's apple pie.

—Harry Reasoner

W e've seen now that we can build a far more interesting regression model by having two predictors and an interaction term. In the same way, we can develop a more interesting analysis of variance (ANOVA) that includes multiple independent (predictor) variables (IVs) and the interactions between those IVs. When an ANOVA has a single IV, it's called a "one-way ANOVA." If the ANOVA has two IVs, it's called a "two-way ANOVA," and so on. In this chapter, I'll introduce a two-way ANOVA using the 24 depression scores from the earlier chapters (see Table 11.1). The one-way ANOVA conducted with these data in Chapter 7 used one IV (Diagnosis) to predict the Depression score. Table 11.1 has two IVs: Sex and Diagnosis. The Sex variable has two possible values: Men or Women. Diagnosis still has two groups: No Dx and Depressed. The two-way ANOVA will use these two IVs (Sex and Diagnosis) to test three questions. First, it will test if men and women had different depression scores on average ("main effect" for Sex). Second, it will test if Depressed subjects score differently on the Depression measure than those with no psychiatric diagnosis (main effect for Diagnosis). Finally, it will test the interaction between Sex and Diagnosis. The interaction reveals whether the *relationship* between Diagnosis and Depressive symptoms is different or the same for men and women.

Table 11.1 Depressive Symptom Scores (DV), the Sex of Each Participant (IV_1), and Whether or Not the Subject Has a Depression Diagnosis (IV_2)

Subject	Symptom Score (DV)	Sex (IV_1)	Diagnosis (IV_2)
1	3	M	None
2	5	M	None
3	6	M	None
4	8	M	None
5	9	M	None
6	11	M	None
7	19	M	Depressed
8	15	M	Depressed
9	16	M	Depressed
10	16	M	Depressed
11	19	M	Depressed
12	17	M	Depressed
13	3	F	None
14	5	F	None
15	4	F	None
16	6	F	None
17	8	F	None
18	10	F	None
19	24	F	Depressed
20	24	F	Depressed
21	22	F	Depressed
22	23	F	Depressed
23	19	F	Depressed
24	20	F	Depressed

GRAND AND GROUP MEANS ♦

The Grand mean Depression score for all 24 subjects ($\overline{Y}_{grand}$) is 13. We also can get means (M) and standard deviations (SD) according to the subject's sex: Men ($M = 12$, $SD = 5.69$); Women ($M = 14$, $SD = 8.66$). Alternatively, we can report means according to diagnosis: Depressed ($M = 19.5$, $SD = 3.18$); No Dx ($M = 6.5$, $SD = 2.68$). Table 11.2 sorts the data according to the four groups defined by the two predictor variables (Depressed Men, Depressed Women, No Dx Men, and No Dx Women).

Table 11.2 Depressive Symptom Scores (Dependent Variable) Arranged by the Independent Variables (Sex and Diagnosis)

	Diagnosis		
	Psych Dx	*No Dx*	*Marginal Sum*
Men	19	3	Σ = 144
	15	5	
	16	6	
	16	8	
	19	9	
	17	11	
Women	24	3	Σ = 168
	24	5	
	22	4	
	23	6	
	19	8	
	20	10	
Marginal Sum	Σ = 234	Σ = 78	

PARTITION THE SUM OF SQUARES ♦

As with the one-way ANOVA, we conduct a two-way ANOVA by partitioning the total sum of squares (*SST*) for Depression scores into (a) the "between" error (SSB) that was explained by the IVs and (b) the residual or "within" error (SSW) that was not explained by the IVs. This time, however, three sources will contribute to SSB: the error explained by Sex, error explained by Diagnosis, and error explained by the interaction between Sex and Diagnosis. To begin, let's find the total error (SST).

Compute SST

The SST, as always, is computed by subtracting the Grand mean of the DV (Depressive symptoms) from each subject's score on the DV ($Y_i - \bar{Y}_{grand}$), squaring the differences, and then summing them. Since the Depression scores are the same as they were in previous chapters, SST too is the same for this two-way ANOVA as it was in previous chapters: SST = $\sum(Y_i - 13.5)^2 = 1204$.

Next, we need the SSB. This time, however, we need three SSB scores—one for each predictor (Sex and Diagnosis) and one for the interaction. We'll begin by finding the SSB for Sex.

SSB for Sex

Steinberg (2011) conceptualized a two-way ANOVA as "a series of one-way ANOVAs—one for each independent variable" (p. 350). Therefore, it's not too surprising that we can use the same formula used in Chapter 7 to compute each SSB (see Equation 11.1). As in Chapter 7, the formula to find SSB_{sex} has two parts: the first being the sum of the averaged squared sum for each group and the second being the correction term (the sum of Y squared and divided by total N):

$$SSB = \sum \left[\frac{\left(\sum Y_{group}\right)^2}{N_{group}} \right] - \frac{\left(\sum Y\right)^2}{N_{total}}. \tag{11.1}$$

The first part of Equation 11.1 requires that we sum the scores within a group, square the value, and divide by the number of subjects in that group. Since Sex has two groups (Men and Women), we complete this process twice:

$$\left[\frac{\left(\sum Y_{men}\right)^2}{N_{men}} \right] + \left[\frac{\left(\sum Y_{women}\right)^2}{N_{women}} \right]. \tag{11.2}$$

We can insert the sum of scores for Men ($\sum Y = 144$), the sum for Women ($\sum Y = 168$), and the N for each group into the equation to get the first part of Equation 11.1:

$$\left[\frac{(144)^2}{12}\right]+\left[\frac{(168)^2}{12}\right]=\left[\frac{20,736}{12}\right]+\left[\frac{28,224}{12}\right]=[1728]+[2352]=4080. \quad (11.3)$$

The first part of Equation 11.1 sums to 4,080. Once we compute the correction term, we can subtract it from this value (4,080). The correction term is the sum of all depression scores squared and divided by total N. The sum of all Depression scores ($\sum Y$) is 312. Square this sum ($312^2 = 97344$), and divide by total sample size ($N = 24$) to get a correction term of 4,056. When we subtract the correction term (4,056) from the first term (4,080), we find that Sex explained 24 SSB (sum of squared errors).

With the SSB for Sex and the SST, we can begin to fill out the summary table needed to complete the two-way ANOVA (Table 11.3).

Table 11.3   Summary Table for Two-Way ANOVA, With Values for SSB$_\text{sex}$ and SST Entered

Source	SS	df	MS	F	p
Sex	24				
Diagnosis					
Sex × Diagnosis					
Error					
Total	1,204				

SSB for Diagnosis

We'll follow the same steps to determine SSB$_\text{Dx}$. Equation 11.4 demonstrates how to insert the group sums for the two diagnosis groups (Depressed = 234, No Dx = 78) to obtain the first part of Equation 11.1 for Diagnosis:

$$\left[\frac{\left(\sum Y_\text{depressed}\right)^2}{N_\text{depressed}}\right]+\left[\frac{\left(\sum Y_\text{NoDx}\right)^2}{N_\text{NoDx}}\right]. \quad (11.4)$$

$$\left[\frac{(234)^2}{12}\right]+\left[\frac{78^2}{12}\right]=\left[\frac{54756}{12}\right]+\left[\frac{6084}{12}\right]=[4563]+[507]=5070.$$

Next, we subtract the correction term (4,056) from the first part of the equation (5,070) to get the SSB for Diagnosis (SSB_{Dx} = 1014). We'll add this value to the summary table (Table 11.4).

Table 11.4   Summary Table for Two-Way ANOVA, With Values for SSB_{sex}, $SSB_{diagnosis}$, and SST Entered

Source	SS	df	MS	F	p
Sex	24				
Diagnosis	1,014				
Sex × Diagnosis					
Error					
Total	1,204				

Interaction of Sex and Diagnosis

When we computed SSB for each IV, we "collapsed" scores across the IV we were *not* looking at. For example, to get SSB for Sex, we used the mean score for all 12 men regardless of their diagnosis, and we used the mean score for all 12 women regardless of their diagnosis. Likewise, to get SSB for Diagnosis, we obtained mean scores for the Depression and the No Dx groups regardless of the subject's sex.

Now, to get the *SS* for the interaction of Sex and Diagnosis ($SS_{sex \times diagnosis}$), we need to attend to Sex and Diagnosis at the same time. To do this, we'll consider each "cell" separately. A cell is a subgroup formed by crossing one IV with the other. Table 11.2 first demonstrated this by presenting the data for men with and without Depression separately and presenting the scores for women with and without Depression separately. In Table 11.5, I've presented these data again, but this time I've included the sum of scores within each cell. Thus, the six men with Depression had a sum of 102, the women with Depression had a sum of 132, the men with no diagnosis had a sum of 42, and the women with no diagnosis had a sum of 36.

Equation 11.5 gives the formula to get the SSB explained by the interaction. The difference between this equation and the formula used to get the SSB for each IV is that this equation has four parts instead of two. The first part is similar to the first part of Equation 11.1—sum the scores in each cell,

Table 11.5 Obtaining Diagonal Means to Calculate the Sum of Squares for the Sex-by-Diagnosis Interaction

		Diagnosis
	Psych Dx	*No Dx*
Men	19	3
	15	5
	16	6
	16	8
	19	9
	17	11
	Σ = 102	Σ = 42
Women	24	3
	24	5
	22	4
	23	6
	19	8
	20	10
	Σ = 132	Σ = 36

square the sum, and divide by the number of subjects in the cell. With four cells, we'll repeat this process four times and sum the results:

$$SS_{\text{sex} \times \text{Dx}} = \Sigma \frac{(\Sigma Y_{\text{cell}})^2}{N_{\text{cell}}} - SSB_{\text{sex}} - SSB_{\text{Psych Dx}} - \frac{(\Sigma Y)^2}{N}. \qquad (11.5)$$

From this sum, we then subtract the SSB found for Sex (24), the SSB found for Diagnosis (1,014), and the correction term (4,056). Table 11.6 gives the sum of Depression scores for each cell, squares the sum, and then divides it by the number of subjects in each cell. The resulting values for each cell are added together, and then the SSB_{sex}, the SSB_{Dx}, and the correction term are subtracted from the sum.

Table 11.6 Sums for Each Cell and the Steps to Compute SSB for the Interaction Between Sex and Diagnosis

Cell 1:	$\dfrac{(\sum Y_{men\ NoDx})^2}{N_{men\ NoDx}} = \dfrac{(42)^2}{6} = \dfrac{1764}{6} = 294$
Cell 2:	$\dfrac{(\sum Y_{men\ depressed})^2}{N_{men\ depressed}} = \dfrac{(102)^2}{6} = \dfrac{10404}{6} = 1734$
Cell 3:	$\dfrac{(\sum Y_{women\ NoDx})^2}{N_{women\ NoDx}} = \dfrac{(36)^2}{6} = \dfrac{1294}{6} = 216$
Cell 4:	$\dfrac{(\sum Y_{women\ depressed})^2}{N_{women\ depressed}} = \dfrac{(132)^2}{6} = \dfrac{17424}{6} = 2904$
Correction term	$\dfrac{(\sum Y)^2}{N} = \dfrac{(312)^2}{24} = \dfrac{97344}{24} = 4056$
$SSB_{sex} = 24$	$SSB_{Dx} = 1014$
$SSB_{interaction} = (Cell\ 1 + Cell\ 2 + Cell\ 3 + Cell\ 4) - SSB_{sex} - SSB_{Dx} - Correction\ term$	
$SSB_{interaction} = (294 + 1734 + 216 + 2904) - 24 - 1014 - 4056$	
$SSB_{interaction} = (5148) - 5094 = 54$	

♦ BEGIN THE SUMMARY TABLE

The SSB explained by the interaction is 54. We can add this information to update the summary table (Table 11.7).

Table 11.7 Summary Table for Two-Way ANOVA, With Values for SSB_{sex}, $SSB_{diagnosis}$, $SSB_{interaction}$, and SST Entered

Source	SS	df	MS	F	p
Sex	24				
Diagnosis	1,014				
Sex × Diagnosis	54				
Error					
Total	1,204				

Residual Sum of Squares

We have almost finished partitioning our total *SS*. All that is left to compute is the residual *SS*. Recall that with ANOVA, the residual *SS* is called the SS "within" (SSW) and it is the difference between SST and the *SSE* explained by the IVs (all SSB).

In fact, we could very simply complete the ANOVA summary table by summing the *SS* explained by Sex (24), Diagnosis (1,014), and the interaction (54) and then subtracting that total (1,092) from the SST (1,204). This simple approach gives a residual error (SSW) of 112:

$$SSW = \sum Y^2 - \sum \left[\frac{\left(\sum Y_{cell}\right)^2}{N_{cell}} \right]. \tag{11.6}$$

Of course, I advocate learning to compute SSW the hard way, without simply subtracting the explained *SS* from SST. Equation 11.6 shows how to compute SSW. This equation also has two parts. The first part is the sum of the squared Depression scores. Table 11.8 gives each Depression score, its squared value, and the sum of those squared values. In this case, $\sum Y^2 = 5260$.

Table 11.8 Depression Scores and Their Squared Values

Subject	Y	Y²
1	3	9
2	5	25
3	6	36
4	8	64
5	9	81
6	11	121
7	19	361
8	15	225
9	16	256
10	16	256

(Continued)

Table 11.8 (Continued)

Subject	Y	Y²
11	19	361
12	17	289
13	3	9
14	5	25
15	4	16
16	6	36
17	8	64
18	10	100
19	24	576
20	24	576
21	22	484
22	23	529
23	19	361
24	20	400
Σ	312	5,260

The second part of Equation 11.6 is identical to the first part of the equation we used to calculate the SSB for the interaction. If you look back at Table 11.6, you'll find that when we summed each cell, squared the value, divided by the N for that cell, and added all four of the resulting values together, the result was 5,148:

$$\left(\sum \left[\frac{\left(\sum Y_{cell} \right)^2}{N_{cell}} \right] \right) = 5,148.$$

When we subtract the value for the second part (5,148) from the value for the first part ($\sum Y^2 = 5260$), we get an SSW of 112:

$$SSW = \sum Y^2 - \sum \left[\frac{\left(\sum Y_{cell} \right)^2}{N_{cell}} \right] = 5260 - 5148 = 112. \tag{11.7}$$

COMPLETE THE SUMMARY TABLE

Fortunately, the SSW calculated with Equation 11.7 is equal to the SSW we obtained when we subtracted SSB from SST. Had they not been equal, then we'd know that we had made a mistake somewhere. We have now partitioned all of the SST into SSB and SSW, and we are just about ready to complete the ANOVA summary table. First we need to determine the degrees of freedom (*df*) for each source. As before, total *df* is $N - 1$, so in this example it is $24 - 1 = 23$. The *df* associated with each IV is 1 less than the number of groups associated with that IV. There are two Sex groups (Men and Women), so the *df* associated with Sex is $2 - 1 = 1$. Likewise, we had two Diagnosis groups, so 1 *df* was used for Diagnosis. The *df* for the interaction is found by multiplying the *df*s for the IVs included in the interaction. Since the interaction is the product of Sex (1 *df*) and Diagnosis (1 *df*), the *df* for the interaction is 1×1, which, of course, is 1. By summing the *df*s used in the ANOVA (1 *df* for Sex, 1 *df* for Diagnosis, and 1 *df* for the interaction), we've used 3 *df*s for this ANOVA. Since we began with 23 *df*s and used 3 *df*s for the ANOVA, the residual or remaining *df*s equal 20. Add these *df*s to the evolving summary table (Table 11.7).

The mean square (*MS*) values for the ANOVA are obtained by dividing the *SS* for each source (the two IVs and the interaction) by the *df* corresponding to that source ($SS \div df = MS$). We calculate an *F* ratio for each source by dividing the *MS* for each source by the MS_{error} (MSE or MS_{within}). For example, $MS_{sex} = 24$, and $MSE = 5.6$. Dividing 24 by 5.6, we obtain $F(1, 20) = 4.286$. The result is three *F* ratios: one for each main effect (Sex and Diagnosis) and one for the interaction. These results are given in Table 11.9.

Table 11.9 Completed Two-Way ANOVA Summary Table

Source	SS	df	MS	F	p
Sex	24	1	24	4.286	.052
Diagnosis	1,014	1	1,014	181.071	<.001
Sex × Diagnosis	54	1	54	9.643	.006
Error	112	20	5.6		
Total	1,206	23			

INTERPRET THE *F* VALUES

Results of a two-way ANOVA are reported separately for each IV and for the interaction. State the *df* used ("between") and remaining ("within") for the specific IV (in this example, df will be 1 and 20 for each IV and the interaction, respectively), report the F ratio, and then give the probability of getting that F ratio if the IV was not related to the DV. For example, we would report the result for the IV Sex as $F(1, 20) = 4.286$, $p = .052$. The result for Diagnosis is $F(1, 20) = 181.071$, $p < .001$ (even the computer doesn't typically get more precise than .001).

The probability of obtaining an F of a certain size can be found either by the computer (the simplest) or by checking a table to see if the obtained F exceeds a critical value. The computer will give you the precise probability: In the case of the main effect for Sex, the precise value of p is .052. Alternatively, you can use an F table—most statistics books will have an F table as an appendix. Table 11.10 is such a table. To use Table 11.10, look down the first column to find the df within (in this example, df within is 20). Next, go across the table to the column for the df between (in this example, df between is 1). Notice that there are two columns for 1 df between—one labeled $p \le .05$ and the other, $p \le .01$. Each column gives critical cutoff values for two different alphas (Type I error probabilities). As I've said before, the conventional probability used by most researchers is .05. Sometimes, however, an occasion requires that we minimize our chance of making a Type I error. On such occasions, we would use a more conservative alpha than .05, such as $p \le .01$. For now, we'll stay with the conventional $p \le .05$. The critical F value for 1 (between) and 20 (within) dfs and $p \le .05$ is 4.35. The obtained F of 4.286 was so very close, but it didn't quite exceed the cutoff value. Holding true to our critical cutoff value, we cannot claim that this main effect (for Sex) was statistically significant.

Table 11.10 Sample of a Table of Critical F Values

	df Between							
	1		2		3		4	
df Within	$p \le .05$	$p \le .01$	$p \le .05$	$p \le .01$	$p \le .05$	$p \le .01$	$p \le .05$	$p \le .01$
1	161	4,052	200	4,999	216	5,403	225	5625
2	18.51	98.49	19.00	99.00	19.16	99.17	19.25	99.25
3	10.13	34.12	9.55	30.82	9.28	29.46	9.12	28.71
4	7.71	21.20	6.94	18.00	6.59	16.69	6.39	15.98

	df Between							
	1		*2*		*3*		*4*	
df Within	*p ≤ .05*	*p ≤ .01*	*p ≤ .05*	*p ≤ .01*	*p ≤ .05*	*p ≤ .01*	*p ≤ .05*	*p ≤ .01*
5	6.61	16.26	5.79	13.27	5.41	12.06	5.19	11.39
6	5.99	13.74	5.14	10.92	4.76	9.78	4.53	9.15
7	5.59	12.25	4.74	9.55	4.35	8.45	4.12	7.85
8	5.32	11.26	4.46	8.65	4.07	7.59	3.84	7.01
9	5.12	10.56	4.26	8.02	3.86	6.99	3.63	6.42
10	4.97	10.04	4.10	7.56	3.71	6.55	3.48	5.99
11	4.84	9.65	3.98	7.20	3.59	6.22	3.36	5.67
12	4.75	9.33	3.89	6.93	3.49	5.95	3.26	5.41
13	4.67	9.07	3.81	6.70	3.41	5.74	3.18	5.20
14	4.60	8.86	3.74	6.51	3.34	5.56	3.11	5.03
15	4.54	8.68	3.68	6.36	3.29	5.42	3.06	4.89
16	4.49	8.53	3.63	6.23	3.24	5.29	3.01	4.77
17	4.45	8.40	3.59	6.11	3.20	5.18	2.97	4.67
18	4.41	8.28	3.56	6.01	3.16	5.09	2.93	4.58
19	4.38	8.18	3.52	5.93	3.13	5.01	2.90	4.50
20	4.35	8.10	3.49	5.85	3.10	4.94	2.87	4.43
21	4.33	8.02	3.47	5.78	3.07	4.87	2.84	4.37
22	4.30	7.94	3.44	5.72	3.05	4.82	2.82	4.31
23	4.28	7.88	3.42	5.66	3.03	4.76	2.80	4.26
24	4.26	7.82	3.40	5.61	3.01	4.72	2.78	4.22
25	4.24	7.77	3.39	5.57	2.99	4.68	2.76	4.18

♦ INTERPRET THE INTERACTION

The interaction between Diagnosis and Sex made this analysis more interesting. An interaction is a conditional statement about the relationship between one of the IVs and the DV. For example, we can state that the relationship between one IV (e.g., Diagnosis) and the DV (Depression score) "depends on" or is "conditional on" the level of the other IV (Sex). Put another way, the relationship between diagnosis and depression scores depends on the subject's sex. Figure 11.1 graphs these relationships. Examining Figure 11.1 reveals that the depression score was lowest for both men and women without depression ($M = 7$ and $M = 6$, respectively); however, the depression score increased more for women who were diagnosed with depression (from $M = 6$ to $M = 22$) than for men diagnosed with depression (from $M = 7$ to $M = 17$). This interaction tells us that the relationship between diagnosis and depressive symptom score depended on the subject's sex.

Figure 11.1 Graph of the Interaction: The Relationship Between Diagnosis and Depression Score, Conditional on the Person's Sex.

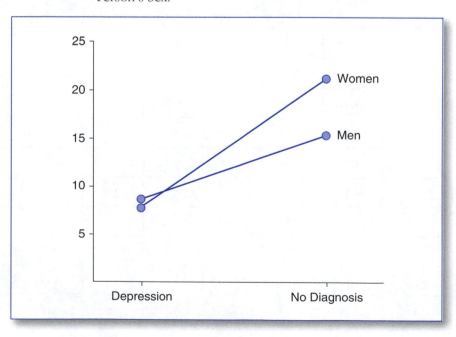

We could just as easily have said that the relationship between sex and depressive symptom scores depends on the person's diagnosis. Figure 11.2 shows this interpretation. This interpretation of the interaction basically says that the effect of Sex on Depression scores is different for people who are diagnosed as depressed versus those who have no diagnosis.

Figure 11.2   Graph of the Interaction: The Relationship Between Sex and Depression Score, Conditional on the Person's Diagnostic Status.

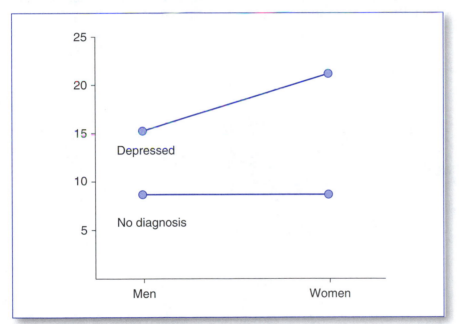

SUMMARY ◆

The two-way ANOVA produced three *F* ratios, and we used those *F* ratios to decide whether or not to reject the null hypotheses associated with both IVs and the interaction. As with the one-way ANOVA, we found the total error in the DV (SST) and then partitioned the SST into variance explained by each IV (SSB for Sex and SSB for Diagnosis), variance explained by the interaction (SSB for Sex × Diagnosis), and variance that is left over (SSW, or residual error). This partitioned variance helped us complete a summary table that generated separate F ratios for each IV and their interaction. The size of F guided our decision whether or not to reject the corresponding H_0. Finally, the interaction gave us an insight as to whether or not the relationship between the DV and one of the IVs might depend on (or be conditional on) the level or score on the other IV.

In Chapters 9 and 10, we performed an analysis similar to a two-way ANOVA, using multiple regression with two predictors and an interaction term. The predictor variables (IVs) in those analyses were continuous variables. We can also conduct a two-way ANOVA using categorical predictors in a multiple regression model comparison. In Chapter 12, I'll demonstrate how to conduct the same two-way ANOVA completed in this chapter by using multiple regression and the model comparison approach.

12

TWO-WAY ANOVA

Model Comparison Approach

. . . Science, in itself, ain't real interesting to the broad audience.

—Randy Olson

Don't Be Such a Scientist

Chapter 11 introduced the traditional two-way analysis of variance (ANOVA). In this chapter, we'll use multiple regression to conduct the same two-way ANOVA. A two-way ANOVA addresses several questions: (a) Is there a relationship between one predictor (IV_1) and the outcome (DV)? (b) Is there a relationship between the other predictor (IV_2) and the DV? and (c) Is there an interaction between IV_1 and IV_2 such that the relationship between IV_1 and the DV depends on the level of IV_2 (or vice versa—Does the relationship between IV_2 and the DV depend on the level of IV_1)? These questions can be answered using multivariate regression model comparisons. A multiple regression with two predictors and their interaction term requires several model comparisons. Table 12.1 presents the comparison for each main effect and the interaction, as well as the *omnibus model* comparison (listed as Comparison "O"). To demonstrate using the regression model comparison approach for a two-way ANOVA, we'll use the same data set that was used to conduct the traditional two-way ANOVA in Chapter 11. We'll begin by conducting the omnibus test and then demonstrate the specific analyses.

But first, we need to assign numerical values to the groups in each IV so that we can enter these numeric values into the regression program.

Table 12.1 Model Comparisons Needed to Isolate the Effects of Each Predictor (IV)

Comparison O: Omnibus Model	
Model A:	Depression $= \beta_0 + \beta_1$ Sex $+ \beta_2$ Diagnosis $+ \beta_3$ Sex $\times$ Diagnosis $+ \varepsilon$
Model C:	Depression $= \beta_0 + \varepsilon$
Difference	β_1 Sex $+ \beta_2$ Diagnosis $+ \beta_3$ Sex $\times$ Diagnosis
Comparison 1: Main Effect for Sex	
Model A:	Depression $= \beta_0 + \beta_1$ Sex $+ \beta_2$ Diagnosis $+ \beta_3$ Sex $\times$ Diagnosis $+ \varepsilon$
Model C_1:	Depression $= \beta_0 + \beta_2$ Diagnosis $+ \beta_3$ Sex $\times$ Diagnosis $+ \varepsilon$
Difference	β_1 Sex
Comparison 2: Main Effect for Diagnosis	
Model A:	Depression $= \beta_0 + \beta_1$ Sex $+ \beta_2$ Diagnosis $+ \beta_3$ Sex $\times$ Diagnosis $+ \varepsilon$
Model C_2:	Depression $= \beta_0 + \beta_1$ Sex$+ \beta_3$ Sex $\times$ Diagnosis $+ \varepsilon$
Difference	β_2 Diagnosis
Comparison 3: Interaction Between Sex and Diagnosis	
Model A:	Depression $= \beta_0 + \beta_1$ Sex $+ \beta_2$ Diagnosis $+ \beta_3$ Sex $\times$ Diagnosis $+ \varepsilon$
Model C_3:	Depression $= \beta_0 + \beta_1$ Sex $+ \beta_2$ Diagnosis $+ \varepsilon$
Difference	β_3 Sex $\times$ Diagnosis

◆ CONTRAST VERSUS DUMMY CODES

This analysis requires that we assign numeric codes to the groups comprising each IV. There are two common approaches to coding categorical variables: (1) *contrast codes* and (2) *dummy codes*. Table 12.2 gives the codes (values) for both of our IVs (Sex and Diagnosis) using these two different coding approaches. The first row gives the values for a "contrast" code. The Sex variable has two groups: (1) Men and (2) Women. Using contrast codes, Men are coded +1 and Women coded −1. The Diagnosis variable also has two groups: (1) Depressed (+1) and (2) No Diagnosis (−1).

Alternatively, we could have used "Dummy" codes. Row two of Table 12.2 shows how to code Sex and Diagnosis using Dummy codes. Dummy codes used for a variable with two levels are 0 and +1. In this example, the Sex variable is coded +1 for Men and 0 for Women; Diagnosis is coded +1 for Depressed and 0 for No Diagnosis.

I prefer to use "contrast codes" because, when the groups have equal N, the numerical values assigned to each group will sum to zero. For example, if we have 12 men coded as +1 and 12 women coded −1, then 12 + (−12) = 0. Obviously the mean score on Sex will then be zero. This contrast coding is equivalent to mean deviating a variable around zero. Remember from previous chapters that I really like to have my predictors/IVs "centered" around zero. Contrast coding accomplishes this for me.

In contrast, were we to use dummy codes, the Sex variable would not center around zero: 12 men (coded +1) and 12 women (coded 0) would sum to 12. The average of these codes (12 ÷ 24) is .5. So using dummy codes with equal N centers the variable around .5. It may seem like a minor difference until you try to interpret an interaction derived using dummy codes.

Once we've coded our two predictors, we still need the interaction variable. We get the interaction variable (as we did in Chapter 10) by multiplying the two IVs together: Sex × Diagnosis. Table 12.3 displays the contrast codes for the interaction term when it is the product of multiplying Diagnosis with Sex. The result is that Men with Depression and Women with no diagnosis were coded +1; Men with no diagnosis and Women with Depression were coded −1.

Table 12.2 Contrast Versus Dummy Codes

	Sex		Diagnosis	
Code	Men	Women	Depressed	No Diagnosis
Contrast	1	−1	1	−1
Dummy	1	0	1	0

Table 12.3 Contrast Codes for the Interaction term

		Diagnosis	
		Depressed	No Diagnosis
	Men	1	−1
Sex	Women	−1	1

◆ CONDUCTING THE OMNIBUS TEST

With our codes established, we can run the multiple regression. The Omnibus regression model (Depression = $\beta_0 + \beta_1$ Sex + β_2 Dx + β_3 Sex × Dx + ε) will be Model A for each of the model comparisons outlined in Table 12.1. The null hypothesis (H_0) for the omnibus test is that *all* of the regression coefficients equal zero (H_0: $\beta_0 = \beta_1 = \beta_2 = \beta_3 = 0$). If we enter our data into a computer statistics package, we'll get the estimated regression shown in Equation 12.1.

$$\text{Depression} = 13 - 1(\text{Sex}) + 6.5(\text{Dx}) - 1.5(\text{Sex} \times \text{Dx}) + \varepsilon. \qquad (12.1)$$

Look at Equation 12.1 for a moment, for it has some impressive characteristics. Remember that the average "score" on Sex is zero, and the average score on Diagnosis also is zero. Therefore, if we hold Sex and Diagnosis constant at their average values (0), all three predictors (Sex, Diagnosis, and Sex × Diagnosis) drop out of the equation, and the predicted score is 13 (the value of the intercept). It's no accident that the model predicts 13 when all predictors are held average—13 is the Grand Mean for depressive symptom scores. That's a benefit of contrast coding. Now imagine that we hold Diagnosis constant at its average value (0) but allow Sex to vary. When Diagnosis is 0, the Diagnosis and the interaction drop out (i.e., equal 0 and therefore do not contribute to the prediction), and we're left with Sex as the only predictor. Our predicted value of Depressive symptoms score for men (+1) is $Y = 13 - 1 \times (+1)$, which is $13 - 1 = 12$. This prediction happens to be the mean depression score for men. Likewise, when we insert the value for women (−1) into the equation, we get the average depression score for the women in the study ($Y = 13 - 1 \times (-1)$, which equals $13 + 1 = 14$).

Now hold Sex constant at its average level (0) and insert the values for Diagnosis. The predicted depressive symptom score for the Depressed group is $Y = 13 + 6.5 \times (+1)$, which is $13 + 6.5 = 19.5$. This score is the average depression score for the depressed group. You shouldn't be surprised to find that inserting the value for the No Dx group (−1) predicts the average depressive symptom score for that group ($Y = 13 + 6.5 \times (-1) = 13 - 6.5 = 6.5$).

◆ CALCULATE THE ERROR OF THE OMNIBUS MODEL

When we insert a person's scores on each IV and interaction into this equation, the regression equation generates a predicted depression score for that subject. To get the *SSE* for the omnibus model, we find the difference between the predicted and actual score $(Y - \hat{Y})$ for every subject and then square and sum the differences $\left(\Sigma (Y - \hat{Y})^2 \right)$. Table 12.4 demonstrates the process of computing the sum of squared errors for the omnibus Model A (SSE_A). The resulting SSE_A is the residual error, which, in ANOVA terms, is called SSW.

Table 12.4   Computing Error With the Omnibus Model

Subject	Symptom Score (DV)	Sex (Men = 1, Women = −1)	Diagnosis (Depressed = 1, No Diagnosis = −1)	Sex × Diagnosis	$\hat{Y}$	$Y - \hat{Y}$	$(Y - \hat{Y})^2$
1	3	1	−1	−1	7	−4	16
2	5	1	−1	−1	7	−2	4
3	6	1	−1	−1	7	−1	1
4	8	1	−1	−1	7	1	1
5	9	1	−1	−1	7	2	4
6	11	1	−1	−1	7	4	16
7	19	1	1	1	17	2	4
8	15	1	1	1	17	−2	4
9	16	1	1	1	17	−1	1
10	16	1	1	1	17	−1	1
11	19	1	1	1	17	2	4
12	17	1	1	1	17	0	0
13	3	−1	−1	1	6	−3	9
14	5	−1	−1	1	6	−1	1
15	4	−1	−1	1	6	−2	4
16	6	−1	−1	1	6	0	0
17	8	−1	−1	1	6	2	4
18	10	−1	−1	1	6	4	16
19	24	−1	1	−1	22	2	4
20	24	−1	1	−1	22	2	4
21	22	−1	1	−1	22	0	0
22	23	−1	1	−1	22	1	1
23	19	−1	1	−1	22	−3	9
24	20	−1	1	−1	22	−2	4
						$\Sigma (Y - \hat{Y})^2 = SSE_A = 112$	

We already know the value of SST—it's been 1,204 in every demonstration with these data, and it won't change now. When we subtract SSE_A (112) from SST (1,204), we have our reduced error, SSR (1,092). SSR tells us that the omnibus Model A, when compared with the simplest compact Model C, explained 1,092 of the total error (SST). The proportion of error reduced by adding both IVs and the interaction to the model is found by dividing SSR by SST (1092 ÷ 1204), which is .907. So this omnibus model explained 90.7% of the total error generated with the simple Model C. The model comparison box (Table 12.5) provides the information we'll need to fill in the summary table (Table 12.6).

The degrees of freedom used for the omnibus model is PA (4) minus PC (1), which is 3. Since we started with 23 total df (df total $= N - 1$), and we used 3 df for the model, we're left with 20 residual (within) df. To get MS for the model, we divide the SS explained by the model (1,092) by the 3 dfs used to create the model: $1,092 ÷ 3 = 364$. Likewise, the MS Error is the residual error, SSE_A (112) divided by the residual df (20): $112 ÷ 20 = 5.6$. The F value is the ratio of the MS for the model (364) divided by MSE (5.6), so $F(3, 20)$ is $364 ÷ 5.6 = 65$ (see Table 12.6).

Table 12.5 Model Comparison Box Displaying the Information Necessary to Complete the Summary Table

Model C:	$Y = 6 + \varepsilon$	PC = 1	SST = 1204
Model A:	$Y = 13 - 1(\text{Sex}) + 6(\text{Dx}) - 1.5(\text{Sex} \times \text{Dx}) + \varepsilon$	PA = 4	SSE_A = 112
			SSR = 1092
	$H_0: \beta_1 = \beta_2 = \beta_3 = 0$		R^2 (PRE) = .907

Table 12.6 Summary Table Testing the Omnibus Model

Source	SS	df	MS	F	p
Sex					
Diagnosis					
Sex × Diagnosis					
Error	112	20	5.6		
Total	1,204	23			

An error reduction of .907 is excellent! And our $F(1, 20) = 65$ would occur fewer than one time out of 1,000 ($p < .001$) if the null hypothesis was true. Obviously with that low a probability of a Type I error, we need to reject H_0! Of course, we now encounter the same problem that we had in Chapter 9— we don't know which of our three predictors contributed to that error reduction. With two predictors and an interaction, there are seven possible alternatives to H_0 (see Table 12.7). To figure out which predictors contributed to the omnibus effect (and therefore which predictors are related to the DV), we need to isolate the effects of each individual predictor.

Table 12.7 The Seven Possible Alternatives on Rejecting H_0 in a Two-Way ANOVA

Possible Alternatives to H_0			
Sex	Diagnosis	Interaction	Interpretation
$b_1 \neq 0$	$b_2 = 0$	$b_3 = 0$	Only sex is significant
$b_1 = 0$	$b_2 \neq 0$	$b_3 = 0$	Only Dx is significant
$b_1 = 0$	$b_2 = 0$	$b_3 \neq 0$	Only the interaction is significant
$b_1 \neq 0$	$b_2 \neq 0$	$b_3 = 0$	Sex and Dx are significant
$b_1 \neq 0$	$b_2 = 0$	$b_3 \neq 0$	Sex and the interaction are significant
$b_1 = 0$	$b_2 \neq 0$	$b_3 \neq 0$	Dx and the interaction are significant
$b_1 \neq 0$	$b_2 \neq 0$	$b_3 \neq 0$	All three predictors are significant

TESTING THE COMPONENTS OF THE MODEL ◆

To isolate the effects of each predictor, we need to modify Model C for each comparison. Look back at Table 12.1 where I listed the modified Model C needed to test (isolate the effects of) each predictor. Let's begin with Comparison 1 (Model C_1), which isolates the main effect for Sex.

Testing the Main Effect of Sex

To isolate the main effect of Sex on Depression score, we follow the same 10 model comparison steps. A summary of the first 8 steps for this comparison is given in Table 12.8.

Table 12.8 First Eight Model Comparison Steps to Test the Relationship Between Sex and Depression Score (β_1)

Step 1	State the compact Model C_1 and an augmented Model A	
	Model C_1:	$\hat{Y} = \beta_0 + \beta_2 Dx + \beta_3 Sex \times Dx$
	Model A:	$\hat{Y} = \beta_0 + \beta_1 \mathbf{Sex} + \beta_2 Dx + \beta_3 Sex \times Dx$
Step 2	Identify the null hypothesis (H_0)	
	H_0:	$\beta_1 = 0$
Step 3	Count the number of parameters estimated by each model	
	PA = 4	
	$PC_1 = 3$	
Step 4	Calculate the regression equation	
	Model C_1:	Dep = 13 + 6.5 (Dx) − 1.5 (Sex × Dx)
	Model A:	Dep = 13 − 1 (Sex) + 6.5 (Dx) − 1.5 (Sex × Dx)
Step 5	Compute sum of squares (SSE_C)	
	$SSE_{C1} = 136$	
Step 6	Compute sum of squares for Model A (SSE_A)	
	$SSE_A = 112$	
Step 7	Compute sum of squares reduced (SSR)	
	SSR = 24	
Step 8	Compute the proportional reduction in error (PRE or R^2)	
	PRE = R^2 = .02	

Step 1 lists the two models to compare, and Step 2 states the null hypothesis of testing these two models. Models A and C_1 are printed below. The difference between these two models is the inclusion of the Sex variable in Model A. Therefore, the null hypothesis is that Sex is unrelated to Depression score, or that $\beta_1 = 0$.

Model A: Depression = $\beta_0 + \beta_1 \mathbf{Sex} + \beta_2 Dx + \beta_3 Sex \times Dx + \varepsilon$.

Model C_2: Depression = $\beta_0 + \beta_2 Dx + \beta_3 Sex \times Dx + \varepsilon$.

Step 3 lists the number of parameters estimated by each model (information that we'll need to determine the *df* when we complete the summary table). The two estimated models (needed to generate a predicted Depression score for each subject) are listed in Step 4, and the error generated by each model is given in Step 5 (Model C_1) and Step 6 (Model A). The *SSE* for Model C_1 is 136. Recall from Table 12.4 that the SSE_A for Model A was 112 (and it will be for every subsequent comparison in this chapter). Step 7 shows the difference in error between Model C_1 and Model A (SSR): 136 − 112, which is 24. Therefore, adding Sex to the regression model reduced the beginning error (*SSE* C_1) by 24. Step 8 converts the reduction in error to a proportion of the total error (SST). Remember, SST was 1,204, so PRE or R^2 is equal to SSR ÷ SST = (24 ÷ 1,204 = .020). We can add this information to the summary table (Table 12.9). Dividing *SS* for Sex (24) by *df* for Sex (1) gives *MS* of 24 for Sex. *MS* for Sex (24) divided by *MSE* (5.6) gives an $F(1, 20) = 4.285$. The probability of this *F*, if H_0 is true, is $p = .052$.

Testing the Main Effect of Diagnosis

Next we'll isolate the effects of adding Diagnosis (Dx) to the model. The process is the same as for testing (isolating) the effects of Sex, and the first eight model comparison steps are listed in Table 12.10. To test the effect of Diagnosis, we'll compare the following models (Step 1):

Model A: Depression = $\beta_0 + \beta_1$ Sex + β_2 **Diagnosis** + β_3 Sex × Diagnosis + ε.

Model C_2: Depression = $\beta_0 + \beta_1$ Sex + β_3 Sex × Diagnosis + ε.

Table 12.9 Summary Table Including the Effects of Including Sex in the Model

Source	SS	df	MS	F	p
Omnibus model	1,092	3	364	65	< .001
Sex	24	1	24	4.285	.052
Diagnosis					
Sex × Diagnosis					
Error	112	20	5.6		
Total	1,204	23			

Table 12.10 Model Comparison Steps to Test the Relationship Between Sex and Depression Score (β_2)

Step 1	State the compact Model C_2 and an augmented Model A	
	Model C_2:	$\hat{Y} = \beta_0 + \beta_1 \text{Sex} + \beta_3 \text{Sex} \times \text{Dx}$
	Model A:	$\hat{Y} = \beta_0 + \beta_1 \text{Sex} + \beta_2 \textbf{Sex} + \beta_3 \text{Sex} \times \text{Dx}$
Step 2	Identify the null hypothesis (H_0)	
	H_0:	$\beta_2 = 0$
Step 3	Count the number of parameters estimated by each model	
	PA = 4	
	$PC_2 = 3$	
Step 4	Calculate the regression equation	
	Model C_2:	Dep = 13 − 1(Sex) − 1.5(Sex × Dx)
	Model A:	Dep = 13 − 1(Sex) + 6.5(Dx) − 1.5(Sex × Dx)
Step 5	Compute sum of squares (SSE_C)	
	$SSE_{C2} = 1,126$	
Step 6	Compute sum of squares for Model A (SSE_A)	
	$SSE_A = 112$	
Step 7	Compute sum of squares reduced (SSR)	
	SSR = 1,014	
Step 8	Compute the proportional reduction in error (PRE or R^2)	
	PRE = R^2 = .842	

The difference between these models is the inclusion of Diagnosis in Model A. The null hypothesis (Step 2) is that there is no relationship between Diagnosis and Depression score ($\beta_2 = 0$). Step 3 presents the parameters estimated for each model, and Step 4 gives the calculated regression equations for both models. Step 5 gives the error of Model C_2 (1,126), and Step 6 gives the error of Model A (still 112). Step 7 tells how much error was reduced by adding Diagnosis to the model ($SSC_2 − SSA = SSR = 1,014$), and Step 8 converts the reduction in error to a proportion of the initial error (PRE = R^2 = SSR ÷ SSC = .842).

So adding Diagnosis to Model C_2 reduced the error of Model C_2 by 84.2%. Very impressive! We add these findings to the summary table (Table 12.11), and we calculate our $F(1, 20) = 181.071$. The probability of this whopping big F, if H_0 is true, is $<.001$. So we reject H_0.

Testing the Interaction of Diagnosis and Sex

Finally, the first eight model comparison steps to test the interaction between Sex and Diagnosis are given in Table 12.12. The interaction is tested by comparing the following models (Step 1):

Model A: Depression = $\beta_0 + \beta_1$ Sex + β_2 Diagnosis + $\boldsymbol{\beta_3}$ **Sex** × **Diagnosis** + ε.

Model C_3: Depression = $\beta_0 + \beta_1$ Sex + β_2 Diagnosis + ε.

By now you should have a sense of the step process, so I'll highlight some of the key findings presented in Table 12.12. The *SSE* for Model C_3 (Step 5) is 166, and the *SSE* for Model A (Step 6) is 112. The difference in error between Models A and C_3 (SSR) is 54 (Step 7). Dividing SSR (54) by SST (1,204) converts the error reduction to a proportion of SST (Step 8): The proportional reduction in error (PRE or R^2) is .045. We can then add this information to Table 12.13 to complete the summary table. The $F(1, 20)$ for the interaction is 9.643, which has a $p = .006$ if H_0 is true. Take a moment to compare this summary table with the summary table we created in Chapter 11. What will you find?

The summary table is now complete. If you were to look back at the final summary table in Chapter 11, you would find that the two are identical (with the exception that Table 12.13 included the omnibus test, which Chapter 11 didn't report).

Table 12.11 Summary Table With Sex and Diagnosis Added

Source	SS	df	MS	F	p
Omnibus model	1,092	3	364	65	< .001
Sex	24	1	24	4.285	.052
Diagnosis	1,014	1	1,014	181.071	<.001
Sex × Diagnosis					
Error	112	20	5.6		
Total	1,204	23			

Table 12.12 First Eight Model Comparison Steps to Test the Relationship Between Sex and Depression Score (β_3)

Step 1	State the compact Model C_3 and an augmented Model A	
	Model C_3:	$\hat{Y} = \beta_0 + \beta_1 \text{Sex} + \beta_2 \text{Dx}$
	Model A:	$\hat{Y} = \beta_0 + \beta_1 \text{Sex} + \beta_2 \text{Dx} + \beta_3 \textbf{Sex} \times \textbf{Dx}$
Step 2	Identify the null hypothesis (H_0)	
	H_0:	$\beta_3 = 0$
Step 3	Count the number of parameters estimated by each model	
	PA = 4	
	$PC_3 = 3$	
Step 4	Calculate the regression equation	
	Model C_3:	Dep = 13 − 1(Sex) + 6.5(Dx)
	Model A:	Dep = 13 − 1 (Sex) + 6.5(Dx) − 1.5(Sex × Dx)
Step 5	Compute sum of squares (SSE_C)	
	$SSE_{C3} = 166$	
Step 6	Compute sum of squares for Model A (SSE_A)	
	$SSE_A = 112$	
Step 7	Compute sum of squares reduced (SSR)	
	SSR = 54	
Step 8	Compute the proportional reduction in error (PRE or R^2)	
	PRE = R^2 = .045	

Table 12.13 Completed Summary Table

Source	SS	df	MS	F	p
Omnibus model	1,092	3	364	65	<.001
Sex	24	1	24	4.285	.052
Diagnosis	1,014	1	1,014	181.071	<.001
Sex × Diagnosis	54	1	54	9.643	.006
Error	112	20	5.6		
Total	1,204	23			

INTERPRETING THE COEFFICIENTS ◆

This chapter and the preceding chapter describe two approaches to conduct a two-way ANOVA. "Why," you may ask, "does someone need *two* ways to conduct a two-way ANOVA?" And that would be a very good question. I can think of at least one answer—the model comparison approach offered something that the traditional ANOVA did not offer—regression coefficients! Regression coefficients tell us *how* the predictors are related to the outcome. Consider the regression model estimated for this example.

$$\text{Depression score} = 13 - 1\,(\text{Sex}) + 6.5\,(\text{Diagnosis}) - 1.5\,(\text{Sex} \times \text{Dx}) + \varepsilon. \tag{12.2}$$

The regression coefficients in Equation 12.2 describe the relationship of Depression scores to each IV and the interaction variable. The coefficient describing the main effect for Sex is −1. This coefficient tells us that as scores on Sex move from a lower value to a higher value (recall that women were coded −1 and men were coded +1), scores on Depression decreased. In other words, our regression predicts lower Depression scores for men than for women.

The coefficient describing the main effect for Diagnosis is +6.5. This coefficient reveals that as scores on Diagnosis move from a lower to a higher value (No Dx subjects were coded −1, Depressed subjects coded +1), Depressive symptom scores increased. In other words, Depressed subjects had higher depressive symptom scores than subjects with no diagnosis.

The interaction coefficient requires a little more consideration to interpret. The interaction tells us whether the relationship between the DV and one of the IVs is conditional on the level of the other IV. In Chapter 10, I rearranged the IVs in the equation in a way that helped me conceptualize this conditional relationship. In Equation 12.3, I've clustered the regression terms so that we can interpret the interaction as the impact that Sex has on the relationship between Diagnosis and Depression score.

$$\text{Depression} = [13 - 1(\text{Sex})] + [6.5(\textbf{Diagnosis} - 1.5(\text{Sex} \times \textbf{Diagnosis}))]. \tag{12.3}$$

By rearranging the regression terms, I can factor Diagnosis out of the equation

$$\text{Depression} = [13 - 1(\text{Sex})] + [6.5 - 1.5(\text{Sex})]\,\textbf{Diagnosis}. \tag{12.4}$$

The terms in the brackets that follow the equal sign **[13 − 1 (Sex)]** describe the intercept term—the initial prediction of Depression scores. Let's call this the "composite intercept." To interpret this "composite intercept," notice that 13 is the grand mean. If I enter the code for women (−1) into the composite intercept, we get the mean depression score for the women's group (13 −1 × (−1) = 13 + 1 = 14). Likewise, if we enter the code for men (+1), we get the average score for the men's group (13 − 1 × (1) = 13 − 1 = 12).

The brackets that precede Diagnosis in the equation **[6.5 −1.5(Sex)]** describe the relationship between Diagnosis and Depression score. If we hold sex constant at its average value (which, since we used contrast codes, is zero), we find that as Diagnosis increases in value, Depressive symptoms scores also increase. If we enter the possible values for Diagnosis, the model predicts the group means for the Depressed subjects (13 + 6.5 × (1) = 13 + 6.5 = 19.5) and the No Dx subjects (13 + 6.5 × (−1) = 13 − 6.5 = 6.5).

Now let's look at the term that describes the relationship between Diagnosis and Depression **[6.5 × 1.5(Sex)]**. The term begins by expressing the relationship between Diagnosis and Depression score as 6.5 and then adjusts that change according to the person's sex. The initial relationship between Diagnosis and Depressive symptom score is lower for men (men were coded +1, so 6.5 − 1.5 × 1 = 5) and higher for women (coded −1, so 6.5 −1.5(−1) = 6.5 + 1.5 = 8). Basically, we've ended up with two different regression coefficients to describe the relationship between Diagnosis and Depression score: (1) one for men (coefficient = 5) and (2) one for women (coefficient = 8).

It's as if we ended up with two different regression models—(1) one for women and (2) one for men. The regression model for men is given in Equation 12.5. The initial predicted Depression score (Y-intercept) for men is 12 and the initial prediction is lowered 5 points for men with No Dx (predicted score = 7) and raised 5 points for men with Depression (predicted score = 17). The regression model for women is given in Equation 12.6. Women begin with a higher initial prediction (14). This initial prediction is adjusted up 8 points for women with Depression (predicted score = 14 + 8 = 22) and adjusted down for women with No Dx (predicted score = 14 − 8 = 6). Notice that the adjustment in predicted scores yields the four group means for these data: (1) men with a psychiatric diagnosis = 17, (2) women with a psychiatric diagnosis = 22, (3) men with no diagnosis = 7, and (4) women with no diagnosis = 6. Again, this nice nuance is due to our use of contrast codes.

$$\text{Depression score} = 12 + 5 \text{ Dx (regression for men).} \qquad (12.5)$$

$$\text{Depression score} = 14 + 8 \text{ Dx (regression for women).} \qquad (12.6)$$

SUMMARY ♦

In this chapter, we have used the multiple regression and model comparison approach to conduct the two-way ANOVA from Chapter 11. We first tested an omnibus Model A that included all of the predictors (both IVs and their interaction term) by comparing the error explained by Model A with the error explained by the simplest compact Model C, which predicted simply the mean depression score for everyone. Then, we defined several modified compact Model Cs that, when compared with Model A, allowed us to isolate the error reduction of each component in Model A.

Using a multiple regression model comparison approach conveys a real understanding of what a traditional ANOVA actually accomplishes—the reduction in error by adding variables (IVs) to a model that improves the prediction of the DV. This approach also revealed the proportion of variance explained by each IV and their interaction. The coefficients in the regression equation (Model A) allowed us to interpret the relationships between the IVs and the DV, as well as to interpret and understand the interaction.

13

ONE-WAY ANOVA WITH THREE GROUPS

Traditional Approach

*If a man will begin with certainties, he shall end in doubts;
but if he will be content to begin with doubts he shall end in
certainties.*

—Sir Francis Bacon

We previously learned how to use a *t* test, one-way analysis of variance (ANOVA), and regression to compare the mean scores from two groups of a dependent variable (DV). On occasion, a researcher might want to compare three (or more) groups. Comparing three or more groups is fundamentally the same as comparing two groups, with some additional considerations. In this chapter, we'll learn how to conduct the traditional one-way ANOVA when the independent variable (IV) has three groups. The next chapter will discuss how to use multiple regression to conduct the same one-way ANOVA when the predictor (IV) has three groups (levels).

For this demonstration, we'll again use the depression data from previous chapters. This time, instead of an IV that has two levels (such as Men vs. Women or Depressed vs. No Diagnosis), we'll test the relationship with an IV, called "Drug Abuse," that has three levels (None, Alcohol, and Poly Drug). Imagine (and remember, these are imaginary data) that each of the 24 subjects can be grouped according to their abuse of alcohol and other drugs. The subjects in the first group, the "None" group (Subjects 1, 2, 3, 4, 13, 14, 15, and 16) do not use alcohol or other drugs. The subjects in the second group, the "Alcohol" group (Subjects 5, 6, 7, 8, 17, 18, 19, and 20) are dependent on alcohol. Those in the third group, the Poly Drug group (Subjects 9, 10, 11, 12, 21, 22, 23, and 24) are dependent on alcohol and at least one other drug. The ANOVA will test if the Depression means (scores on the DV) are different for these three Drug Abuse (DA) groups. These data are presented in Table 13.1. The group means and standard deviations are presented in Table 13.2, and the data are graphed in Figure 13.1.

The null hypothesis (H_0) is that the means are not different. The means in Table 13.2 and Figure 13.1 certainly look different, which raises two questions. First, are the means statistically different (i.e., can we reject the H_0 that the means are the same)? This question is equivalent to the omnibus test. It is also the same as the first fundamental statistical questions (Are the two variables, Depression score and DA, related?). If the omnibus test reveals that the means are different (and therefore that the IV and DV are related), we're still left wondering *which* means are different. Therefore, the second question asks whether all three means are different from each other or whether one is different from the other two (e.g., Is Alcohol different from both None *and* Poly Drug? Are None and Poly Drug different from each other?). The one-way ANOVA with three groups (levels) will answer the first question. If the ANOVA leads us to reject the H_0 and conclude that the means are different, then we'll need a follow-up analysis (called a "post hoc" test) to determine which means differed. But before we get into post hocs, let's conduct the ANOVA.

◆ CONDUCTING THE ANALYSIS OF VARIANCE

Total Variance

The one-way ANOVA that compares three groups is very similar to the one-way ANOVA from Chapter 7, which compared two groups on these same Depression scores. We need to determine the total variance of the DV (sum of squares [*SS*] or total sum of squares [SST]) and then partition SST into (a) variance explained by the IV (the "between" variance, SSB) and (b) residual variance (the "within" variance, SSW). Since the Depression scores haven't changed since Chapter 7, SST is still 1,204.

Table 13.1 Depression Scores (*Y*), the Sex of Each Participant (*X*), and Grand (13.5) and Group Mean Scores

Subject	Symptom Score (DV)	Drug Abuse (IV$_3$)
1	3	None
2	5	None
3	6	None
4	8	None
5	9	Alcohol
6	11	Alcohol
7	19	Alcohol
8	15	Alcohol
9	16	Poly Drug
10	16	Poly Drug
11	19	Poly Drug
12	17	Poly Drug
13	3	None
14	5	None
15	4	None
16	6	None
17	8	Alcohol
18	10	Alcohol
19	24	Alcohol
20	24	Alcohol
21	22	Poly Drug
22	23	Poly Drug
23	19	Poly Drug
24	20	Poly Drug

NOTE: IV = independent variable; DV = dependent variable.

Table 13.2 Depression Means for Each of the Three Drug Abuse Groups

Drug Abuse Groups		
None	*Alcohol*	*Poly Drug*
5.00 (1.69)	15.00 (6.59)	19.00 (2.62)

Figure 13.1 Line Graph Displaying Group Means.

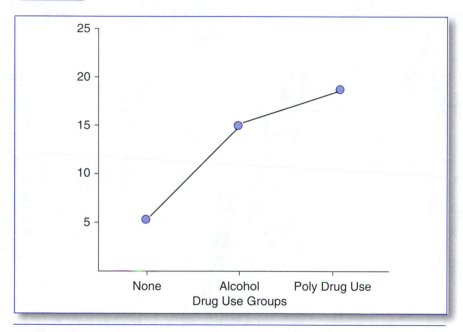

NOTE: Depressive symptom scores are noted along the y-axis, and Drug Abuse independent variable groups along the x-axis.

Variance Explained

SSB is calculated just as it was in Chapter 7, only this time with 3 rather than two groups. The formula used to calculate SSB is represented in Equation 13.1:

$$\text{SSB} = \sum \left(n_{\text{group}} (\overline{Y}_{\text{group}} - \overline{Y}_{\text{grand}})^2 \right). \tag{13.1}$$

To demonstrate how to get SSB, let's use Equation 13.1 to first find the contribution to SSB from the group with no DA (None group). The Grand mean for Depressive symptom scores is 13. The None group had an average depression score of 5. Subtracting the Grand mean from the group mean (5 − 13) gives a difference of −8. We square that difference (−8² = 64) and multiply it by the number of subjects in the None group ($n = 8$; 8(64) = 512) to get the contribution to SSB from the None group (512). Next, we'll repeat the process for the Alcohol group by subtracting the Grand mean from the group mean for the Alcohol group (15 − 13 = 2), squaring the difference (2² = 4), and multiplying the squared difference by the number of subjects in the Alcohol group ($n = 8$; 8(4) = 32). The SSB for alcohol-dependent subjects is 32. Finally, we'll repeat the process to get the SSB for the Poly Drug group. The mean for the Drug group (19) minus the Grand mean (13) is 6. The difference squared (36) is multiplied by the number of subjects in the Poly Drug group ($n = 8$) to get the SSB associated with the Poly Drug group (8(36) = 288). Once we have repeated this process for all three groups, we sum each group's contribution to get the SSB associated with the IV (512 + 32 + 288 = 832). Table 13.3 summarizes this process.

Compute the Residual Variance

The residual variance (SSW) is the difference between the SST and the SSB associated with the IV (DA groups). Knowing SST (1,204) and SSB (832), it's a snap to figure out that SSW is 372 by subtracting SSB from SST (1,204 − 832 = 372). But, to be thorough, let's see how to calculate SSW by using Equation 13.2:

$$SSE_W = \Sigma(Y_{Group} - \overline{Y}_{Group})^2. \tag{13.2}$$

SSW is computed by subtracting the group mean from the score of each subject within that group, squaring the differences, and then summing the squared differences obtained from each subject. Table 13.4 applies

Table 13.3 Steps for Calculating SSB (the "Between" Variance) for These Data

Group	$\overline{Y}_{group} - \overline{Y}_{grand}$	$(\overline{Y}_{group} - \overline{Y}_{grand})^2$	$n(\overline{Y}_{group} - \overline{Y}_{grand})^2$		SSB
None	5 − 13 = −8	64	8 × 64	=	512
Alcohol	15 − 13 = 2	4	8 × 4	=	32
Poly Drug	19 − 13 = 6	36	8 × 36	=	288
			SSB	=	832

Table 13.4 Steps to Calculate SSW (the Residual Variance) for These Data

Subject	Symptom Score (DV)	Group Mean	$Y - \bar{Y}_{group}$	$(Y - \bar{Y}_{group})^2$
1	3	5	−2	4
2	5	5	0	0
3	6	5	1	1
4	8	5	3	9
5	9	15	−6	36
6	11	15	−4	16
7	19	15	4	16
8	15	15	0	0
9	16	19	−3	9
10	16	19	−3	9
11	19	19	0	0
12	17	19	−2	4
13	3	5	−2	4
14	5	5	0	0
15	4	5	−1	1
16	6	5	1	1
17	8	15	−7	49
18	10	15	−5	25
19	24	15	9	81
20	24	15	9	81
21	22	19	3	9
22	23	19	4	16
23	19	19	0	0
24	20	19	1	1
			SSW =	372

Equation 13.2 to compute SSW for this example. Look at Subject 1, who is in the None group and has a Depression score of 3. The mean symptom score for the None group is 5, so we subtract 5 from 3 and get a difference of −2. Squaring that difference (-2^2) gives us a squared difference of 4 for Subject 1. We repeat this process for all 24 subjects, then sum the squared differences to get SSW. Table 13.4 produced an SSW of 372, which fortunately is the value we expected when we subtracted SSB from SST.

COMPLETE THE SUMMARY TABLE ◆

Now that we've partitioned SST into SSB (explained variance) and SSW (unexplained or residual variance), we can complete the ANOVA summary table (Table 13.5) to arrive at *F*. Notice how the degrees of freedom (*df*s) are determined in Table 13.5. Total *df* is still the total number of subjects ($N = 24$) minus 1 ($N − 1 = 23$). The between *df* is calculated by subtracting 1 from the *number of groups* we're comparing. When we only compared two groups, $df_{between}$ was $2 − 1 = 1$. This time, however, we have three groups to compare (None, Alcohol, and Poly Drug), so $df_{between}$ is $3 − 1 = 2$. We began with 23 *df*s and used 2 for the analysis ($df_{between}$), leaving us with 21 df_{within} (residual).

Having partitioned the *SS* and *df*s, we can calculate the "between" mean squares, $MS_{between}$ or MSB (MSB = SSB ÷ $df_{between}$ = 832 ÷ 2 = 416), and "within" mean squares, MS_{within} or MSW (MSW = SSW ÷ df_{within} = 372 ÷ 21 = 17.714). Dividing MSB by MSW gives us the *F* value. The result, 23.484, is fairly large—in fact, the chances are fewer than 1 in 1,000 ($p < .001$) that we would get an *F* that large when H_0 is true, so it's best that we reject H_0 and conclude that the DA groups have different means.

Table 13.5 ANOVA Summary Table

Source	SS	df	MS	F	p
Drug Abuse	832	2	416	23.484	<.001
Within	372	21	17.714		
Total	1,204	23			

♦ POST HOC ANALYSIS: WHERE'S THE DIFFERENCE?

The results of the ANOVA led us to reject H_0 and infer that the Depression means for the None, Alcohol, and Poly Drug groups are different. What the ANOVA didn't tell us is which means are different. It could be that all three groups are different. Or it could be that the None group is different from both the Alcohol and the Poly Drug groups, that the Poly Drug group is different from both the None and the Alcohol groups, or that the Alcohol group is different from both the None and the Poly Drug groups. To resolve this question, we'll conduct a *post hoc analysis* to determine which means are different.

It would be nice if we could simply conduct a t test for each pair of means we need to compare. Unfortunately, every time we run a t test, we increase the risk of making a Type I error. Therefore, we need a post hoc test that will not increase our Type I error risk.

There are many different post hoc tests, each with its own advantages and disadvantages. My purpose here is to demonstrate the post hoc process, not to review all possible post hoc tests. So I'll describe just one of the more common post hocs—the least significant difference (LSD) test. The LSD is somewhat like a t test, just slightly altered to compensate for the increased risk of a Type I error due to conducting multiple tests. Let's take a second to understand just what I mean by an increased risk of a Type I error due to multiple comparisons.

Risk of Multiple Tests

This example has three means, and we want to know which pairs of means are different from each other. To accomplish that, we'll have to conduct three analyses to compare means. Table 13.6 lists the mean comparisons we need to test. So why would it be such a big deal if we just conducted three t tests

Table 13.6 Summary of Mean Comparisons

Comparison	Mean 1		Mean 2
1	None	vs.	Alcohol
2	None	vs.	Poly Drug
3	Alcohol	vs.	Poly Drug

for those comparisons? Remember that every time we conduct a statistical analysis and reject a null hypothesis (H_0), we accept a 5% chance of incorrectly rejecting a true H_0 (a Type I error).

These probabilities of a Type I error accumulate with each t test. Therefore, if we conducted 20 t tests, there would be a good chance that one of the tests would result in a Type I error (5% of 20 is 1). If we ran 50 t tests, we would likely make 2 to 3 Type I errors (5% of 50 is 2.5). One hundred t tests would result in 5 Type I errors. So the more t tests we run, the more chances we have of making a Type I error. Now 3 t tests to compare the three means doesn't seem like a lot, but even with 3 comparisons the chance of a Type I error increases from 5% to 15%. I'm not comfortable with that probability of a Type I error. Fortunately, the LSD test corrects for this problem in two ways. First, LSD is calculated using the mean square error (MSW) from the ANOVA rather than the pooled variance, as is used by the t test. Second, LSD bases the comparison on fewer dfs ($21\ df_{within}$) than the t test used ($N - 2 = 22\ dfs$).

$$LSD = t_{critical} \sqrt{MSW \left[\frac{1}{N_{group1}} + \frac{1}{N_{group2}} \right]}. \qquad (13.3)$$

Calculate the LSD

Enough of conceptualizing—let's compute the LSD. Equation 13.3 gives the formula for the LSD. To calculate LSD, all we need is a *critical t* value, MSW from the ANOVA, and the sample size for each of the two groups we're comparing. Critical t is the smallest value of t that allows us to reject a H_0. In Chapter 6, we found the critical t from a table (reproduced as Table 13.7 below). We'll use critical t based on 21 dfs (the df_{within}), which is 2.08 (see Table 13.7, 21 dfs, two-tailed test). The summary table (Table 13.5) gives us MSW (17.714).

We have everything we need to calculate LSD (critical $t = 2.08$, MSW = 17.714, and the n of each group is 8). We simply plug the values into the formula:

$$LSD = t_{critical} \sqrt{MSE \left[\frac{1}{N_{group1}} + \frac{1}{N_{group2}} \right]}. \qquad (13.4)$$

$$LSD = 2.08 \sqrt{17.714 \left[\frac{1}{8} + \frac{1}{8} \right]},$$

$$LSD = 2.08\sqrt{17.714(0.25)} = 2.08\sqrt{4.4285,}$$

$$LSD = 2.08(2.104) = 4.377.$$

The LSD is 4.377. Recall that LSD stands for least significant difference, which means that for any two means to be statistically different (at $p < .05$ alpha), their difference must be at least 4.377. Table 13.8 compares the differences between each pair of means against the LSD to see which pairs are significantly different. The difference between the None group ($M = 5$) and the Alcohol group ($M = 15$) is 10, and 10 certainly is greater than 4.377. So

Table 13.7 Table of Critical t Values for Alpha Probability, $p \le .05$

df	One-Tailed	Two-Tailed	df	One-Tailed	Two-Tailed
1	6.31	12.71	18	1.73	2.09
2	2.92	4.30	19	1.73	2.10
3	2.35	3.18	20	1.73	2.09
4	2.13	2.78	21	1.72	2.08
5	2.02	2.57	22	1.72	2.07
6	1.94	2.45	23	1.71	2.07
7	1.90	2.37	24	1.71	2.06
8	1.86	2.31	25	1.71	2.06
9	1.83	2.26	26	1.71	2.06
10	1.81	2.23	27	1.71	2.05
11	1.80	2.20	28	1.70	2.05
12	1.78	2.18	29	1.70	2.05
13	1.77	2.16	30	1.69	2.04
14	1.76	2.15	40	1.68	2.02
15	1.75	2.13	60	1.67	2.00
16	1.75	2.12	120	1.66	1.98
17	1.74	2.11	oo	1.65	1.96

Table 13.8 Results of Mean Comparisons

Comparison	Mean 1		Mean 2	Difference	LSD	Decision
1	None	vs.	Alcohol			
	5		15	10	4.377	None ≠ Alcohol
2	None	vs.	Drug			
	5		19	14	4.377	None ≠ Poly Drug
3	Alcohol	vs.	Drug			
	15		19	4	4.377	Alcohol = Poly Drug

we conclude that the None group scored lower than the Alcohol group on the Depressive symptom score. Likewise, the difference between the None group ($M = 5$) and the Poly Drug group ($M = 19$) is 14, which again is greater than the LSD, so the None group scored reliably lower than the Poly Drug group. Finally, the difference between the mean scores for the Alcohol group ($M = 15$) and the Poly Drug group ($M = 19$) is 4, which is less than the LSD. So the difference in mean scores for the Alcohol and Poly Drug groups is not large enough to conclude that they are statistically different. Our conclusion is that the non–drug abusers (None group) scored differently than the other two groups but those groups (Alcohol and Poly Drug) were not different.

We report that the results of the ANOVA revealed that DA (the IV) was related to Depressive symptom scores, $F(1, 21) = 23.484$, $p < .001$. Post hoc analyses revealed that those who used no drugs (the None group) scored lower on Depressive symptoms, on average, than both the Alcohol and the Poly Drug groups. The Alcohol and Poly Drug groups were not significantly different from each other.

◆ SUMMARY

This chapter demonstrated the use of ANOVA to test the relationship between two variables (a DV and an IV) when the IV is a categorical variable with three groups or levels. The same procedure could be used to test an IV that has four groups, or five, or more. The null hypothesis (H_0) was that DA is not related to Depressive symptom score or, put another way, that the Depression score means for each group are not reliably different. If the

ANOVA produces an F ratio that would be unusually large if H_0 was true, we would reject H_0. Rejecting H_0 implies that at least one of the mean scores is different from the others; however, the F ratio alone did not tell us which means were different. To determine which means were different, we conducted a post hoc analysis, the LSD test. The LSD compared each combination of pairs of group means without increasing our risk of making a Type I error.

By now it is no surprise to learn that there is a way to use regression to conduct this same analysis. An advantage of the regression model comparison approach is that it folds the post hoc analysis into the model comparison, thus eliminating the need for a separate post hoc test. The next chapter introduces the regression approach for conducting an ANOVA when the IV has more than two groups.

14

ANOVA WITH THREE GROUPS

Model Comparison Approach

It didn't matter how much you knew—it wasn't real if it didn't appear in a scientific journal.

—Christopher Moore

Fluke: Or I Know Why the Winged Whale Sings[1]

By now you should have the idea that you can use regression to conduct any analysis of variance (ANOVA). In this chapter, I'll demonstrate how to use multiple regression to conduct the same one-way ANOVA with three groups that we conducted in Chapter 13. The model comparison is the same as before: We'll identify two models, a compact (Model C) and an augmented (Model A), compare the models to see if they are different, and (if they are different) isolate the predictors to learn what makes the models different.

ISOLATING EFFECTS: CONCEPTUALIZING ♦ LINEAR COMPARISONS OF THREE GROUPS

You may have already noticed a critical difference between the regression approach to a one-way ANOVA in this chapter (where the independent

1. Moore, C. (2003). *Fluke: Or I know why the winged whale sings*. New York: William Morrow & Company. Reprinted with permission.

variable [IV] has three levels) and the regression approach to a one-way ANOVA in Chapter 8 (where the IV had only two levels). In Chapter 8, we didn't need to "isolate" effects because we had only one IV. So why, in this example where we again have only one IV, am I talking about isolating the effects?

That's a good question, and I wish I had a simple answer. When an IV has three or more groups, assigning numeric codes as "labels" for the groups is somewhat trickier than when the IV had only two groups. When we had one IV with two groups, we created one predictor that coded one group −1 and coded the other group +1. This time, with one IV that has three groups, we'll create *two* predictors.

The reason things get tricky is because assigning numeric values to the groups forces a numerical relationship between those groups. With two groups, it simply meant that one group was higher or lower than the other. The order didn't matter. The challenge, however, is that as the number of groups increases, the number of possible numeric relationships between the groups also increases. For example, using a single code for three groups will force one group to be higher than another, while the third group falls in between. But what if that order is wrong? What if the middle group was really higher than both of the other groups? Obviously, we need to account for this increased number of possible relationships when assigning codes. In the one-way ANOVA from the last chapter, we had three Drug Abuse (DA) groups (None, Alcohol, Poly Drug). One way to code the groups is to make Alcohol lowest (−1), the None group in the middle (0), and Poly Drug the highest (1). These codes even meet my desire for contrast codes—the codes sum to zero!

But!—and it's a big "but"—that code assumes that the three variables have a linear relationship in which the Alcohol group is the lowest, the Poly Drug group is the highest, and the None group falls conveniently in between. What if the None group is the lowest and the Alcohol and Poly Drug groups are equal? We need a second code that accounts for that possibility.

Look at Figure 14.1, Panel a, which is a line graph of the Depressive Symptom group means. The groups are organized (and coded) along the X-axis from None (−1) to Alcohol (0) to Poly Drug (+1). When the groups are arranged in this linear order, the resulting regression equation is $\hat{Y} = 13 + 7X$. The straight line is the regression line superimposed on the graph of the means. Now look at Panel b in Figure 14.1. These are the identical means that were graphed in Panel a; however, the order of the groups along the X-axis (and their codes) was altered to progress from Alcohol (−1) to None (0) to Poly Drug (+1). This change produced quite a difference in the line graph

Figure 14.1 Line Graphs Comparing Group Mean Depressive Symptom Scores.

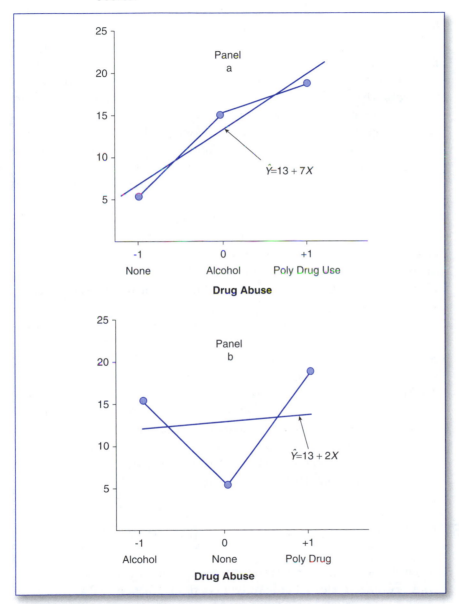

NOTES: Panel a shows the means with None coded -1, Alcohol coded 0, and Poly Drug coded +1. The line indicates the regression equation for these codes. Panel b shows the means if codes for None and Alcohol are switched. Notice that the regression line in Panel b looks flatter (has less slope) than the line in Panel a.

and regression equation. When groups are placed in this order, the regression equation is $\hat{Y} = 13 + 2X$. This regression line is superimposed on the graph. The point is that the codes we assign to the IV groups is arbitrary, yet the order can affect the regression equation if we only use a single set of codes. Clearly, more than one set of codes is required to represent the possible relationships between groups.

So to test a single IV with more than two groups, we will need multiple predictors. The rule for determining the number of predictor variables is to count the number of IV groups and subtract 1. Thus, when the IV had two groups (as in Chapter 8), we needed only one predictor (2 groups − 1 = 1 predictor). But this time, with three groups, we'll need two predictor variables in the regression (3 groups − 1 = 2 predictors). If we had four groups, we'd need three predictors; five groups would require four predictors; and so on.

On the up side, the inclusion of multiple predictors eliminates the need for post hoc analyses. This is because the multiple predictors actually serve as preplanned group comparisons. We can actually decide what comparisons make theoretical sense a priori (before the fact). Isolating the effects of each predictor gives us a good sense of which means are different from each other.

Using two predictor variables for an IV with three groups will not cover every possible comparison of means. Therefore, we need to "preplan" our comparisons so that they address our specific hypotheses. In the present example where we're testing the relationship between Depression scores (dependent variable [DV]) and DA (IV), we may hypothesize that both Alcohol abuse and Poly Drug abuse will produce higher Depressive Symptom scores than when there is no alcohol or drug abuse. Therefore, we will select codes that reflect this preplanned, a priori hypothesis (i.e., test if the mean scores for both the Alcohol and Poly Drug groups are different from the mean for the None group).

◆ CONTRAST CODES WITH MORE THAN TWO GROUPS

The challenge to mastering this chapter will be in understanding the concept of contrast codes. There are two conditions necessary for successful contrast codes. The first condition (we've already seen) is that the codes for each group on an IV must sum to zero. This concept was easy when we had two groups and therefore only needed one predictor: one group was coded −1 and the other group was coded +1. Simple: $1 + (-1) = 0$, and the condition was met.

But now we have three groups, so we need two predictors. Let's label the first predictor λ_1. I've already suggested one set of codes above that meets the first contrast code condition: Alcohol group = −1, None = 0, and Poly Drug = +1. These three values form a linear relationship, and they sum to zero. Using these codes, the "None" group essentially drops out (because it was coded zero), so the contrast tests whether the Alcohol and Poly Drug groups are different.

Picking the set of codes for the second predictor (we'll label it λ_2) is where the second condition for contrast codes becomes important. To understand the second condition for selecting codes, realize that each DA group will have two codes: one for the first predictor (λ_1) and the other for the second predictor (λ_2). Therefore, subjects in the None group have two scores or codes: $\lambda_{1(none)}$ and $\lambda_{2(none)}$. Likewise, Alcohol subjects have two scores ($\lambda_{1(alcohol)}$ and $\lambda_{2(alcohol)}$) as do the Poly Drug subjects ($\lambda_{1(poly)}$ and $\lambda_{2(poly)}$). If we multiply the first code for a group with the second code for that group ($\lambda_1 \times \lambda_2$), and we do this for all three groups, we'll have three products ($\lambda_1 \times \lambda_2$ for None; $\lambda_1 \times \lambda_2$ for Alcohol; and $\lambda_1 \times \lambda_2$ for Poly Drug). The second condition requires that those three products sum to zero (see Equation 14.1). Doing this makes the two predictors *orthogonal*, which means that they do not overlap (Keppel & Zedeck, 2002).

$$\lambda_{1(none)}\lambda_{2(none)} + \lambda_{1(alcohol)}\lambda_{2(alcohol)} + \lambda_{1(poly)}\lambda_{2(poly)} = 0. \qquad (14.1)$$

Look at Table 14.1. The contrast codes for the linear predictor (λ_1) are given for the Alcohol, None, and Poly Drug groups. In the "Sum" column to the far right, we see that these codes meet Condition 1 by summing to zero. Below λ_1 and the linear codes is the quadratic predictor (λ_2). It's called the quadratic code because it resembles a quadratic function in which the "middle" group has a different code than the two "end" groups, and the "end" groups are equal (in this case, the middle code, −2, is lower than the two end codes, +1 each). These codes (+1, −2, +1) sum to zero, and therefore, λ_2 meets Condition 1 of contrast codes.

On the bottom row of Table 14.1, the products of the two codes ($\lambda_1\lambda_2$) are given for each group. For example, the Alcohol group has two codes: −1 and +1. The product of these two codes (−1 × 1) is −1. The None group has two codes, 0 and −2, and their product is 0. Finally, the product of the Poly Drug group's code is 1. The second condition of contrast codes requires that those three products sums to zero. At the bottom of the far right "Sum" column, we see that they do (−1 + 0 + 1 = 0)!

Table 14.1 Example of Orthogonal Contrast Codes

Contrast Code	Groups			Sum
	Alcohol	None	Poly Drug	
Predictor				
Linear (λ_1)	−1	0	+1	−1 + 0 + 1 = 0
Quadratic (λ_2)	+1	−2	+1	1 − 2 + 1 = 0
Product (λ_1, λ_2) (Linear × Quadratic)	−1 × 1 = −1	−2 × 0 = 0	1 × 1 = 1	−1 + 0 + 1 = 0

Before we leave the process of assigning contrast codes, let's take a look at what the codes actually represent. I mentioned above that using these codes amounts to a "preplanned comparison" that reduces the need for a post hoc analysis. Consider λ_1, the linear contrast, in which the Alcohol group was coded −1 and the Poly Drug group was coded +1. Essentially, this contrast tests whether the Alcohol and Poly Drug groups are different. When we test the regression model and isolate the effects of the two predictors, if the linear predictor (λ_1) is statistically significant (F is unusually large), then we can conclude that the mean scores for the Alcohol and Poly Drug groups are not equal.

Now look at the quadratic contrasts. In this contrast, we've set the Alcohol and Drug groups equal to each other (both coded +1), and contrasted them against the None group (coded −2). If the model comparison finds that the quadratic contrast is statistically significant, then we can conclude that the mean for the None group is different from the means for the Alcohol and Poly Drug groups.

Figure 14.2 graphs the mean Depressive Symptom scores for the three groups using the second set of contrast codes (λ_2). Recall that for λ_2, the Alcohol and Poly Drug groups are both coded +1, and the None group is coded −2. The regression line based on these codes is $\hat{Y} = 13 + 4X$, which is superimposed on the graph. Essentially, these codes contrast the mean for the None group against the average of the means of the other two groups (Poly Drug and Alcohol).

Contrast coding is a fairly sophisticated process, and I have only given a brief pragmatic overview. I encourage you to consult Judd et al. (2009), Keppel and Zedeck (2002), or Kahane (2001) to learn more.

Figure 14.2   Line Graph Comparing Drug Abuse Group Mean Depressive Symptom Scores.

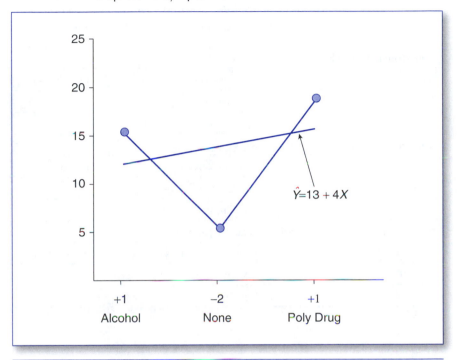

NOTE: Quadratic group codes are demonstrated here: None = –2, and Alcohol = Poly Drug = +1.

COMPARING MODELS TO TEST THE ONE-WAY ANOVA ◆

Now that we've established that we need two predictors (λ_1 and λ_2) for a one-way ANOVA with three levels, and we've defined the contrast codes for λ_1 and λ_2, we can conduct the regression analyses to test the relationship between the IV (DA) and the DV (Depression score). Table 14.2 summarizes the three model comparisons needed for this analysis. First we'll conduct a model comparison that tests whether Model A is different from the omnibus Model C_0. After conducting the omnibus test, we'll isolate the effects of each predictor to see which comparisons (if any) explain the relationship between DA and Depression scores. The data for these comparisons are presented in Table 14 3, including the contrast codes for the two DA predictors.

Table 14.2 Summary of the Three Comparisons to Test the One-Way ANOVA With Three Levels (Groups): Omnibus Test, Comparison of Alcohol Versus Drug Groups, and Comparison of the None Group Versus the Alcohol and Drug Groups

Comparison O: Omnibus model	
Model A:	Depression = $\beta_0 + \beta_1$ Linear + β_2 Quadratic + ε
Model C:	Depression = $\beta_0 + \varepsilon$
Difference:	β_1 Linear + β_2 Quadratic
Comparison 1: Alcohol versus Drug groups	
Model A:	Depression = $\beta_0 + \beta_1$ Linear + β_2 Quadratic + ε
Model C:	Depression = $\beta_0 + \beta_2$ Quadratic + ε
Difference:	β_1 Linear
Comparison 2: None group versus Alcohol/Drug groups	
Model A:	Depression = $\beta_0 + \beta_1$ Linear + β_2 Quadratic + ε
Model C:	Depression = $\beta_0 + \beta_1$ Linear + ε
Difference:	β_1 Quadratic

Table 14.3 Depression Scores (DV) and the Two Contrast Codes for the Three Drug Abuse Groups

Subject	Symptom Score (DV)	Drug Abuse Groups	λ_1 Linear Code	λ_2 Quadratic Code
1	3	None	0	−2
2	5	None	0	−2
3	6	None	0	−2
4	8	None	0	−2
5	9	Alcohol	−1	1
6	11	Alcohol	−1	1
7	19	Alcohol	−1	1
8	15	Alcohol	−1	1
9	16	Poly Drug	1	1
10	16	Poly Drug	1	1
11	19	Poly Drug	1	1

Subject	Symptom Score (DV)	Drug Abuse Groups	λ_1 Linear Code	λ_2 Quadratic Code
12	17	Poly Drug	1	1
13	3	None	0	−2
14	5	None	0	−2
15	4	None	0	−2
16	6	None	0	−2
17	8	Alcohol	−1	1
18	10	Alcohol	−1	1
19	24	Alcohol	−1	1
20	24	Alcohol	−1	1
21	22	Poly Drug	1	1
22	23	Poly Drug	1	1
23	19	Poly Drug	1	1
24	20	Poly Drug	1	1

CONDUCTING THE OMNIBUS TEST

The first eight steps to compare Model A, which includes both predictors (λ_1 and λ_2) with the simplest Model C_0 (which includes neither predictor) are summarized in Table 14.4. The H_0 is that neither predictor improves the model. Model C_0 estimated one parameter (β_0), so $PC_0 = 1$. Model A estimated three parameters ($\beta_0, \beta_1, \beta_2$), so PA = 3. Therefore, this is a 2 *df* test (PA − PC = 2). The error for Model C_0 is 1,204 (Step 5) and the error for Model A is 372 (Step 6), so the reduction in error (SSR) is 832 (Step 7). Dividing SSR by SST gives a proportional reduction in error (PRE) of .691 (Step 8). These results are entered in the summary table (see Table 14.5). We complete the summary table by dividing each *SS* by its corresponding *df* to get MSB (mean square between) for the omnibus Model A and MSW (mean square within) for the residual error. We divide MSB by MSW to get *F* for the omnibus model. The $F(2, 21)$ for the omnibus model is 23.484, which has a $p < .001$ if H_0 is true. We'll reject H_0, so we know that either β_1, β_2, or both $\neq 0$.

Compare the results of this omnibus test with the one-way ANOVA from Chapter 13. You'll find that the results are identical. This test suggests that the three DA group means are not equal ($F(2, 21) = 23.484, p < .001$), and therefore, DA (the IV) is related to Depression score (the DV). But the test

Table 14.4 First Eight Model Comparison Steps to Test the Omnibus Relationship Between Drug Abuse Groups and Depression Score

Step 1	State the compact Model C_0 and an augmented Model A
	Model C_0: $\hat{Y} = \beta_0$
	Model A: $\hat{Y} = \beta_0 + \beta_1$ Linear $+ \beta_2$ Quadratic
Step 2	Identify the null hypothesis (H_0)
	H_0: $\beta_1 = \beta_2 = 0$
Step 3	Count the number of parameters estimated by each model
	PA = 3
	$PC_0 = 1$
Step 4	Calculate the regression equation
	Model C_0: Depression = 13 + ε
	Model A: Depression = 13 + 2 Linear + 4 Quadratic + ε
Step 5	Compute sum of squares (SSE_C)
	$SSE_{C0} = SST = 1,204$
Step 6	Compute sum of squares for Model A (SSE_A)
	$SSE_A = 372$
Step 7	Compute sum of squares reduced (SSR)
	SSR = 832
Step 8	Compute the proportional reduction in error (PRE or R^2)
	PRE = R^2 = .691

Table 14.5 Results for Omnibus Test Added to the Summary Table

Source	SS	df	MS	F	p	R^2
Model A	832	2	416	23.484	<.001	.691
Residual (SSE_A)	372	21	17.714			
Total	1,204	23				

doesn't tell us which means are different. In Chapter 13, this was as far as the one-way ANOVA took us, so we used a post hoc analysis to figure out which means were different. In this model comparison approach, however, we can conduct two more model comparisons to decide which groups are different from each other. First, let's isolate the effects of the linear predictor (λ_1), which compares the Alcohol and the Drug groups.

ISOLATING THE EFFECTS OF THE LINEAR PREDICTOR ◆

To isolate the effects of the linear predictor, we'll compare the omnibus Model A with a compact Model C_1 that includes only the quadratic predictor (C_1: Depressive Symptoms $= \beta_0 + \beta_2 \times$ Quadratic). The steps and results for isolating the effects of adding the linear predictor to the model are summarized in Table 14.6. The difference between Model A and Model C_1 is that

Table 14.6 First Eight Model Comparison Steps to Test the Relationship Between the Linear Predictor and Depression Score ($\beta 1$)

Step 1	State the compact Model C_1 and an augmented Model A
	Model C_1: $\hat{Y} = \beta_0 + \beta_2$ Quadratic
	Model A: $\hat{Y} = \beta_0 + \beta_1$ Linear $+ \beta_2$ Quadratic
	H_0: $\beta_1 = 0$
Step 3	Count the number of parameters estimated by each model
	PA = 3
	$PC_1 = 2$
Step 4	Calculate the regression equation
	Model C_1: Depression $= 13 + 4$ Quadratic $+ \varepsilon$
	Model A: Depression $= 13 + 2$ Linear $+ 4$ Quadratic $+ \varepsilon$
Step 5	Compute sum of squares (SSE_C)
	$SSE_{C1} = 436$
Step 6	Compute sum of squares for Model A (SSE_A)
	$SSE_A = 372$
Step 7	Compute sum of squares reduced (SSR)
	SSR = 64
Step 8	Compute the proportional reduction in error (PRE or R^2)
	PRE $= R^2 = .053$

Model A includes the linear contrast code, whereas Model C_1 does not. H_0 is that the linear predictor does not improve Model A over Model C_1 (H_0: $\beta_1 = 0$). Model C_1 estimated two parameters (β_0 and β_1), and Model A estimated three, so this is a 1 *df* test (PA − PC = 1)[2]. The error for Model C_1 is 436 (Step 5) and the error for Model A is 372 (Step 6), so the SSR is 64 (Step 7). Dividing SSR by SST gives a PRE of .053 attributed to the linear effect (Step 8). These results are then added to the summary table (see Table 14.7). As usual, MSB for the linear predictor is calculated by dividing SSB_{linear} by 1 *df*. F for this test is calculated by dividing MSB_{linear} by MSW.

The resulting $F(1, 21)$ is 3.613, and the probability of getting this F if H_0 is true is .071. As this probability is greater than .05, we don't reject H_0. The results of this comparison suggest that the Alcohol and Poly Drug group means were not statistically different.

Next let's isolate the effects of the quadratic predictor on Depression scores.

Table 14.7 Results for the Comparison to Isolate the Linear Model

Source	SS	df	MS	F	p	R^2
Model A	832	2	416	23.484	<.001	.691
Linear predictor	64	1	64	3.613	.071	.053
Residual (SSE_A)	372	21	17.714			
Total	1,204	23				

◆ ISOLATING THE EFFECTS OF THE QUADRATIC PREDICTOR

The steps and results for isolating the effects of adding the quadratic predictor to the model are summarized in Table 14.8. The difference between the Model A and Model C_2 is the inclusion of the quadratic contrast code in Model A. H_0 is that the quadratic predictor does not improve the model ($\beta_1 = 0$). Model C_2 estimated two parameters, and Model A estimated three, so this again is a 1 *df* test (PA − PC = 1). The error for Model C_2 is 1,140 (Step 5) and the error for Model A is 372 (Step 6), so the SSR is 768 (Step 7). Dividing SSR by SST gives a PRE of .638 (Step 8). These results are entered into the summary table (see Table 14.9).

---

2. Remember from Chapter 9 that a 1 *df* test is best because it will tell us which means are different.

| Table 14.8 | First Eight Model Comparison Steps to Test the Relationship Between the Quadratic Predictor and Depression Score ($\beta2$) |

Step 1	State the compact Model C_2 and an augmented Model A
	Model C_2: $\hat{Y} = \beta_0 + \beta_1$ Linear
	Model A: $\hat{Y} = \beta_0 + \beta_1$ Linear $+ \beta_2$ Quadratic
Step 2	Identify the null hypothesis (H_0)
	H_0: $\beta_2 = 0$
Step 3	Count the number of parameters estimated by each model
	PA = 3
	$PC_2 = 2$
Step 4	Calculate the regression equation
	Model C_2: Depression = 13 + 2 Linear + ε
	Model A: Depression = 13 + 2 Linear + 4 Quadratic + ε
Step 5	Compute sum of squares (SSE_C)
	$SSE_{C2} = 1,140$
Step 6	Compute sum of squares for Model A (SSE_A)
	$SSE_A = 372$
Step 7	Compute sum of squares reduced (SSR)
	SSR = 768
Step 8	Compute the proportional reduction in error (PRE or R^2)
	PRE = R^2 = .638

Dividing $SSB_{quadratic}$ by 1 *df* gives $MSB_{quadratic}$. $MSB_{quadratic}$ divided by MSW gives us $F(1, 21)$ of 43.356. The probability of this *F*, if H_0 is true, is very small ($< .001$), so we reject H_0 and infer that the quadratic predictor improved prediction of Depressive Symptoms.

The quadratic predictor contrasted the None group against the Alcohol and Drug groups. Since the model comparison led us to reject the H_0, we interpret this finding to mean that Depressive scores for those who did not abuse alcohol or other drugs (None group) were different (lower) than for subjects in the Alcohol and Poly Drug groups.

Taken together, these two model comparisons suggest that the Alcohol and Poly Drug groups did not have different Depressive Symptom means, but those two groups were different from the None group. These results are the

Table 14.9 Results for the Comparison to Isolate the Linear Model

Source	SS	df	MS	F	p	R^2
Model A	832	2	416	23.484	<.001	.691
Linear predictor	64	1	64	3.613	.071	.053
Quadratic predictor	768	1	768	43.356	<.001	.638
Residual (SSE_A)	372	21	17.714			
Total	1,204	23				

same as we found with the post hoc analysis in Chapter 13: the "None" group scored different on average than the other two groups.

◆ SUMMARY

In this chapter, we used multiple regression and the model comparison approach to conduct a one-way ANOVA where the IV had three levels. The most critical concept in this chapter was that a single categorical predictor (IV) with more than two groups (levels) required multiple predictor variables. We determined how many predictor variables we needed by subtracting 1 from the number of groups. Having three groups in the IV, we needed two predictor variables. We also used contrast codes that allowed for preplanned, a priori ("before the fact") group comparisons. These contrast coded predictors saved us the step of conducting a post hoc analysis to determine which group means were different.

Once we had created the two predictor variables for this one-way ANOVA, the model comparisons were the same as before. The results of this analysis were identical to the traditional one-way ANOVA with three levels conducted in Chapter 13. An advantage of the model comparison approach was that isolating the effects of each predictor reduced our need to conduct a post hoc analysis subsequent to finishing the ANOVA.

15

TWO-BY-THREE ANOVA

Complex Categorical Models

It is commonly believed that anyone who tabulates numbers is a statistician. This is like believing that anyone who owns a scalpel is a surgeon. A statistician is one who has learned how to get valid evidence from statistics and how (usually) to avoid being misled by irrelevant facts.

—Robert Hooke

How to Tell the Liars From the Statisticians

Research advances by our embracing the ever-expanding complexity of our theoretical and statistical models. We've seen that we can test a categorical variable with two groups (levels) and a categorical variable with three (or more) levels. We've also seen that our models aren't restricted to a single predictor variable (independent variable, IV). We built a two-way analysis of variance (ANOVA) model that had two IVs, each with two levels. In this chapter, we'll test a two-way ANOVA where one of the IVs has three levels. This model is called a 2 × 3 ("two-by-three") ANOVA, to specify the number of levels or groups in each IV. By now you realize that we can conduct this ANOVA both in the traditional manner and by using the multiple regression model comparison approach. This chapter presents the traditional model; Chapter 16 will show how to conduct the same analysis using the model comparison approach.

A two-way ANOVA has two IVs predicting the dependent variable (DV). Consequently, the two-way ANOVA model tests three components: (1) the main effect for one IV, (2) the main effect for the second IV, and (3) the interaction of the two IVs. Regardless of whether the IVs have two or three (or more) groups, a two-way ANOVA (meaning two IVs) always tests three null hypotheses that correspond to the components of the omnibus model: (1) the group means of the first IV are equal, (2) the group means of the second IV are equal, and (3) the IVs do not interact. For this example, we'll use Depressive symptom data and two IVs already familiar to us: Sex and Drug Abuse (DA). To conduct the ANOVA, we will again partition the total variance (total sum of squared errors, SST) into variance explained by the two main effects (sum of squares between for DA and Sex, SSB_{DA} and SSB_{sex}, respectively), variance explained by the interaction ($SS_{DA \times sex}$), and unexplained (residual) variance (sum of squares within, SSW). We already know that the SST of these Depression scores is 1,204 and that the total degrees of freedom (*dfs*) is total N minus 1 ($24 - 1 = 23$). Now to determine the SSB.

◆ SUM OF SQUARES BETWEEN

SSB is the part of the SST that is explained by the main effects and interaction of the two IVs. To get the SSB, we need to find the "main effects" contribution to SSB from each IV (Sex and DA). We use the same formula we used in Chapter 7 and Chapter 11 to compute each part of SSB:

$$SSB_{group} = \Sigma \frac{\left(\Sigma Y_{group}\right)^2}{N_{group}} - \frac{\left(\Sigma Y\right)^2}{N}. \tag{15.1}$$

Equation 15.1 can be split into two parts. Part I (shown in Equation 15.2) is the average squared sum for each group:

$$\Sigma \frac{\left(\Sigma Y_{group}\right)^2}{N_{group}}. \tag{15.2}$$

Part II is called the "correction term" and is given again in Equation 15.3:

$$\text{Correction term} = \left(\frac{\left(\Sigma Y\right)^2}{N}\right). \tag{15.3}$$

Sum of Squares Between for Sex

To use Equation 15.1 to get the SSB for Sex (SSB_{sex}), we need the sum of scores for each Sex group regardless of their drug use. To get these sums, I've organized the data by Sex and DA (see Table 15.1). Let's begin with Part I; first we sum the Depression scores for all the men, square the sum, and divide by the number of men in the study. We repeat this process for the women: sum the scores for all the women, square the sum, and divide by the number of women in the study. The sum of all the men's scores is 144. That value squared (20,736) and divided by the number of men (12) gives the contribution to SSB_{sex} for men (1,728). The sum of women's scores (168) squared (28,224) and divided by the number of women (12) gives the contribution to SSB_{sex} for women (2,352). The sum of the contribution from men (1,728) and from women (2,352) is 4,080 gives us Part I of Equation 15.1.

Now we need the correction term. To get the correction term, we sum all of the scores (regardless of group), square that sum, and divide by the total number of subjects. The sum of all of the scores is 312. We square that value (97,344) and divide by the total number of subjects ($N = 24$) to get the correction term (4,056). Now we have both parts of Equation 15.1: the

Table 15.1 Depression Scores According to Participants' Sex and Drug Abuse Group

	Drug Abuse			
	None	*Alcohol*	*Poly Drug*	*Marginal*
Men	3	9	16	
	5	11	16	
	6	19	19	Σ for Men = 144
	8	15	17	M = 12
	Σ = 22	Σ = 54	Σ = 68	
Women	3	8	22	
	5	10	23	
	4	24	19	Σ for Women = 168
	6	24	20	M = 14
	Σ = 18	Σ = 66	Σ = 84	
Marginal	Σ for None = 40	Σ for Alcohol = 120	Σ for Poly Drug = 152	Grand mean = 13
	M = 5	M = 15	M = 19	

correction term (4,056) and the value of Part I (4,080). We get the SS explained by the IV Sex by subtracting Part II from Part I. The result is $SSB_{sex} = 24$.

The IV Sex reduced the total error (SST) by 24. Because the variable Sex has two levels (Men and Women), testing Sex used 1 df (between df [$df_{between}$] = No. of groups − 1). This information for the Sex variable is added to the summary table (Table 15.2). The SSB_{sex} (24) divided by the df for Sex (1) gives a mean square value for Sex (MS_{sex}) of 24.

Sum of Squares Between for Drug Abuse

We follow the same process to get the SS explained by the DA variable (SSB_{DA}). Since DA has three group means, this time we'll find the contribution to SS from each of the three DA groups: None, Alcohol, and Poly Drug. Look back at Table 15.1. The sum of scores for the None group is 40, the sum for the Alcohol group is 120, and the sum for the Poly Drug group is 152. To get Part I (the contribution to SSB_{DA} from each group), we square each of those sums and divide by the number of subjects in each group (in this demonstration, $N = 8$ for each group). Equation 15.4 works through this process:

$$\text{Part I: } \frac{\left(\Sigma Y_{DA:none}\right)^2}{N_{DA:none}} + \frac{\left(\Sigma Y_{DA:alcohol}\right)^2}{N_{DA:alcohol}} + \frac{\left(\Sigma Y_{DA:polydrug}\right)^2}{N_{DA:polydrug}}. \quad (15.4)$$

$$\text{Part I: } \frac{(40)^2}{8} + \frac{(120)^2}{8} + \frac{(152)^2}{8}$$

$$= \frac{1600}{8} + \frac{14400}{8} + \frac{23104}{8}$$
$$= 200 + 1800 + 2888$$
$$= 4888.$$

We already know that the correction term (Part II of the equation) is 4,056. When we subtract the correction term from 4,888 (Part I), we have SSB_{DA} (832). We add the SSB_{DA} findings to the summary table (Table 15.3). Since the DA variable has three levels (None, Alcohol, and Poly Drug), testing the main effect for DA used 2 dfs (No. of groups − 1). Dividing the SSB_{DA} (832) by the df for DA (2) gives a MS_{DA} of 416.

Table 15.2 Summary Table for Two-Way ANOVA With SSB_{sex} and SST Values Entered

Source	SS	df	MS	F	p
Sex	24	1	24		
Drug Abuse					
Sex × Drug Abuse					
Error					
Total	1,204	23			

Table 15.3 Summary Table for Two-Way ANOVA With Values for SSB_{sex}, SSB_{DA}, and SST Entered

Source	SS	df	MS	F	p
Sex	24	1	24		
Drug Abuse	832	2	416		
Sex × Drug Abuse					
Error					
Total	1,204	23			

INTERACTION OF SEX AND DRUG ABUSE ◆

To get the main effect for Sex, we collapsed scores across DA: We summed the scores for all of the men regardless of which DA group they were in, and we summed the scores for all of the Women regardless of their DA group. Likewise, to get the main effect for DA, we collapsed scores across the Sex variable by summing the scores for each DA group regardless of the sex of the subject.

When we determine the *SS* explained by the interaction of Sex and DA ($SS_{sex×DA}$), we won't collapse scores across any of the groups. Instead, we'll use all six cells created by the two IVs (2 Sex × 3 DA). First we'll sum the scores within a cell, then we'll square that sum, and finally we'll divide this squared sum by the number of subjects in that cell. Since we have six cells, we'll do this six times, once for each cell, and when we have these six values, we'll sum them. From that sum, we'll subtract three values: the SSB_{sex} (24), the SSB_{DA} (832), and the correction term (4,056). This formula for the interaction is given in Equation 15.5:

$$SS_{sex \times DA} = \frac{\left(\sum Y_{men \times none}\right)^2}{N_{men \times none}} + \frac{\left(\sum Y_{men \times alcohol}\right)^2}{N_{men \times alcohol}} + \frac{\left(\sum Y_{men \times polydrug}\right)^2}{N_{men \times polydrug}}$$

$$+ \frac{\left(\sum Y_{women \times none}\right)^2}{N_{women \times none}} + \frac{\left(\sum Y_{women \times alcohol}\right)^2}{N_{women \times alcohol}} + \frac{\left(\sum Y_{women \times polydrug}\right)^2}{N_{women \times polydrug}} \quad (15.5)$$

$$- SSB_{sex} - SSB_{DA} - \frac{\left(\sum Y\right)^2}{N}.$$

In Table 15.4, I've computed the squared sum for each cell (divided by the cell's N). I've also given the correction term (4,056), SSB_{sex} (24), and SSB_{DA} (832). I now have everything I need to complete Equation 15.5 and get the $SSB_{sex \times DA}$. The result is $SSB_{sex \times DA} = 28$. The interaction explained 28 SS. To compute the df for the interaction, we multiply the number of dfs for each predictor (IV) in the interaction. Sex used 1 df, and DA used 2, so the df for the interaction is 2 × 1, which of course equals 2.

Table 15.4 Computation of Sums of Squares Explained by the Interaction of Sex and Dug Abuse

Cell 1:	$\dfrac{\left(\sum Y_{men \times none}\right)^2}{N_{men \times none}} = \dfrac{(22)^2}{4} = \dfrac{484}{4} = 121$
Cell 2:	$\dfrac{\left(\sum Y_{men \times alcohol}\right)^2}{N_{men \times alcohol}} = \dfrac{(54)^2}{4} = \dfrac{2916}{4} = 729$
Cell 3:	$\dfrac{\left(\sum Y_{men \times polydrug}\right)^2}{N_{men \times polydrug}} = \dfrac{(68)^2}{4} = \dfrac{4624}{4} = 1156$
Cell 4:	$\dfrac{\left(\sum Y_{women \times none}\right)^2}{N_{women \times none}} = \dfrac{(18)^2}{4} = \dfrac{324}{4} = 81$
Cell 5:	$\dfrac{\left(\sum Y_{women \times alcohol}\right)^2}{N_{women \times alcohol}} = \dfrac{(66)^2}{4} = \dfrac{4356}{4} = 1089$

Cell 6:	$\dfrac{\left(\Sigma Y_{\text{women}\times\text{polydrug}}\right)^2}{N_{\text{women}\times\text{polydrug}}} = \dfrac{(84)^2}{4} = \dfrac{7056}{4} = 1764$
Correction term:	$\dfrac{\left(\Sigma Y\right)^2}{N} = \dfrac{(312)^2}{24} = \dfrac{97344}{24} = 4056$

$SSB_{\text{sex}} = 24 \qquad SSB_{\text{DA}} = 832$

$SSB_{\text{sex}\times\text{DA}} = (\text{Cell 1} + \text{Cell 2} + \text{Cell 3} + \text{Cell 4} + \text{Cell 5} + \text{Cell 6}) - SSB_{\text{sex}} - SSB_{\text{DA}} - \text{Correction term}$

$SSB_{\text{sex}\times\text{DA}} = (121 + 729 + 1156 + 81 + 1089 + 1764) - 24 - 832 - 4056$

$SSB_{\text{sex}\times\text{DA}} = (4940) - 4912 = 28$

We've calculated all of the explained *SS* and partitioned it according to the two IVs (Sex and DA) and the interaction. Adding this information to the summary table (Table 15.5), we can calculate the *MS* for the interaction ($SS_{\text{sex}\times\text{DA}} \div df_{\text{sex}\times\text{DA}}$). The *df* for the interaction is the product of the *df* for Sex (1) and the *df* for DA (2). The results is that 2 *df* were used for the interaction. Dividing the $SS_{\text{sex}\times\text{DA}}$ for the interaction (28) by the *df* for the interaction (2) gives us a $MS_{\text{sex}\times\text{DA}}$ of 14.

Table 15.5 Summary Table for Two-Way ANOVA With Values for SSB_{sex}, SSB_{DA}, $SSB_{\text{sex}\times\text{DA}}$, and SST Entered

Source	SS	df	MS	F	p
Sex	24	1	24		
Drug Abuse	832	2	416		
Sex × Drug Abuse	28	2	14		
Error					
Total	1,204	23			

SUM OF SQUARES WITHIN ◆

We have almost finished partitioning the SST. All that's left to compute is the residual error (SS_{residual}). Recall that in ANOVA, the residual SS is called the "SS within" (SSW) and it is the difference between the SST and the SS explained ($SSB_{\text{sex}} + SSB_{\text{DA}} + SS_{\text{sex}\times\text{DA}}$).

We could very easily complete the ANOVA summary table by summing the *SS* explained by Sex, DA, and the interaction (24 + 832 + 28 = 884) and then subtracting the explained *SS* from the SST (1,204). The difference between the total error and explained error gives us a residual error (SSW) of $1204 - 884 = 320$. Of course, I feel obliged to demonstrate how to compute SSW the hard way, without simply subtracting explained *SS* from SST. The formula for computing SSW is given in Equation 15.6. The first part of the equation is the sum of the squared values of all 24 depression scores (ΣY^2):

$$\text{SSW} = \Sigma Y^2 - \Sigma \left[\frac{(\Sigma Y_{\text{cell}})^2}{N_{\text{cell}}} \right]. \qquad (15.6)$$

ΣY^2 is computed in Table 15.6 by squaring each Depression score and then summing the squared scores. The result is 5,260.

Table 15.6 Depression Scores and Their Squared Values

Subject	Y	Y²
1	3	9
2	5	25
3	6	36
4	8	64
5	9	81
6	11	121
7	19	361
8	15	225
9	16	256
10	16	256
11	19	361
12	17	289
13	3	9
14	5	25
15	4	16
16	6	36
17	8	64
18	10	100
19	24	576
20	24	576

Subject	Y	Y^2
21	22	484
22	23	529
23	19	361
24	20	400
	312	5,260

NOTE: The sum of scores (ΣY) is 312, and the sum of squared scores (ΣY^2) is 5,260.

To get the second part of Equation 15.6, we first sum the scores within each cell. Once again, since we have six cells, we'll have six values. The sums for each cell were reported in Table 15.1. In Table 15.7, I've squared each sum and divided by the number of observations in that cell (in this example there were four scores in each cell). I then add the six resulting values. The sum, shown in Table 15.7, is 4,940.

Finally, to get SSW, we subtract the sum obtained in Table 15.7 (4,940) from the ΣY^2 obtained in Table 15.6 (5,260). This difference (5260 − 4940) is 320.

Fortunately, the SSW calculated using Equation 15.5 (320) is equal to the SSW we got when we subtracted SSB from SST. It's always a good thing when two values that are supposed to be equal turn out to be equal! We can now add the SSW information to the ANOVA summary table (Table 15.8). The within *df* (df_{within}) is the difference between total *df* (23) and the *df* used in the model. In this example, we used 1 *df* for Sex, 2 *df* for DA, and 2 *df* for the interaction. The difference, 23 − 1 − 2 − 2 is 18.

Dividing SSW (320) by df_{within} (18) gives the mean square within (MSW), which is 17.778. Now that we have MSW, we can compute an *F* ratio for each main effect (Sex and DA) and for the interaction. You know how to get *F* by now. These *F* values are included in the summary table (Table 15.8).

Table 15.7 Computing the Sum of Each Cell

Cell	Sex	Drug Abuse	$(\Sigma Y)^2$	$(\Sigma Y)^2/N_{cell}$
1	Men	None	484	121
2	Men	Alcohol	2,916	729
3	Men	Poly Drug	4,624	1,156
4	Women	None	324	81
5	Women	Alcohol	4,356	1,089
6	Women	Poly Drug	7,056	1,764
Σ				4,940

Table 15.8 Completed Summary Table for Two-Way ANOVA

Source	SS	df	MS	F	p
Sex	24	1	24	1.350	.260
Drug Abuse	832	2	416	23.400	<.001
Sex x Drug Abuse	28	2	14	0.788	.470
Error	320	18	17.778		
Total	1,204	23			

◆ INTERPRETING THE RESULTS

The results of this 2×3 ANOVA are reported separately for each main effect and for the interaction. Neither the main effect for Sex, $F(1, 18) = 1.35, p = .26$, nor the interaction between Sex and DA, $F(1, 18) = 0.79$, $p = .470$, were statistically significant. There was a main effect for DA, $F(2, 18) = 23.40, p < .001$. Since DA has three groups, we need to conduct a post hoc analysis to decide which groups are different. The least significant difference (LSD) analysis introduced in Chapter 13 is presented again in Equation 15.7. The two-tail critical t for 18 df is 2.09, MSE is 17.778, and each group had 8 subjects. Putting these values into Equation 15.7, we get LSD = 4.406. This value tells us that for any two Mean scores to be statistically different from each other, they must be at least 4.406 points apart. For which of our three group means does this condition hold?

$$\text{LSD} = t_{\text{critical}} \sqrt{MSE \left[\frac{1}{N_{\text{group1}}} + \frac{1}{N_{\text{group2}}} \right]}.$$

(15.7)

$$
\begin{aligned}
\text{LSD} &= 2.09 \sqrt{17.778 \left[\frac{1}{8} + \frac{1}{8} \right]} \\
&= 2.09 \sqrt{17.778 (0.25)} \\
&= 2.09 \sqrt{4.4445} \\
&= 2.09 (2.108) \\
&= 4.406.
\end{aligned}
$$

Table 15.9 presents the differences between each of the DA mean scores. The difference between the None group ($M = 5$) and the Alcohol group ($M = 15$) is 10, which of course is greater than 4.406, so the None group scored reliably (statistically significantly) lower than the Alcohol group on the Depression measure. The 14-point difference between the None group and the Poly Drug group also is greater than the LSD, so the None group scored reliably lower than the Poly Drug group. Finally, the 4-point difference between the Alcohol and the Poly Drug groups is not large enough to conclude that those two groups scored differently.

Table 15.9 Results of Mean Comparisons

Comparison	Mean 1		Mean 2	Difference	LSD	Decision
1	None	vs.	Alcohol			
	5		15	10	4.406	None ≠ Alcohol
2	None	vs.	Drug			
	5		19	14	4.406	None ≠ Poly Drug
3	Alcohol	vs.	Drug			
	15		19	4	4.406	Alcohol = Poly Drug

SUMMARY ◆

This chapter revisited the two-way ANOVA; however, the chapter focused on a two-way ANOVA in which one of the IVs had three groups (levels). We called this analysis a 2×3 ("two-by-three") ANOVA to indicate the number of groups in the IVs (two levels of Sex, three levels of DA). Then, using various formulas, we partitioned the total sum of squared errors (SST) into between *SS* (that explained by each IV), *SS* explained by the interaction, and within (residual) error. In the next chapter, we'll use the model comparison approach to conduct the 2×3 ANOVA.

16

TWO-BY-THREE ANOVA

Model Comparison Approach

Far better an approximate answer to the right question, which is often vague, than an exact answer to the wrong question, which can always be made precise.

—John Tukey

In the previous chapter, we used a two-way ANOVA in which one of the independent variables (IVs) had three groups (levels). It was called a 2×3 ("two-by-three") ANOVA to indicate the number of groups in the IVs (two Sex groups and three Drug Abuse [DA] groups). Then, using various formulas, we partitioned the total sum of squared errors (SST) into SS explained by each IV, SS explained by the interaction, and the within (residual) error (SSW). In this chapter, we'll repeat the 2×3 ANOVA, this time using the model comparison approach.

OMNIBUS MODEL ◆

The model comparison approach to a 2×3 ANOVA is very similar to the model comparison approach for a 2×2 ANOVA, with just a few differences. The only challenge is defining the omnibus Model A. As we did in Chapter 14, we'll again need two predictors for the DA variable (linear and quadratic), and because DA needs two predictors, the interaction will also need two predictors. The good news is that by using contrast codes to define the variables, we won't need post hoc tests.

First, we should define the omnibus model (Model A) that tests our 2×3 ANOVA. Model A includes both predictor variables (Sex and DA) and their interaction (Sex × DA). Table 16.1 presents the contrast codes for both IVs. Model A has three predictor variables for the two main effects—one for Sex and two for Drug Abuse (DA_{linear} and $DA_{quadratic}$). The model has two predictors for the Sex × DA interactions (Sex × DA_{linear} and Sex × $DA_{quadratic}$). This analysis will require five model comparisons to isolate the individual components.

Table 16.1 Contrast Codes for the Two Independent Variables: Drug Abuse (DA) and Sex

	DA		
Predictor	*Alcohol*	*None*	*Drug*
DA_{linear} (Alcohol vs. Poly Drug)	−1	0	+1
$DA_{quadratic}$ (None vs. Alcohol and Poly Drug)	+1	−2	+1
	Sex		
	Women	*Men*	
Men vs. Women	−1	−1	

The interaction variables are defined by multiplying the two IVs together. This time, however, since DA required two predictors, we multiply each DA predictor separately with Sex (Sex × DA_{linear} and Sex × $DA_{quadratic}$), producing two predictors for the Sex × DA interaction. Table 16.2 presents the contrast codes for these interaction terms.

Table 16.2 Contrast Codes for the Interaction Between Drug Abuse (DA) and Sex: Sex × DA_{linear} (*top*) and Sex × $DA_{quadratic}$ (*bottom*)

		Drug Abuse (DA_{linear})		
		Alcohol	*None*	*Poly Drug*
		−1	0	1
Men	1	−1	0	1
Women	−1	1	0	−1

		Alcohol	None	Poly Drug
		1	−2	1
Men	1	1	−2	1
Women	−1	−1	2	−1

Drug Abuse ($DA_{quadratic}$)

We have created the codes for all five of the predictors needed for this 2×3 model comparison ANOVA. Model A is presented in Equation 16.1. Submitting the model to a statistical program estimates the regression coefficients for Model A (see Equation 16.2).

$$\text{Depression score} = \beta_0 + \beta_1 \text{ Sex} + \beta_2 \text{ DA}_{linear} + \beta_3 \text{ DA}_{quadratic}$$

$$+ \beta_4 \text{ Sex} \times \text{DA}_{linear} + \beta_5 \text{ Sex} \times \text{DA}_{quadratic} + \varepsilon. \quad (16.1)$$

$$\text{Depression score} = 13 + (-1.00) \text{ Sex} + (2.00) \text{ DA}_{linear} + (4.00) \text{ DA}_{quadratic}$$

$$+ (-0.25) \text{ Sex} \times \text{DA}_{linear} + (-.75) \text{ Sex} \times \text{DA}_{quadratic} + \varepsilon. \quad (16.2)$$

COMPUTE ERROR FOR MODEL A ◆

With Model A defined and estimated, we can calculate the error of this omnibus model (see Table 16.3). Model A predicts a score for each subject. We find the differences between the predicted and actual scores for each subject $(Y - \hat{Y})$ and then square and sum those differences: $\sum (Y - \hat{Y})^2$ The result is a sum of squared errors of 320 for Model A (SSE_A). The SSE_A is the residual error (SSW) for all five of our model comparisons in this 2×3 ANOVA.

ISOLATE THE EFFECTS OF EACH MODEL A PREDICTOR ◆

We know from the earlier chapters that total error for these data (SST) is 1,204, and we now know that SSE_A is 320. Therefore, the omnibus Model A reduced the total error by $1,204 - 320 = 884$, which is a 73.4% reduction in error ($R^2 = .734$). We don't know, however, which predictors actually reduced error—it might have been all five predictors, or it might have been only one

Table 16.3 Process of Computing the Sum of Squared Errors for Model A (SSE_A)

Subject	Depression Score (Y)	$\hat{Y}$	$(Y - \hat{Y})$	$(Y - \hat{Y})^2$
1	3	5.5	−2.5	6.25
2	5	5.5	−0.5	0.25
3	6	5.5	0.5	0.25
4	8	5.5	2.5	6.25
5	9	13.5	−4.5	20.25
6	11	13.5	−2.5	6.25
7	19	13.5	5.5	30.25
8	15	13.5	1.5	2.25
9	16	17	−1	1
10	16	17	−1	1
11	19	17	2	4
12	17	17	0	0
13	3	4.5	−1.5	2.25
14	5	4.5	0.5	0.25
15	4	4.5	−0.5	0.25
16	6	4.5	1.5	2.25
17	8	16.5	−8.5	72.25
18	10	16.5	−6.5	42.25
19	24	16.5	7.5	56.25
20	24	16.5	7.5	56.25
21	22	21	1	1
22	23	21	2	4
23	19	21	−2	4
24	20	21	−1	1
			$SSE_A = 320$	

predictor. To determine which predictors were statistically significant contributors to the error reduction, we'll conduct a series of model comparisons to isolate the individual effects. The five comparisons are given in Table 16.4.

Table 16.4 Summary of the Model Comparisons to Test the 2 × 3 ANOVA

Comparison 1: Main Effect for Sex	
Model A:	$Depression = \beta_0 + \beta_1\, Sex + \beta_2\, DA_{linear} + \beta_3\, DA_{quadratic} + \beta_4\, Sex \times DA_{linear} + \beta_5\, Sex \times DA_{quadratic} + \varepsilon$
Model C$_1$:	$Depression = \beta_0 + \beta_2\, DA_{linear} + \beta_3\, DA_{quadratic} + \beta_4\, Sex \times DA_{linear} + \beta_5\, Sex \times DA_{quadratic} + \varepsilon$
Comparison 2: Main Effect for DA$_{linear}$	
Model A:	$Depression = \beta_0 + \beta_1\, Sex + \beta_2\, DA_{linear} + \beta_3\, DA_{quadratic} + \beta_4\, Sex \times DA_{linear} + \beta5\, Sex \times DA_{quadratic} + \varepsilon$
Model C$_1$:	$Depression = \beta_0 + \beta_1\, Sex + \beta_3\, DA_{quadratic} + \beta_4\, Sex \times DA_{linear} + \beta_5\, Sex \times DA_{quadratic} + \varepsilon$
Comparison 3: Main Effect for DA$_{quadratic}$	
Model A:	$Depression = \beta_0 + \beta_1\, Sex + \beta_2\, DA_{linear} + \beta_3\, DA_{quadratic} + \beta_4\, Sex \times DA_{linear} + \beta_5\, Sex \times DA_{quadratic} + \varepsilon$
Model C$_1$:	$Depression = \beta_0 + \beta_1\, Sex + \beta_2\, DA_{linear} + \beta_4\, Sex \times DA_{linear} + \beta_5\, Sex \times DA_{quadratic} + \varepsilon$
Comparison 4: Interaction, Sex × DA$_{linear}$	
Model A:	$Depression = \beta_0 + \beta_1\, Sex + \beta_2\, DA_{linear} + \beta_3\, DA_{quadratic} + \beta_4\, Sex \times DA_{linear} + \beta5\, Sex \times DA_{quadratic} + \varepsilon$
Model C$_1$:	$Depression = \beta_0 + \beta_1\, Sex + \beta_2\, DA_{linear} + \beta_3\, DA_{quadratic} + \beta_5\, Sex \times DA_{quadratic} + \varepsilon$
Comparison 5: Interaction, Sex × DA$_{linear}$	
Model A:	$Depression = \beta_0 + \beta_1\, Sex + \beta_2\, DA_{linear} + \beta_3\, DA_{quadratic} + \beta_4\, Sex \times DA_{linear} + \beta_5\, Sex \times DA_{quadratic} + \varepsilon$
Model C$_1$:	$Depression = \beta_0 + \beta_1\, Sex + \beta_2\, DA_{linear} + \beta_3\, DA_{quadratic} + \beta_4\, Sex \times DA_{linear} + \varepsilon$

Comparison 1: Main Effect for Sex

The first comparison isolates the main effect of Sex on Depression score. This analysis compares Model A with a Model C_1 that looks identical to Model A with the exception that it does not include the Sex variable. Equation 16.3 presents Model C_1:

$$\text{Depression score} = 13 + 2\ DA_{linear} + 4\ DA_{quadratic} + (-0.25)\ \text{Sex} \times DA_{linear} + (-0.75)\ \text{Sex} \times DA_{quadratic} + \varepsilon. \quad (16.3)$$

By now you know the steps of a model comparison. The critical information (the parameters estimated by each model, the *SSE* for each model, the SSR [sum of squares reduced], and the H_0) is presented in the model comparison box (Table 16.5). To compute SSE_{C1}, we use Model C_1 to predict a Depression score for each subject. Next, we subtract the predicted from the actual Depression scores for each subject and then square and sum the differences to get a sum of squared errors for Model C_1, SSE_{C1}, which is 344. The difference in error between Model C_1 (344) and Model A (320) is the sum of squares reduced (SSR = 24) from adding Sex to the model. In other words, when the model included Sex as a predictor (Model A), the error of the model was 320; however, when Sex was excluded from the model (Model C_1), the error wasn't much different ($SSE_{C1} = 344$). In fact, adding Sex to the model only reduced the total error (remember that SST = 1204) by 2%: The proportion of total error (1,204) explained by Sex (24) was .02 (24 ÷ 1204).

Table 16.5 Model Comparison to Test the Main Effect of Sex (Model C_1)

Model C_1:	Depression = 13 + 2 (DA_{linear}) + 4 $(DA_{quadratic})$ + (−.25) (Sex × DA_{linear}) + (−.75) (Sex × $DA_{quadratic}$) + ε
Model A:	Depression = 13 + (−1) Sex + 2 (DA_{linear}) + 4 $(DA_{quadratic})$ + (−.25) (Sex × DA_{linear}) + (−.75) (Sex × $DA_{quadratic}$) + ε
$PC_1 = 5$	$SSE_{C1} = 344.00$
PA = 6	$SSE_A = 320.00$
Difference = 1	SSR = 24
H_0: $\beta_1 = 0$	R^2 (PRE) = .020

Comparison 2: Linear Main Effect for Drug Abuse (DA$_{linear}$)

The second comparison isolates the main effect of DA on Depression score. This analysis compares the linear contrast for DA (Model C$_2$) with the omnibus Model A. Model C$_2$ is identical to Model A with the exception that it does not include the DA$_{linear}$ variable. The error for Model C$_2$ (SSE_{C2}) is 384. The difference in error (SSR) between Model C$_2$ (384) and Model A (320) is 64. As with Comparison 1, leaving DA$_{linear}$ out of the model didn't result in much more error. The proportion of the total error (SST = 1204) reduced by the linear DA predictor (64) was .053 (64 ÷ 1204). The linear contrast for DA (comparing Alcohol abusers with Poly Drug abusers) reduced the error of the model by 5.3% (see model comparison box, Table 16.6).

Table 16.6 Model Comparison to Test the Linear Main Effect of Drug Abuse (Model C$_2$)

Model C$_2$:	Depression = 13 + (−1) Sex + 4 (DA$_{quadratic}$) + (−.25) (Sex × DA$_{linear}$) + (−.75) (Sex × DA$_{quadratic}$) + ε
Model A:	Depression = 13 + (−1) Sex + 2 (DA$_{linear}$) + 4 (DA$_{quadratic}$) + (−.25) (Sex × DA$_{linear}$) + (−.75) (Sex × DA$_{quadratic}$) + ε
PC$_2$ = 5	SSE_{C2} = 384.00
PA = 6	SSE_A = 320.00
Difference = 1	SSR = 64
H$_0$: β$_2$ = 0	R^2 (PRE) = .053

Comparison 3: Quadratic Main Effect for Drug Abuse (DA$_{quadratic}$)

The third comparison isolates the quadratic main effect of DA on Depression score. The quadratic contrast compared both drug-abusing groups (Alcohol and Poly Drug) with the nonabusing group (None). Model C$_3$ looks identical to Model A with the exception that it does not include the DA$_{quadratic}$ predictor (see the model comparison box, Table 16.7). The error for Model C$_3$ (SSE_{C3}) is 1,088. This time, the difference between SSE_A and SSE_{C3} is larger than the reduction we found with the first two comparisons (SSR = 768). The proportion of the SST reduced by the quadratic DA

| Table 16.7 | Model Comparison to Test the Quadratic Main Effect of Drug Abuse (Model C_3) |

Model C_3:	Depression = 13 + (−1) Sex + 2 (DA_{linear}) + (−.25) $(Sex \times DA_{linear})$ + (−.75) $(Sex \times DA_{quadratic})$ + ε
Model A:	Depression = 13 + (−1) Sex + 2 (DA_{linear}) + 4 $(DA_{quadratic})$ + (−.25) $(Sex \times DA_{linear})$ + (−.75) $(Sex \times DA_{quadratic})$ + ε
$PC_3 = 5$	$SSE_{C3} = 1088.00$
PA = 6	$SSE_A = 320.00$
Difference = 1	SSR = 768
$H_0: \beta_3 = 0$	R^2 (PRE) = .638

predictor is .638 (768 ÷ 1204), so the quadratic contrast for DA reduced the error of the model by 63.8%.

If you look back at the final summary table in Chapter 15 (Table 15.8), you'll find that the *SS* explained by the main effect for DA was 832. Now look at the *SS* explained by the two DA predictors in this chapter. The *SS* reduced by the linear comparison (DA_{linear}) was 64, and the *SS* reduced by the quadratic comparison $(DA_{quadratic})$ was 768. If we add these two values, we conveniently get 832, which is identical to the *SS* explained by DA using the traditional 2 × 3 ANOVA.

These first three comparisons provided information that tested the main effects of this 2 × 3 ANOVA. Now it's time to test the interaction effects (Comparisons 4 and 5 from Table 16.4).

Comparison 4: Interaction Between Sex and Linear Contrast for Drug Abuse (DA_{linear})

The fourth comparison isolates the effect of the interaction between Sex and the linear contrast of the DA groups. To isolate the effect, Model C_4 excludes the Sex × DA_{linear} predictor. The model comparison information is presented in the model comparison box (Table 16.8). The error for Model C_4 is 321 (SSE_{C4}). Hence, leaving the Sex × DA_{linear} interaction of the model resulted in almost no difference between SSE_A and SSE_{C4}. SSR is 1, which is pretty small compared with the SST of 1,204; R^2 is less than .001 (to be exact, it is .0008). This interaction term explained less than .1% of the error in Depression scores.

Table 16.8 Model Comparison to Test the First Interaction Term: Sex × DA_{linear} (Model C_4)

Model C_4:	Depression = 13 + (−1) Sex + 2 (DA_{linear}) + 4 ($DA_{quadratic}$) + (−.75) (Sex × $DA_{quadratic}$) + ε
Model A:	Depression = 13 + (−1) Sex + 2 (DA_{linear}) + 4 ($DA_{quadratic}$) + (−.25) (Sex × DA_{linear}) + (−.75) (Sex × $DA_{quadratic}$) + ε
$PC_4 = 5$	$SSE_{C4} = 321.00$
$PA = 6$	$SSE_A = 320.00$
Difference = 1	SSR = 1.00
$H_0: \beta_4 = 0$	R^2 (PRE) = .001

Comparison 5: Interaction Between Sex and Quadratic Contrast for Drug Abuse (DA_{linear})

Finally, the fifth comparison isolates the effect of the interaction between Sex and the quadratic contrast of the DA groups. Model C_5 differs from Model A by excluding the Sex × $DA_{quadratic}$ predictor. The model comparison information is presented in the model comparison box (Table 16.9). The error for Model C_5, which excluded the quadratic interaction term, is 347. Subtracting SSE_A from SSE_{C5} gives an SSR of 27. Notice once again that the combined SSR for the two interaction terms in this chapter (1 + 27 = 28) is equal to the SSR for the Sex × DA interaction in the final summary table (Table 15.8) in Chapter 15. The SSR of 27, compared against the SST of 1,204, gives an R^2 of .022, so this interaction term explained 2.2% of the error in Depression scores.

Table 16.9 Model Comparison to Test the First Interaction Term: Sex × $DA_{quadratic}$ (Model C_5)

Model C_5:	Depression = 13 + (−1) Sex + 2 (DA_{linear}) + 4 ($DA_{quadratic}$) + (−.25) (Sex × DA_{linear}) + ε
Model A:	Depression = 13 + (−1) Sex + 2 (DA_{linear}) + 4 ($DA_{quadratic}$) + (−.25) (Sex × DA_{linear}) + (−.75) (Sex × $DA_{quadratic}$) + ε
$PC_5 = 5$	$SSE_{C5} = 347.00$
$PA = 6$	$SSE_A = 320.00$
Difference = 1	SSR = 27.00
$H_0: \beta_5 = 0$	R^2 (PRE) = .022

◆ COMPLETE THE SUMMARY TABLE

Now that all five comparisons are completed, we can fill in the summary table (Table 16.10). SST is 1,204, and the total df is still $N - 1 = 23$. Model A, which included every predictor, left 320 unexplained SS, so the residual error is 320 (which is consistent with the SSW in Chapter 15). The error explained by each predictor (SSR) is added to the table. Each predictor also used only 1 df (the number of parameters estimated by Model A less the number of parameters estimated by Model C, i.e., PA – PC, was 6 – 5 for each comparison). After adding each predictor's SSR and df to the summary table, we compute the mean squares (MS) for each predictor (SSR ÷ df). Finally, we divide the MS for each predictor by the residual mean square error (MSE) to get an F value for each predictor.

Once again, the model comparison approach has replicated the traditional approach to an ANOVA. The only F value with a probability of a Type I error below .05 is the quadratic main effect comparison for the DA variable. We report this finding as follows: There was a main effect for the quadratic DA predictor that contrasted the nonabusers (the None group) with the two abusing groups (Alcohol and Poly Drug), $F(1, 18) = 4.39, p < .001$. There is no need to conduct a post hoc analysis since the contrast codes for this predictor already revealed which DA groups were ($DA_{quadratic}$) and were not (DA_{linear}) different.

Table 16.10 Final Summary Table Including the Effects of Each Predictor in Model A

Source	SS	df	MS	F	p	R^2
Omnibus model	884	5	176.8	9.94		
Sex	24	1	24	1.35	.260	.020
DA_{linear}	64	1	64	3.6	.074	.053
$DA_{quadratic}$	768	1	768	43.20	<.001	.638
Sex × DA_{linear}	1	1	1	0.06	.815	<.001
Sex × $DA_{quadratic}$	27	1	27	1.52	.234	.022
Error	320	18	17.78			
Total	1,204	23				

SUMMARY ◆

This chapter applied the model comparison approach to our Depression symptoms scores to conduct a 2 × 3 ANOVA. The results were identical to those from the traditional ANOVA approach used in Chapter 15. Because of the three groups in the DA variable, this analysis required five model comparisons. Each comparison tested the difference between the omnibus Model A and the modified Models C that resembled Model A with one predictor removed.

It is possible to use the same model comparison approach to test a model in which both IVs have three groups (a 3 × 3 ANOVA). Of course, with such a model, each IV would require two predictors, and the interaction would require four predictors (two predictors for one IV × two predictors for the second IV). Try sketching out what a 3 × 3 regression model would look like.

Rather than proceed down that path, the next chapter will introduce the concept of analysis of covariance.

17

ANALYSIS OF COVARIANCE

Continuous and Categorical Predictors

If there is a 50–50 chance that something can go wrong, then nine times out of ten it will.

—Paul Harvey
Paul Harvey News

So far, the predictors in our models have been either continuous or categorical variables. In this chapter, I'll present a model that mixes categorical with continuous predictors to create a multiple regression model with one categorical predictor and one continuous predictor variable. The steps to test this model are the same as those we used to test a multiple regression in Chapter 9.

An obvious reason for this mixed model is the increased flexibility of the statistical analysis. It just might be that one predictor we're interested in is a continuous variable and another variable of interest is categorical. It makes sense, then, that we'd want to include both predictors, regardless of the type of variable, in our statistical analysis.

There is also a more subtle design issue that this model might resolve: the problem that arises when a third variable confounds the association between an independent variable (IV) and a dependent variable (DV). The confounding influence of a third variable can be corrected by statistically *covarying* for the confounding variable. Before demonstrating how to test a model with both continuous and categorical IVs, I'll briefly review the concept of statistical covariation.

◆ CONCEPT OF STATISTICAL COVARIATION

Sometimes when we look at the relationship between two variables, a third variable can confound the findings. For example, "Age" might be related to the DV such that older subjects score lower on average than younger subjects. Age might therefore cause a problem if our sampling produced younger male subjects and older female subjects. Age, as a confounding variable, could mask a real relationship between Sex and the DV.

In an experimental design, where the researcher randomly assigns subjects to research groups, we assume that potential confounding variables are randomly distributed across the groups. But even a true experimental design is not immune to chance differences that occur during random assignment (Keppel & Zedeck, 2002). Quasi-experimental designs, however, are more vulnerable to uncontrolled sources of variation because the subjects are not randomly assigned to groups (Lomax, 2001). Therefore, when using quasi-experimental designs, we can't assume that these confounding variables are equally distributed. When we can't control these variables through an experimental design, we have to control for them statistically.

Suppose that you tested the relationship between an IV and a DV and found no association. In our data, for example, Sex (the IV) and Depression symptom scores (the DV) appear unrelated. The mean score for Men is 12 (standard deviation [SD] = 5.689) and the mean score for Women is 14 (SD = 8.655). Comparing these means statistically produced a t test value (degrees of freedom [df] = 22) of 0.669 (p = .511) and an $F(1, 22)$ of 0.447 (p = .511). Based on these results, we should conclude that Sex and Depression symptoms are not related (i.e., there is no statistically significant difference between the mean scores for Men and Women).

What if in fact there is a relationship between Sex and Depression scores but another variable, such as Age, is masking it? Ideally, we would have tried to design the study to control for the meddling influences of other variables, but sometimes those pesky "third" variables are just beyond our control. Fortunately, we can statistically control for meddling third variables by using the model comparison approach and entering "Age" into the model as a *covariate*. A covariate is a variable that is not directly of interest to the researcher but does affect how subjects score on the DV, and it wasn't (or couldn't be) controlled for by the research design (Lomax, 2001). To conduct an analysis of covariance (ANCOVA), we simply create a statistical model (Model A) that includes both the covariate (Age) and the IV (Sex), and then we compare that Model A with a model (Model C) that isolates the effects of the IV Sex (see the model comparison box, Table 17.1). This ANCOVA partitions out (or "controls for") the variance in Depression scores that was reduced or explained by the covariate Age.

Table 17.1 Model Comparison Box Conceptualizing the Second Comparison, Which Isolates the Contribution of the Covariate, Age

Model C:	Depression $= \beta_0 + Z_1$ (Age) $+ \varepsilon$	PC $= 2$	SSE$_C =$
Model A:	Depression $= \beta_0 + Z_1$ (Age) $+ \beta_1$ (Sex) $+ \varepsilon$	PA $= 3$	SSE$_A =$
	Differences $+ \beta_1$ (Sex)	PA $-$ PC $= 1$	SSR $=$
	H_0: $\beta_1 = 0$	R^2 (PRE) $=$	

A covariate explains or reduces a portion of the total error in the DV (SST). When we reduce the error variance by including one (or more) covariates in Model C, the covariates reduce the residual error. Less residual error produces a smaller mean square error (*MSE*), and since *MSE* is the denominator of *F*, a smaller *MSE* will produce a larger *F*. Therefore, the greater the error reduced by the covariate, the smaller is the *MSE* and the larger the *F*. And as *F* increases, our chance of rejecting H_0 (our "power" to reject a false H_0) increases. To demonstrate this ANCOVA, we'll use the Depression score data (see Table 17.2).

Table 17.2 Depression Scores and Ages for Each Subject

Subject	Symptom Score (DV)	Age (Covariate)
1	3	21
2	5	22
3	6	22
4	8	22
5	9	21
6	11	19
7	19	20
8	15	19
9	16	18
10	16	17

(Continued)

Table 17.2 (Continued)

Subject	Symptom Score (DV)	Age (Covariate)
11	19	21
12	17	22
13	3	23
14	5	24
15	4	25
16	6	23
17	8	22
18	10	21
19	24	18
20	24	18
21	22	19
22	23	20
23	19	20
24	20	21

Throughout this book, we have always known that the total error variance for the Depression symptom scores (SST) is 1,204. This SST is the error associated with a Model C that predicted only the Grand mean score for every subject (Equation 17.1).

$$\text{Old Model C: Depression symptoms} = \beta_0 + \varepsilon. \quad (17.1)$$

To conduct an ANCOVA, we are going to reduce that total error (SST) by subtracting the variance in Depression symptom scores that we can explain based on the subjects' ages. Our new Model C for this ANCOVA is given in Equation 17.2.

$$\text{New Model C: Depression symptoms} = \beta_0 + Z_1 (\text{Age}) + \varepsilon. \quad (17.2)$$

Equation 17.2 is simply a bivariate regression in which Age is a predictor variable and Depression symptoms is the outcome variable. The slope of the regression line is Z_1. Z_1 is a regression coefficient, just as β_1 was in our prior regression equations. The reason for using Z instead of β is merely to help us remember that Age is a covariate.

TESTING THE EFFECTS OF SEX, CONTROLLING FOR AGE ◆

Table 17.1 provided the two models (A and C) for the ANCOVA. Our null hypothesis is that there is no relationship between Sex and Depression symptoms. Since β_1 describes the relationship between Sex and Depression symptoms, the null hypothesis is that $\beta_1 = 0$. The results of the first eight model comparison steps are presented in Table 17.3. The models are reported in Step 1, and the null hypothesis is stated in Step 2. Counting the parameters estimated by each model (Step 3), we find that the number of

Table 17.3 Summary of the First Eight Steps Comparing the Omnibus Model A With Model C

Step 1	State the compact Model C and an augmented Model A
	Model C: $\hat{Y} = \beta_0 + Z_1(\text{Age})$
	Model A: $\hat{Y} = \beta_0 + Z_1(\text{Age}) + \beta_1(\text{Sex})$
Step 2	Identify the null hypothesis (H_0)
	H_0: $\beta_1 = 0$
Step 3	Count the number of parameters estimated by Model A (PA) and Model C (PC)
	PA = 3
	PC = 2
Step 4	Calculate the regression equation
	Model C: $\hat{Y} = 13 - 2.561(\text{Age})$
	Model A: $\hat{Y} = 13 - 2.79(\text{Age}) - 2.162(\text{Sex})$
Step 5	Compute the sum of squares for Model C (SSE_C)
	$SSE_C = 584.275$
Step 6	Compute the sum of squares for Model A (SSE_A)
	$SSE_A = 477.004$
Step 7	Compute the sum of squares reduced (SSR)
	SSR = 107.271
Step 8	Compute the proportional reduction in error (PRE or R^2)
	PRE = R^2 = .184

parameters estimated by Model A (PA) = 3 and PC = 2 (Z is counted as a parameter). Therefore, we know that this will be a 1-*df* test (PA − PC = 1). The regression equations are given in Step 4. Using the equation for Model C, we can predict a score for each subject, find the differences between the predicted and actual scores, square the differences, and sum the squared differences to get the error for Model C (Step 5). We follow the same process to get the error for Model A (Step 6), and then we subtract the sum of squared errors for Model A (SSE_A) from SSE_C to get the sum of squares reduced (SSR) (Step 7). Finally, dividing SSR by SSE_C gives us the proportional reduction in error (PRE or R^2).

We enter the information from Table 17.3 into a summary table (Table 17.4) to complete the analysis and calculate F. Since SSR for this comparison was 107.271 and the comparison used 1 *df*, *MS* is 107.271. Dividing the residual error (SSE_A = 477.004) by the 21 residual *df*s gives an *MSE* of 22.714. Then, dividing *MS* for Sex (107.714) by *MSE* (22.714), we get $F(1, 21) = 4.745$. The probability of obtaining an F of this size if H_0 was true is less than 5 out of 100 ($p = .04$). Therefore, we reject H_0 and conclude that Sex is related to Depression symptoms, after controlling for Age.

Table 17.4 Summary Table for the ANCOVA Testing the Relationship Between Sex (IV) and Depression Symptom Scores (DV), Controlling for Age (Covariate)

Source	SS	df	MS	F	p	R^2
Sex	107.271	1	107.271	4.745	0.04	
Error	477.004	21	22.714			
Total (SSE_C)	584.275	22				

◆ THEY WEREN'T RELATED, BUT NOW THEY ARE!

At the beginning of this chapter, I pointed out that Sex and Depression symptoms were not statistically related, yet now I am claiming that there is a statistically significant relationship between them. Am I changing my mind faster than a presidential hopeful with an Etch A Sketch? No. The reason for the difference is that initially we compared a model (Model A) that included only Sex with a simple model (Model C) that predicted only the Grand mean. The total error for that simple Model C was 1,204. When we partitioned out error that could be explained by age, we had a new Model C whose error was much smaller (584.275). With less total error to begin with, we also had less residual error when we compared the models. Less residual error gave us a smaller *MSE*, and since *MSE* is the denominator of *F*, a smaller *MSE* produced a larger *F*. Therefore, after first removing error variance explained by Age, we are able to discover that Sex in fact is related to Depression symptom scores.

◆ SUMMARY

Many factors contribute to the error variance in an outcome variable. As researchers, our goal is to find the factors that contribute to error. When we find a factor that contributes to error, it is legitimate to remove the error variance explained by that variable. In the example from this chapter, Age was a factor that contributed to the error variance in Depression scores. After we removed the variance explained by Age, we were able to use Sex to explain the remaining (residual) error variance in Depression symptoms.

18

REPEATED MEASURES

My dear Prue, we are the inheritors of a wonderful world, a beautiful world, full of life and mystery, goodness and pain. But likewise are we the children of an indifferent universe.

—Colin Meloy
Wildwood[1]

To this point, we have built statistical models that used one of more independent (predictor) variables to predict scores on a single dependent (outcome) variable. Our ongoing example has been to create increasingly complex models that predict a depression score. Imagine, however, that we want to test if a person's depression score changes over time. For example, we might want to know if, on average, depression scores decreased after receiving treatment. We could administer a pretest to get the person's "baseline" or pretreatment depression level. Then, after the person completes treatment, we could administer a posttest assessment to measure his or her depression level after treatment. We now have two depression scores for each subject: the baseline score at Time 1 (T_1) and the follow-up score at Time 2 (T_2). So far, our models have only had a single DV; now we have two DVs for our model. The research question asks whether the two scores (T_1 and T_2) are different, and the H_0 is that the two scores are *not* different.

1. Meloy, C. (2011). *Wildwood*. New York: Balzer + Bray. Used by permission of HarperCollins Publishers.

We have two scores on the dependent variable (DV) for each subject. Analyzing these data gets tricky because these two repeated measurements are not *independent* of each other—a person's score at T_1 influences how she or he will score at T_2. Independence of observations (measurements) is an important assumption of statistical analyses. "Independent measurements" assumes that a person's score is free to vary (i.e., a person can obtain any score on a measure) *regardless of other scores*. When a person takes a measure twice, however, many of the same characteristics that influenced the first score (T_1) will continue to influence the score at T_2. Seemingly irrelevant factors such as attention, interest, motivation, cognitive processing speed, reading ability, and so on (you name it!) exert their influences at T_1 and T_2. Thus, two scores taken from the same person violates our statistical assumption that scores are independent.

Fortunately, we have statistical approaches that control for the dilemma of nonindependence by using each subject as her or his own control. In this chapter, we'll learn how to conduct a repeated measures analysis using a "matched pairs" t test. Then, not surprisingly, I'll demonstrate that we can conduct the same matched pairs t test using the model comparison approach ("repeated measures analysis of variance" or ANOVA).

◆ REPEATED MEASURES "MATCHED PAIRS" t TEST

One approach to the problem of nonindependent scores is to match each subject's first score (T_1) with her or his second score (T_2). Pairing a subject's two scores together controls for individual differences that influence scores. Essentially, you're using each subject as her or his own control. The first technique we'll use to deal with multiple observations is the *matched pairs* t *test*. The formula for computing a matched pairs t test is given in Equation 18.1. As with the standard t test, the matched pairs t test contrasts (a) the mean of the differences between two (nonindependent) scores (numerator) with (b) the standard error of the mean differences between scores (denominator). In Equation 18.1, "D" is the difference between the two scores ($D = T_1 - T_2$) and μ_D is the (null-) hypothesized difference between the two scores. In almost every repeated measures test, the null hypothesis is that the repeated scores are not different. If H_0 predicts that the repeated scores are not different, then μ_D will equal zero. μ_D is basically a placeholder for our null hypothesis of what the difference in means will be. Thus, μ_D is almost always zero, and for practical purposes, we can ignore μ_D in our formula:

$$t = \frac{\bar{D} - \mu_D}{\sqrt{\dfrac{\sum D^2 - \dfrac{(\sum D)^2}{n}}{n(n-1)}}}. \qquad (18.1)$$

We'll use our depression data to demonstrate a matched pairs *t* test. Until now, we've looked at a single depression score for each subject. Let's consider that score the Symptom Score at Time 1 (T_1). Suppose that we then measured each person's depression again 3 months after T_1 (call this T_2). We want to know if, on average, subjects' depression scores changed over time. Our H_0 predicts that depression score at T_1 is equal to the score at T_2 ($\mu_D = 0$). If the scores do not change over time, as our H_0 predicts, then T_1 will equal T_2, and $T_1 - T_2 = 0$. Depression data, with the second (T_2) depression score, are presented in Table 18.1.

The numerator of the matched pairs *t* test is the average of the differences between subjects' depression scores at T_1 and at T_2 minus μ_D. Of course, since our H_0 is that the means are not different, $\mu_D = 0$ and can be dropped from the equation. The fourth column in Table 18.1 gives the difference between T_1 and T_2 scores for each subject. The average of these differences ($\bar{D}$) is shown at the bottom of Column 4 ($\bar{D} = 3$).

The denominator of the matched pairs *t* test is the standard error of the mean difference between scores at T_1 and T_2 ($S_{\bar{D}}$). The standard error of $\bar{D}$ is computed using the computational formula, reproduced in Equation 18.2. For this formula, we use the following values found in Table 18.1: the sum of the differences ($\sum D = 72$), the squared sum of the differences (($\sum D)^2 = 72^2 = 5,184$), and the sum of the squared differences ($\sum D^2 = 668$). By inserting these values into Equation 18.2, we get the standard error of the mean differences, which is .905.

$$SE_D = \sqrt{\frac{\sum D^2 - \dfrac{(\sum D)^2}{n}}{n(n-1)}} = \sqrt{\frac{668 - \dfrac{5184}{24}}{24(24-1)}} = \sqrt{\frac{668 - 216}{24 \times 23}} = \sqrt{\frac{452}{552}} = \sqrt{.819} = .905. \quad (18.2)$$

When we divide the average difference in scores ($\bar{D} = 3$) by the standard error of the mean differences ($SE_D = .905$), we get the matched pairs *t* test value ($3 \div .905 = 3.315$).

Table 18.1 Initial Depression Scores (T_1) and Follow-Up Depression Scores (T_2)

I	II	III	IV	V
Subject	Symptom Score (T_1)	Symptom Score (T_2)	Difference (D)	D^2
1	3	5	-2	4
2	5	4	1	1
3	6	4	2	4
4	8	5	3	9
5	9	10	-1	1
6	11	8	3	9
7	19	14	5	25
8	15	15	0	0
9	16	16	0	0
10	16	7	9	81
11	19	8	11	121
12	17	9	8	64
13	3	3	0	0
14	5	5	0	0
15	4	6	-2	4
16	6	8	-2	4
17	8	9	-1	1
18	10	11	-1	1
19	24	19	5	25
20	24	20	4	16
21	22	21	1	1
22	23	10	13	169
23	19	11	8	64
24	20	12	8	64
Σ			72	668
Average	13	10	3	

Remember that with a regular *t* test, if H_0 is true, the calculated *t* value usually equals or is close to zero. This is true as well for a matched pairs *t* test. If there is truly no difference between the two scores, then the numerator of *t* (and therefore the *t* itself) should be zero. It is likely that random error will produce a *t* that is slightly different from zero; however, if the calculated *t* is unusually different from zero (i.e., we would rarely get a *t* that size if $T_1 = T_2$), we reject H_0. As before, determining if a *t*-test value is unusually different from zero requires that we know the probability of getting a *t* that size if there is no real difference between scores (H_0 is true: $\overline{T}_1 = \overline{T}_2$). If we conducted this analysis 1,000 times with separate data sets, and the true difference between means is zero (H_0 is true), we could expect by chance to get a *t*-test value of 3.315 or larger only 3 times (i.e., $p = .003$). Those odds are small (certainly $p \le .05$), so we conclude that 3.315 is unusually large, we reject H_0, and we infer that the depression scores changed between T_1 and T_2.

REPEATED MEASURES ANOVA: ♦ MODEL COMPARISON APPROACH

By this time, in this book, I hope you're not surprised to learn that we can conduct this same analysis using the model comparison approach. To use this approach, we need a way to combine the two dependent measure scores (depression at T_1 and T_2) into a single outcome (DV) score. There are two basic ways to combine scores: (1) we can add them together or (2) we can subtract one from the other to find the difference between them. Because we're interested in the change (differences) in depression scores from T_1 to T_2, we'll use the differences approach. Finding the differences, however, is not as simple as it would seem it should be.

Finding the Difference Between the Two DVs

Although finding a difference between two scores seems straightforward, how we actually do it is a little tricky. What we will do is actually *combine* the two scores after we first multiply each score by a contrasted weight. We'll designate these weights with the Greek letter lambda (λ), and they will resemble the contrast codes we used previously when we compared groups. Recall that when we had two groups, we assigned −1 and +1 to the different groups. Likewise, in this example (and whenever we compare only two repeated measure scores), the contrasted weights (λs) also are +1 and −1 (λ_1 = +1 and λ_2 = −1). We are going to multiply each subject's T_1 score by λ_1 (+1) and each subject's T_2 score by λ_2 (−1), and then we'll add the weighted products. The result ($\lambda_1 T_1 + \lambda_2 T_2$) can be restated as (+1)(T_1) + (−1)(T_2), which reduces to $T_1 - T_2$ and *looks* a lot like we simply subtracted one score from the other. While the effect is the same as subtracting one score from the other, the concept of contrasting weights is a critical difference. This concept will become especially important in the next chapter when we deal with *three* repeated measures.

The two depression scores for each subject are again presented in Table 18.2. Look at Subject 1, whose first depression score (T_1) is 3. We multiply that score by the contrasted (λ_1) weight of 1, which gives us a weighted score of 3. The second depression score (T_2) for Subject 1 is 5. When we multiply 5 by the λ_2 weight of −1, we get the weighted score of −5. Now when we add these two "weighted" scores (3 and −5), we get the weighted combination for Subject 1 (3 + (−5 = −2). Repeating this process for every subject gives us the values listed in Column IV of Table 18.2.

Unfortunately, the process of combining the two scores isn't yet complete. Remember how we multiplied each score by a λ weight (either +1 or −1) before we combined the weighted products to get the values in Column IV? Well, now we need to return these scores to their original metric (i.e., before we multiplied them by their λ weights). Although it seems obvious that since we added two scores to get Column IV, we should divide by 2, it's unfortunately not that straight forward. In fact, we divide our Column IV scores by the "combined weights" (λs) that we used. But since our used two weights (λ_1 and λ_2) had values of +1 and −1, if we add these weights together, we of course get zero, and we can't divide by zero. So as we typically do to resolve the problem of negative values, we square the contrasted weights to make them both positive. Then we add these squared contrasted weights together ($1^2 + (−1^2) = 1 + 1$), which gives us a value of 2.

But now, since we squared the contrasted weights to make them both positive, we must "unsquare" them by taking the square root of the combined contrasted weights. The square root of 2 is 1.414, so we have to divide each of the weighted combined scores in Column IV by 1.414. Look again at the first subject, whose weighted sum was −2. We divide the combined sum (−2) by $\sqrt{2}$ to get the subject's final weighted score (−2 ÷ 1.414 = −1.414).

Table 18.2 Combining the Two Depression Scores (T_1 and T_2) Into a Single "Difference" Score

I	II	III	IV	V
Subject	Symptom Score (T_1)	Symptom Score (T_2)	$T_1 - T_2$	$(T_1 - T_2) \div \sqrt{2}$
1	3	5	−2	−1.41
2	5	4	1	0.71
3	6	4	2	1.41
4	8	5	3	2.12
5	9	10	−1	−0.71
6	11	8	3	2.12
7	19	14	5	3.54
8	15	15	0	0.00
9	16	16	0	0.00
10	16	7	9	6.36
11	19	8	11	7.78
12	17	9	8	5.66
13	3	3	0	0.00
14	5	5	0	0.00
15	4	6	−2	−1.41
16	6	8	−2	−1.41
17	8	9	−1	−0.71
18	10	11	−1	−0.71
19	24	19	5	3.54
20	24	20	4	2.83
21	22	21	1	0.71
22	23	10	13	9.19
23	19	11	8	5.66
24	20	12	8	5.66
Average	13	10	3	2.122

Equation 18.3 summarizes the process of combining two nonindependent scores. Since we computed a combined weighted score for each subject based on their scores at T_1 and T_2, and then divided that combined weighted score by $\sqrt{2}$, we need a new label for the final combined score. Given that the combined scores were based on "weighted" values, we'll label this new combined variable with the letter "W" (W_1).

$$W_1 = \frac{(\lambda_1 T_1 + \lambda_2 T_2)}{\sqrt{\lambda_1^2 + \lambda_2^2}}. \tag{18.3}$$

In this example, λ_1 equals +1 and λ_2 equals −1, so the formula to combine two nonindependent scores can be reduced to Equation 18.4. Using Equation 18.4, we can get a combined weighted (W_1) score for each subject. These scores can be found in Column V of Table 18.2.

$$W_1 = \frac{(+1)T_1 + (-1)T_2}{\sqrt{2}}. \tag{18.4}$$

The combined weighted scores from Table 18.2 are conceptually similar to the difference (D) scores used for the t test. If H_0 is true and there is no difference between the T_1 and T_2 scores, then each W_1 score should be zero. Therefore, H_0 predicts that the average of the W_1 scores ($\overline{W}_1$) is zero. In fact, as Table 18.2 shows, the average W_1 score was 2.122, which is not zero. The repeated measures statistical question, then, is whether 2.122 is enough different from zero for us to reject H_0, or if 2.122 is close enough to zero that we can "fail to reject H_0."

To test if 2.122 is significantly different from zero, we'll use the model comparison approach. For a model comparison, we need two models. Model C predicts the H_0 for each subject, which is that $W_1 = 0$. Therefore, Model C is $\hat{W}_1 = 0$. Model A represents our research hypothesis—that is, that T_1 and T_2 scores are not equal. Model A therefore predicts the average W_1 score for each subject (Model A: $\hat{W}_1 = \overline{W}_1$). Since we know that the average of W_1 is 2.122, we know that Model A is $\hat{W}_1 = 2.122$. We'll test if Model A is much different from Model C by computing the error for Model C (SSE_C) and the error for Model A (SSE_A). To calculate these errors, we compare the actual measured W_1 for each subject with the scores predicted by Models C and A. If SSE_A is significantly less than SSE_C, then we can reject H_0. These models are shown in Table 18.3.

Table 18.3	Model Comparison Box, Which Provides the Information Necessary to Compare a Model Predicting Difference of Zero With a Model Predicting the Average of W_1

Model C:	$W_1 = 0 + \varepsilon$	
Model A:	$W_1 = 2.122 + \varepsilon$	
	PC = 0	SSC =
	PA = 1	SSA =
	PA − PC = 1	SSR =
H_0:	$\beta_0 = 0$	R^2 (PRE) =

PA = 1 and PC = 0 because we estimated one parameter for Model A ($\overline{W}_1$), but we didn't estimate any parameters for Model C. The difference (PA − PC) gives us 1 *df* (degree of freedom) used for this test.

Next we'll calculate the error of Model C. We get SSE_C the same way as always—subtract the predicted score (0) from each subject's actual W_1 score, square that difference, and sum the squared differences. Table 18.4 works through this process for each subject. The resulting error for Model C (SSE_A) is 334.

Table 18.4	Calculating the Error of Model C

Subject	W_1	$W_1 - 0$	$(W_1 - 0)^2$
1	−1.41	−1.41	2.00
2	0.71	0.71	0.50
3	1.41	1.41	2.00
4	2.12	2.12	4.50
5	−0.71	−0.71	0.50
6	2.12	2.12	4.50

(Continued)

Table 18.4 (Continued)

Subject	W_1	$W_1 - 0$	$(W_1 - 0)^2$
7	3.54	3.54	12.50
8	0.00	0.00	0.00
9	0.00	0.00	0.00
10	6.36	6.36	40.50
11	7.78	7.78	60.50
12	5.66	5.66	32.00
13	0.00	0.00	0.00
14	0.00	0.00	0.00
15	−1.41	−1.41	2.00
16	−1.41	−1.41	2.00
17	−0.71	−0.71	0.50
18	−0.71	−0.71	0.50
19	3.54	3.54	12.50
20	2.83	2.83	8.00
21	0.71	0.71	0.50
22	9.19	9.19	84.49
23	5.66	5.66	32.00
24	5.66	5.66	32.00
			SSC = 334.00

We'll repeat this process to calculate the error for Model A (see Table 18.5). The error for Model A is 226.

We next subtract SSE_A (226) from SSE_C (334) to get the reduction in error (SSR). What we find is that Model A reduced the error of our prediction by 108. The ratio of the reduction in error (SSR = 108) to the total error (SSE_C = 334) gives us the proportional reduction in error (PRE) of .323 (108 ÷ 334 = .323).

Using the data gathered in the model comparison box (Table 18.6), we now can complete a summary table to calculate F (Table 18.7). SSE_C (334) is

Table 18.5 Calculating the Error of Model A

Subject	W_1	$W_1 - 2.12$	$(W_1 - 2.12)^2$
1	−1.41	−3.54	12.50
2	0.71	−1.42	2.00
3	1.41	−0.71	0.50
4	2.12	0.00	0.00
5	−0.71	−2.83	8.00
6	2.12	0.00	0.00
7	3.54	1.41	2.00
8	0.00	−2.12	4.50
9	0.00	−2.12	4.50
10	6.36	4.24	17.99
11	7.78	5.66	31.99
12	5.66	3.54	12.50
13	0.00	−2.12	4.50
14	0.00	−2.12	4.50
15	−1.41	−3.54	12.50
16	−1.41	−3.54	12.50
17	−0.71	−2.83	8.00
18	−0.71	−2.83	8.00
19	3.54	1.41	2.00
20	2.83	0.71	0.50
21	0.71	−1.42	2.00
22	9.19	7.07	49.98
23	5.66	3.54	12.50
24	5.66	3.54	12.50
			SSC = 226.00

entered as the total error, and SSE_A (226) as the residual error. The difference (SSR = 108) is the reduction in error attributed to changes in depression scores. Total df is N − PC. Remember, Model C predicted 0 for everyone, so we did not estimate a parameter for Model C. Therefore, Total df is 24 − 0 or 24. We used 1 df for the comparison (PA − PC = 1 − 0 = 1), so the residual df (24 − 1) is 23. Dividing each SS by its corresponding df, the MS (mean square) for the repeated measure score (W_1) is 108 ÷ 1 = 108, and the MS for the error term (MSE) is 226 ÷ 23 = 9.826. To get F, we divide MS for the repeated measures model (108) by the MSE (9.826). The resulting F (1, 23) = 10.991.

To decide whether or not to reject H_0, we need to decide if F (1, 23) = 10.991 is unusually large (if H_0 is true). We could either use an F table to see if 10.991 exceeds the critical value for a probability less than or equal to .05, or we could let a computer statistics program give us the exact probability. If H_0 is true, the exact probability of getting an F of 10.991 (with 1 used and 23 residual df) is .003. This small probability suggests that F is unusually

Table 18.6   Model Comparison Box Comparing a Predicted Difference of Zero With a Predicted Difference Based on the Average of W_1

Model C:	Depression = 0 + ε	
Model A:	Depression = 2.122 + ε	
	PC = 0	SSC = 334
	PA = 1	SSA = 226
Difference:	1	SSR = 108
H_0:	$\beta_0 = 0$	R^2 (PRE) = .323

Table 18.7   Summary Table for the Repeated Measures ANOVA Comparing Depression Scores at Time 1 and Time 2

Source	SS	df	MS	F	p	R^2
Repeated Score	108	1	108	10.991	.003	.323
Error	226	23	9.826			
Total	334	24				

large ($p = .003$ is certainly smaller than $p \leq .05$), so we reject the null hypothesis that depression scores are the same at Time 1 and Time 2 and infer that they are different.

We can also calculate the PRE or the variance explained by dividing the error reduced by this repeated measures model (108) by the total error (334). The PRE or R^2 is .323. In other words, 32.3% of the error variance was reduced by allowing T_1 and T_2 to be different ($T_1 \neq T_2$) as predicted by Model A rather than forcing T_1 to equal T_2 as predicted by Model C.

Finally, remember that $F = t^2$. We can check that this ANOVA generated the same result as the matched pairs t test by taking the square root of the F generated by the model comparison (10.991). It should (and in fact does) match the repeated measures t-test value calculated earlier in the chapter ($t = \sqrt{F} = \sqrt{10.991} = 3.315$).

Results for this analysis would be reported using the following language:

> A repeated measures analysis of variance (ANOVA) was used to test whether depression scores prior to treatment were different from scores following treatment. There was a statistically significant difference between pre- and posttreatment depression scores, $F(1, 23) = 10.991$, $p = .003$.

SUMMARY ◆

Sometimes we might collect a score on a DV more than one time from each subject. Such repeated measures data are conceptualized and analyzed a little differently than analyses looked at thus far. Repeated multiple measure analyses test whether two scores from the same subject, on average across subjects in the sample, are different. If the scores reflect measurements at two different times, the repeated measures analysis will test whether the scores changed over time. Alternatively, two scores can be measured for each subject at about the same time but under different conditions. In that case, this repeated/multiple measures analysis will test if subjects score the same in the two different conditions. This chapter presented two approaches to analyze multiple or repeated scores: matched pairs t test and model comparison. Keep in mind that these repeated measure analyses are used to test for differences between two DV scores collected from the same subject. We could not use a repeated measure ANOVA, or a matched-pairs t test, if we were comparing two independent groups.

You should now be able to create a Model C that tests the null hypothesis that a person's score on a measure at Time 1 is not different from how she or he scores at Time 2. Likewise, you should be able to define a Model A that suggests that Time 1 and Time 2 scores are different. This chapter expanded on our depression data example by providing two depression scores from each subject. You may also have two nonindependent scores from two different sources. Consider an alternative example. Imagine that you are interested in the percent of time that couples spend arguing. You realize that you can't just ask one member of the dyad how often they fight, so you ask both. Now you have two "% time arguing" scores for each couple. The scores are likely to be similar (therefore, not independent), but not identical. In fact, an interesting question might be how much two partners agree or differ in how often they fight. How would you design a study and analyze these data, using repeated measures, to test whether couples generate different estimates of the time they spend fighting? You should be able to write the regression equation for Model C and Model A.

This chapter dealt with a situation where a researcher had only two dependent variable scores for each subject. It's possible that a researcher might have three (or more) DV scores for each subject. The model comparison approach can be used to test whether the mean of three (or more) DV scores are different. The next chapter will demonstrate how to manage three DV scores.

19

MULTIPLE REPEATED MEASURES

It is only with the heart that one can see rightly; what is essential is invisible to the eye.

—Antoine de Saint-Exupery

hapter 18 addressed the challenge of comparing scores when each subject had two scores on the dependent variable (DV). When we test whether those two scores (on average) are different, we are testing to see if there are differences in scores that occur within the subject. Therefore, we call a repeated measures analysis a *within* test.

When a researcher has three (or more) scores on the DV, we can use a repeated measures *within* ANOVA to test whether these mean scores are different. This chapter will demonstrate how to use model comparison to test for differences in scores when we have three scores on the DV for each subject.

THREE REPEATED MEASURES: WEIGHTING EACH SCORE ◆

When we had two scores for each subject, we assigned a weight (λ) to each score. At Time 1, $\lambda = +1$, and at Time 2, $\lambda = -1$. These λ weights helped us compare whether T_1 score was different from T_2 score. At the time you probably thought that it was silly to "weight" the scores since it amounted to merely subtracting T_1 from T_2. Worse yet, I then divided by $\sqrt{\lambda_{time1}^2 + \lambda_{time2}^2} = \sqrt{2}$ rather than 2!

The importance of these weights is clearer when we have more than two scores. With a pair of scores (T_1 and T_2), we needed *one* set of contrasted weights to compare the two scores. With three scores, we'll need *two* sets of contrasted weights that allow us to compare all of the scores. This concept is identical to our use of "contrast codes" in Chapter 14 when we compared three groups. The difference is that in Chapter 14 the contrast codes were used to compare three groups that made up the IV. In this triple repeated measure design, the contrast codes/weights are used to compare three scores on the DV. The contrast weights, however, are the same. We'll have a linear comparison and a quadratic comparison.

In Chapter 18, we compared two depression scores. We now have depression scores taken three times for each subject (T_1, T_2, and T_3). We could create three weights to contrast those scores (+1, 0, −1). These weights or codes, however, impose a linear trend on the three scores (i.e., the codes impose an assumption that $T_1 > T_2 > T_3$). It is possible that the linear trend reflects (or models) the true relationship between the scores, but a linear relationship is not the only possibility. Suppose that treatment worked quickly and the change in depression scores happened between T_1 and T_2, but there was no change between T_2 and T_3. Alternatively, what if treatment effects were slow? We might not see a change from T_1 to T_2, but we might see a difference between T_2 and T_3. Worse yet, what if treatment effects were transitory? We might find improvement from T_1 to T_2, but then discover that scores at Time 3 had returned to Time 1 levels ($T_1 = T_3 \neq T_2$). These four possibilities are graphed in Figure 19.1.

In Figure 19.1, Panel A depicts a linear relationship in which scores at T_1 are greater than scores at T_2, and scores at T_2 are greater than scores at T_3. Panel B shows a situation in which the mean score at T_1 is different from the second two mean scores, which are approximately equal ($\bar{T}_2 \cong \bar{T}_3$). Similarly, Panel C depicts a condition where the first two means are similar ($\bar{T}_1 \cong \bar{T}_2$), but the third score is different. Finally, Panel D presents a condition where the first and last scores are equal ($\bar{T}_1 \cong \bar{T}_3$), but the middle score is different. Panel A depicts a linear relationship between depression means ($\bar{T}_1 \geq \bar{T}_2 \geq \bar{T}_3$), and Panel D depicts a quadratic relationship between scores. Panels B and C reflect a combined linear and quadratic effect.

Table 19.1 shows the two basic relationships that the three scores can have: (1) a linear relationship or (2) a quadratic relationship. We'll use these two possible relationships to create two different sets of contrasted weights: (1) one models a linear relationship and (2) the other models a quadratic relationship. Table 19.1 gives the codes used to create these two weighted variables.

Figure 19.1 Possible Relationships Between Depression Scores at Time 1, Time 2, and Time 3.

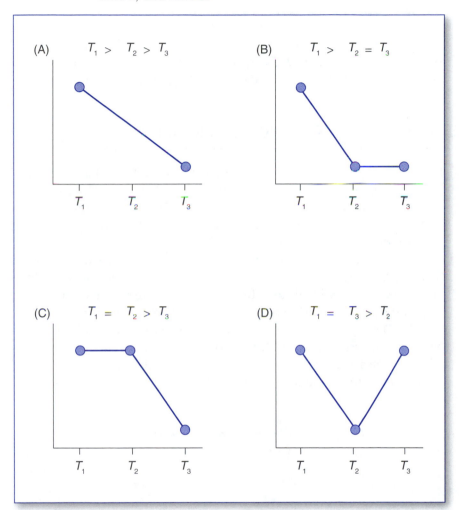

(A) $T_1 > T_2 > T_3$

(B) $T_1 > T_2 = T_3$

(C) $T_1 = T_2 > T_3$

(D) $T_1 = T_3 > T_2$

Table 19.1 Contrast-Coded Weights Used to Compare Scores at Time 1, Time 2, and Time 3

	Time 1	Time 2	Time 3
λ_{linear}	1	0	−1
$\lambda_{quadratic}$	1	−2	1

Since there are two weighted variables (W_{linear} and $W_{quadratic}$), this analysis will require two model comparisons—one to test whether W_{linear} is different from zero, and the second to test if $W_{quadratic}$ is different from zero. As in Chapter 18, each analysis will compare a Model A that predicts the average W ($\overline{W}_{linear}$ or $\overline{W}_{quadratic}$) score against a Model C that simply predicts zero (the H_0) for each observation. H_0 for each comparison is that $\overline{W} = 0$ (Model A is not better than Model C). Let's begin by testing the linear relationship.

◆ LINEAR CHANGE IN MEAN SCORES OVER TIME

For this comparison, T_2 is assigned a weight of zero. By having a weight of zero, T_2 Depression scores literally contribute nothing to the W_{linear} scores. As a result, this linear contrast essentially compares Depression scores at T_1 and T_3. If those two scores are not significantly different, then $\overline{W}_{linear}$ should be close to zero.

Table 19.2 lists the depression scores collected from each subject at Times 1, 2, and 3. In the fifth column of Table 19.2, the combined weighted depression score is calculated. To create a W_{linear} score for each subject, T_1 Depression score is multiplied by 1, T_2 Depression score is multiplied by 0, and T_3 Depression score is multiplied by –1. Look at Subject 6. This subject had a T_1 Depression score of 11, a T_2 score of 8, and a T_3 score of 7. In Equation 19.1, the scores for Subject 6 are multiplied by their respective weights, then summed to get the W_{linear} score of 4 for Subject 6.

$$\begin{aligned}
(\lambda_{linear-T1} \times T_{1\text{-Subj 6}}) &+ (\lambda_{linear-T2} \times T_{2\text{-Subj 6}}) + \\
(\lambda_{linear-T3} \times T_{3\text{-Subj 6}}) &= (1 \times 11) + (0 \times 8) + (-1 \times 7) \\
&= (11) + (-7) \\
&= 4.
\end{aligned} \tag{19.1}$$

Table 19.2 Depression Scores at Time 1, Time 2, and Time 3

Subject	Symptom Score (T1)	Symptom Score (T2)	Symptom Score (T3)	W_1 $T_1 + (0 \times T_2) + (-1 \times T_3)$	W_1 $T_1 + (0 \times T_2) + (-1 \times T_3) \div \sqrt{2}$
1	3	5	6	–3	–2.12
2	5	4	3	2	1.41
3	6	4	3	3	2.12

Subject	Symptom Score (T1)	Symptom Score (T2)	Symptom Score (T3)	W_1 $T_1 + (0 \times T_2) + (-1 \times T_3)$	W_1 $T_1 + (0 \times T_2) + (-1 \times T_3) \div \sqrt{2}$
4	8	5	6	2	1.41
5	9	10	11	−2	−1.41
6	11	8	7	4	2.83
7	19	14	13	6	4.24
8	15	15	16	−1	−0.71
9	16	16	17	−1	−0.71
10	16	7	6	10	7.07
11	19	8	7	12	8.49
12	17	9	10	7	4.95
13	3	3	2	1	0.71
14	5	5	6	−1	−0.71
15	4	6	7	−3	−2.12
16	6	8	7	−1	−0.71
17	8	9	8	0	0.00
18	10	11	12	−2	−1.41
19	24	19	20	4	2.83
20	24	20	19	5	3.54
21	22	21	20	2	1.41
22	23	10	11	12	8.49
23	19	11	12	7	4.95
24	20	12	11	9	6.36
Average	13	10	10	3	2.122

In Chapter 18, we divided the weighted sum (Column 5 of Table 19.2) by a value determined by the λ weights to get the "average" contrasted value. The "value" we used was the square root of the sum of the squared weights. For this linear contrast example, we have three weights (λs): (1) $\lambda_{\text{linear-}T1} = 1$,

(2) $\lambda_{\text{linear-}T2} = 0$, and (3) $\lambda_{\text{linear-}T3} = -1$. The formula to get this value is given in Equation 19.2.

$$\sqrt{\lambda^2_{\text{linear-}T1} + \lambda^2_{\text{linear-}T2} + \lambda^2_{\text{linear-}T3}} = \sqrt{1^2 + 0^2 + (-1^2)} = \sqrt{1+1} = \sqrt{2} = 1.414. \quad 19.2)$$

We divide the sum of the weighted scores (Column 5 of Table 19.2) by the value calculated in Equation 19.2 (1.414) to get each subject's W_{linear} score. Look again at Subject 6. His weighted sum is 4. Dividing 4 by 1.414 produces his W_{linear} score (2.83).

◆ MODEL A AND THE AVERAGE W_{linear} SCORE

After we've computed the W_{linear} score for each subject, we calculate the average W_{linear} score, which is 2.122. $\overline{W}_{\text{linear}}$ (i.e., 2.122) is the Model A score we will predict for each subject. H_0 is that the scores did not change at all. If H_0 is true (i.e., $T_1 = T_3$), then $\overline{W}_{\text{linear}}$ would equal or be close to zero $(H_0 : \overline{W}_{\text{linear}} = 0)$. Model C represents the null hypothesis and therefore predicts zero for every subject. We know that our estimated $\overline{W}_{\text{linear}}$ is 2.122, which obviously is different from zero. This analysis will tell us whether 2.122 is far enough different from zero that we can reject H_0, or if 2.122 is close enough to zero that we fail to reject H_0. The model comparison for this analysis is presented in the model comparison box (Table 19.3).

We estimated one parameter for Model A (β_0, which was $\overline{W}_{\text{linear}}$ or 2.122). PA therefore is 1. We did not calculate a parameter for Model C (we used the constant, zero), so PC is 0. The difference (PA − PC) is 1; therefore, this comparison used 1 df for this part of the analysis. The next step is to calculate the errors of Model C and Model A.

Table 19.3 Model Comparison Box Comparing a Predicted Difference of Zero With a Predicted Difference Based on the Average of W_{linear}

Model C:	$W_{\text{linear}} =$	$0 + \varepsilon$	PC = 0	SSC =
Model A:	$W_{\text{linear}} =$	$\beta_0 + \varepsilon = 2.122 + \varepsilon$	PA = 1	SSA =
	Difference =	1		SSR =
	$H_0: \beta_0 =$	0		R^2 (PRE) =

To get the error of Model C, we subtract each subject's predicted W_{linear} score (which for Model C is zero) from the subject's actual W_{linear} score ($W_{linear} - 0$), square the difference ($W_{linear} - 0$)^2, and sum these squared differences ($\Sigma(W_{linear} - 0)^2$). Table 19.4 shows the steps to calculate the individual error scores for each subject and then sums them. The result is an *SSE* of 356 for Model C.

Table 19.4 Calculating the Error of Model C

Subject	W_1	$W_1 - 0$	$(W_1 - 0)^2$
1	−2.121	−2.121	4.499
2	1.414	1.414	1.999
3	2.121	2.121	4.499
4	1.414	1.414	1.999
5	−1.414	−1.414	1.999
6	2.828	2.828	7.998
7	4.243	4.243	18.003
8	−0.707	−0.707	0.500
9	−0.707	−0.707	0.500
10	7.071	7.071	49.999
11	8.485	8.485	71.995
12	4.950	4.950	24.503
13	0.707	0.707	0.500
14	−0.707	−0.707	0.500
15	−2.121	−2.121	4.499
16	−0.707	−0.707	0.500
17	0.000	0.000	0.000
18	−1.414	−1.414	1.999
19	2.828	2.828	7.998
20	3.536	3.536	12.503
21	1.414	1.414	1.999
22	8.485	8.485	71.995
23	4.950	4.950	24.503
24	6.364	6.364	40.500
			SSC = 356.000

We repeat this process to get the error for Model A (see Table 19.5). This time we subtract the score predicted by Model A (2.122) from each subject's actual score, square the differences, and sum the individual squared errors. The resulting *SSE* of Model A is 248. The difference between the SSE_C (356) and SSE_A (248) is 108. I've added these values to the model comparison box (Table 19.6).

Table 19.5 Calculating the Error of Model A

Subject	W_1	$(W_1 - 2.12)$	$(W_1 - 2.12)^2$
1	−2.121	−4.243	18.003
2	1.414	−0.708	0.501
3	2.121	−0.001	0.000
4	1.414	−0.708	0.501
5	−1.414	−3.536	12.503
6	2.828	0.706	0.498
7	4.243	2.121	4.499
8	−0.707	−2.829	8.003
9	−0.707	−2.829	8.003
10	7.071	4.949	24.493
11	8.485	6.363	40.488
12	4.950	2.828	7.998
13	0.707	−1.415	2.002
14	−0.707	−2.829	8.003
15	−2.121	−4.243	18.003
16	−0.707	−2.829	8.003
17	0.000	−2.122	4.503
18	−1.414	−3.536	12.503
19	2.828	0.706	0.498
20	3.536	1.414	1.999
21	1.414	−0.708	0.501

Subject	W_1	$(W_1 - 2.12)$	$(W_1 - 2.12)^2$
22	8.485	6.363	40.488
23	4.950	2.828	7.998
24	6.364	4.242	17.995
			SSA = 248.00

Table 19.6 Model Comparison Box Comparing a Predicted Difference of Zero With a Predicted Difference Based on the Average of W_1

Model C:	Depression	$= 0 + \varepsilon$	PC = 0	SSC = 356
Model A:	Depression	$= 2.122 + \varepsilon$	PA = 1	SSA = 248
	Difference	$= 1$		SSR = 108

We'll use the information from the model comparison box to start the ANOVA summary table (Table 19.7). Total *df* is 24 (Total *df*: $N - PC = 24 - 0$). This comparison used 1 *df* (PA − PC: $1 - 0 = 1$), leaving 23 residual *df*s. Dividing each *SS* by its corresponding *df* gives us an *MS* of 108 for the linear test and 10.783 for the error term. Dividing the *MS* for the linear effect by the *MS* Error produces an *F* of 10.016. The probability that we would get an $F(1, 23)$ of 10.016 is .004. Since the probability of an *F* this large is unusual ($p \le .05$), we reject the H_0 that depression scores are the same at Times 1 and 3, and instead infer that there is a linear difference between these means.

Of course, we don't know where T_2 depression scores fit because we essentially ignored them in this linear contrast by multiplying them by zero. Now that we know that $T_1 \ne T_3$, we'll next test the quadratic relationship to see how T_2 fits into the mix.

Table 19.7 Summary Table for the Linear Effect of the Repeated Measures ANOVA Comparing Depression Scores at Times 1, 2, and 3

Source	SS	df	MS	F	p	R^2
Linear effect (W_1)	108	1	108	10.016	.004	.303
Error	248	23	10.783			
Total	356	24				

Figure 19.2 graphs the mean Depression scores at each time point. Notice that the mean scores do decline across time points; however, they also don't form a straight line. Our significant linear effect suggests that a linear effect works, but since this figure resembles Panel B in Figure 19.1, it's possible that the quadratic relationship fits as well. To complete this repeated measures (within) ANOVA, the next step is to test for the quadratic effect.

Figure 19.2 Mean Depression Scores at Time 1, Time 2, and Time 3

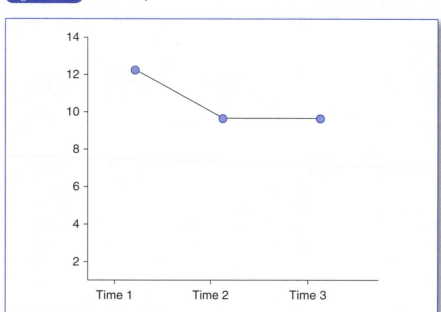

◆ QUADRATIC CHANGE IN MEAN SCORES OVER TIME

The depression scores collected from each subject at Times 1, 2, and 3 are presented again in Table 19.8. As we did with the linear test, we'll calculate a weighted sum of these scores ($W_{quadratic}$) that tests their quadratic relationship. The quadratic contrast codes treat T_1 and T_3 as equal and compare them against T_2. This contrast, therefore, tests if T_2 is different from T_1 and T_3.

Column 5 of Table 19.8 provides the weighted sum for each person. The weights used to conduct the quadratic contrast were $\lambda_{quad\text{-}T1} = 1$, $\lambda_{quad\text{-}T2} = -2$, and $\lambda_{quad\text{-}T3} = 1$. Using these weights, Equation 19.3 determines the value that we will divide the weighted sums by (2.4495). Dividing each weighted sum in

Table 19.8   Calculation of the Combined Weighted Depression Scores for the Quadratic Effect

Subject	Symptom Score (T_1)	Symptom Score (T_2)	Symptom Score (T_3)	W_2 $T_1 + (-2 \times T_2) + (1 \times T_3)$	W_2 $T_1 + (-2 \times T_2) + (1 \times T_3) \div \sqrt{6}$
1	3	5	6	−1	−0.408
2	5	4	3	0	0.000
3	6	4	3	1	0.408
4	8	5	6	4	1.633
5	9	10	11	0	0.000
6	11	8	7	2	0.816
7	19	14	13	4	1.633
8	15	15	16	1	0.408
9	16	16	17	1	0.408
10	16	7	6	8	3.266
11	19	8	7	10	4.082
12	17	9	10	9	3.674
13	3	3	2	−1	−0.408
14	5	5	6	1	0.408
15	4	6	7	−1	−0.408
16	6	8	7	−3	−1.225
17	8	9	8	−2	−0.816
18	10	11	12	0	0.000
19	24	19	20	6	2.449
20	24	20	19	3	1.225
21	22	21	20	0	0.000
22	23	10	11	14	5.715
23	19	11	12	9	3.674
24	20	12	11	7	2.858
Average	13	10	10	3	1.225

Column 5 by 2.4495 gives us a $W_{quadratic}$ score for each subject (see Column 6, Table 19.8). $\overline{W}_{quadratic}$ for all 24 subjects is 1.225.

$$\sqrt{\lambda^2_{quad\text{-}T1} + \lambda^2_{quad\text{-}T2} + \lambda^2_{quad\text{-}T3}} = \sqrt{1^2 + (-2^2) + 1^2} = \sqrt{1 + 4 + 1} = \sqrt{6} = 2.4495. \quad (19.3)$$

If T_2 Depression score is not different from T_1 and T_3 (or, more precisely, $2T_2 = T_1 + T_3$), then $\overline{W}_{quadratic}$ should be zero. Therefore, the H_0 for this quadratic test is that $\overline{W}_{quadratic} = 0$, so Model C predicts a score of zero for each subject. The error of Model C is found by subtracting zero from every score, squaring the difference, and summing the squared differences. In Table 19.9, the error is calculated for each subject, squared, then summed, and the resulting squared and summed error for Model C (SSE_C) is 112.

Table 19.9 Calculation of the Sum of Squared Errors for Model C

Subject	W_2	$W_2 - 0$	$(W_2 - 0)^2$
1	−0.408	−0.408	0.166
2	0.000	0.000	0.000
3	0.408	0.408	0.166
4	1.633	1.633	2.667
5	0.000	0.000	0.000
6	0.816	0.816	0.666
7	1.633	1.633	2.667
8	0.408	0.408	0.166
9	0.408	0.408	0.166
10	3.266	3.266	10.667
11	4.082	4.082	16.663
12	3.674	3.674	13.498
13	−0.408	−0.408	0.166
14	0.408	0.408	0.166
15	−0.408	−0.408	0.166

Subject	W_2	$W_2 - 0$	$(W_2 - 0)^2$
16	−1.225	−1.225	1.501
17	−0.816	−0.816	0.666
18	0.000	0.000	0.000
19	2.449	2.449	5.998
20	1.225	1.225	1.501
21	0.000	0.000	0.000
22	5.715	5.715	32.661
23	3.674	3.674	13.498
24	2.858	2.858	8.168
			SSC = 112.00

Model A predicts the actual $\overline{W}_{quadratic}$ (1.225) for every subject. The error of Model A is computed by subtracting 1.225 from every actual score, squaring those differences, and summing the squared differences. Table 19.10 demonstrates how to calculate the sum of squared error for Model A. The resulting $SSE_A = 76$.

Table 19.10 Calculation of the Sum of Squared Errors for Model A

Subject	W_2	$W_2 - 1.225$	$(W_2 - 1.225)^2$
1	−0.408	−1.633	2.667
2	0.000	−1.225	1.501
3	0.408	−0.817	0.667
4	1.633	0.408	0.166
5	0.000	−1.225	1.501
6	0.816	−0.409	0.167
7	1.633	0.408	0.166
8	0.408	−0.817	0.667
9	0.408	−0.817	0.667

(Continued)

Table 19.10 (Continued)

Subject	W_2	$W_2 - 1.225$	$(W_2 - 1.225)^2$
10	3.266	2.041	4.166
11	4.082	2.857	8.162
12	3.674	2.449	5.998
13	−0.408	−1.633	2.667
14	0.408	−0.817	0.667
15	−0.408	−1.633	2.667
16	−1.225	−2.450	6.003
17	−0.816	−2.041	4.166
18	0.000	−1.225	1.501
19	2.449	1.224	1.498
20	1.225	0.000	0.000
21	0.000	−1.225	1.501
22	5.715	4.490	20.160
23	3.674	2.449	5.998
24	2.858	1.633	2.667
			SSA = 76.00

The difference in error between Models A and C (SSR) is 112 − 76 or 36. I've added this information to the model comparison box (Table 19.11), which now has the information we need to complete the summary table to test the quadratic effect (Table 19.12).

Table 19.11 Model Comparison Box Comparing a Predicted Difference of Zero With a Predicted Difference Based on the Average of W_1

Model C:	Depression =	$0 + \varepsilon$	PC = 0	SSC = 36
Model A:	Depression =	$\beta_0 + \varepsilon = 1.225 + \varepsilon$	PA = 1	SSA = 76
	Difference =	1		SSR = 112
	$H_0: \beta_0 = 0$			R^2 (PRE) = .321

The summary table produced an $F(1, 23)$ of 10.896. If H_0 is true, this F would be unusually large ($p \leq .003$), so we'll reject H_0 and infer that T_2 Depression scores were different, on average, from the combined T_1 and T_3 Depression scores.[1] This finding indicates that, in addition to the linear relationship, these means also show a quadratic relationship.

♦ COMBINE THE TWO ANALYSES INTO A SINGLE SUMMARY TABLE

This repeated measures analysis produced two summary tables. We can combine the two into a single summary table (Table 19.13). By including both the linear and quadratic tests in the same table, we can conduct an "omnibus" test. Sum of squares reduced by both the linear (108) and the quadratic (36) tests sum to 144 (the omnibus SSR). Omnibus *df*s is 2 (1 *df* for the linear effect plus 1 *df* for the quadratic effect). The omnibus *MS* effect is found by dividing the total SSR (144) by the *df* used (2), which produces an *MS* Reduced of 72.

The residual error of the linear test was 248, and residual error for the quadratic test was 76. Therefore, total residual error is 324 (248 + 76). Residual *df*s are 46 (23 for the linear test and 23 for the quadratic test). *MSE* for the omnibus test is found by dividing the total residual error (324) by total residual *df* (46), which gives us an *MSE* of 7.043.

Dividing the omnibus *MS* Residual (72) by the omnibus *MSE* (7.043) produces the omnibus $F(2, 46\ df)$ of 10.223. The probability of getting an $F(2, 46)$ of 10.223, if H_0 is true, is less than one in 1,000. Therefore, we'll reject H_0 and conclude that the mean depression scores changed over time.

Table 19.12   Summary Table for the Repeated Measures ANOVA Comparing Depression Scores Across Times 1, 2, and 3

Source	SS	df	MS	F	p	R²
$W_{quadratic}$	36	1	36	10.896	.003	.321
Error	76	23	3.304			
Total	112	24				

---

1. To be precise, $2T_2 \neq T_1 + T_3$. Look back at Figure 19.2 and you can see that T_2 and T_3 appear equal. So technically it would be wrong to infer that $T_2 \neq T_3$.

Table 19.13 Summary Table Combining the Results for Testing W_{linear} and $W_{quadratic}$

Source	SS	df	MS	F	p	R^2
Omnibus	144	2	72	10.223	.000	.444
W_{linear}	108	1	108	10.016	.004	.303
$W_{quadratic}$	36	1	36	10.896	.003	.321
Error W_{linear}	248	23	9.826			
Error $W_{quadratic}$	76	23	3.304			
Total error	324	46	7.043			
Total	468	24				

♦ SUMMARY

This chapter advanced the concept of testing differences in repeated/multiple DV scores. The focus of this chapter was managing three repeated measures. Having three DVs for each subject required that we combine the DVs into two contrast-weighted scores. The first (W_{linear}) tested a linear relationship between scores (specifically, if $T_1 \neq T_3$). The second contrast ($W_{quadratic}$) tested if T_2 was different from T_1 and T_3. Four different relationships were possible: a linear relationship ($T_1 > T_2 > T_3$ or $T_1 < T_2 < T_3$), a quadratic relationship ($T_2 \neq T_1$ or T_3), and two combined linear and quadratic effects ($T_1 \neq T_2 = T_3$ or $T_1 = T_2 \neq T_3$).

The information covered in this chapter should help you conceptualize and analyze a research design in which you measured an outcome variable (DV) three times. At the end of Chapter 18, I challenged you to conceptualize the repeated measures approach with a different scenario in which you estimated how often a couple argues by obtaining an argument score from both members. You could include a third argument score by asking a child of the couple to indicate how often her or his parents argue. Considering these three argument scores (father, mother, child), How many contrast codes (λ) would you need? What codes would you use? What are your null hypotheses? and What Models A and C would you create to test your hypotheses?

This chapter considered only three scores for each subject. It is possible to follow the same model comparison steps to compare four or more scores; however, the weighted contrasts become trickier. For example, if you had four scores for each subject, you'd need three weighted contrasts (linear, quadratic, and cubic). This level of complexity is beyond the scope of this book. Those interested in comparing four DVs should refer to textbooks that cover these more complex analyses (e.g., Cohen et al., 2003; Judd et al., 2009).

Now that we've seen how to test repeated/multiple scores, we can consider the final level of complexity to be covered in this book: the *mixed model*. In a mixed model, we combine the within effects (repeated measures) with between group comparisons. Chapter 20 introduces this model comparison.

20

MIXED BETWEEN AND WITHIN DESIGNS

"She's in that state of mind," said the White Queen, "that she wants to deny something—only she doesn't know what to deny!"

—Lewis Carroll

Through the Looking-Glass and What Alice Found There

We have built statistical models that use one or more independent variables (IVs) to predict a single dependent variable (DV). We called this a "between" effects ANOVA because it tested the differences between the groups that made up the IV. We have also built models that test for differences between multiple related (i.e., nonindependent) DVs. We called this a "within" effects model because it tested for differences or change "within" the subjects. It's time now to combine these two types of models into a single "mixed" design that includes both the predictor (independent) variable and multiple (two or more) outcome DVs.

It's possible that we would be interested in whether scores on a DV change differently for subjects depending on what group a person is in. Imagine that some of our depressed subjects received treatment for depression and the others did not. We'd have two "between" groups: (1) those who were treated (Tx) and (2) those who were not (No Tx). If we look at their depression score prior to treatment (Time 1) and their score after treatment (Time 2), we'd have two dependent scores for each.

With these data, we can test the within (repeated measures) main effect. If scores change from T_1 to T_2, regardless of which treatment Group the subjects are in (i.e., we "collapse" or average the treatment IV), we'd have a "within" main effect. We can also compare the depression scores between the treatment groups: those who received treatment (Tx) versus those who did not receive treatment (No Tx), after combining the T_1 and T_2 depression scores into one single depression score. Since we are then comparing between groups (as opposed to within an individual), we call this analysis a *between* test. It tells us whether or not the group that received treatment scored lower, higher, or the same on a depression measure as the group that did not receive treatment.

Perhaps the most interesting question, however, is whether we can find a *within* effect (change in scores) that is different *between* the groups. It asks if the change in scores from T_1 to T_2 (within effect) *depends* on which group a subject is in. Put another way, we can use this mixed design to test if depression scores declined for subjects who received treatment but not for those without treatment. To answer this question, we test the *interaction* of the within and between effects.

Ideally, we hope to find that depression scores decreased for the Tx group but did not change for the No Tx group. We can conduct this analysis using a "mixed design analysis of variance." We call it mixed because it tests (a) the main effect of the between comparison (No Tx vs. Tx groups), (b) the main effect of the within test (T_1 vs. T_2 Depression scores), and (c) tests the interaction between the within and between effects.

◆ MAIN EFFECT BETWEEN GROUPS

Collapsing across measurement times T_1 and T_2, the average group depression score for subjects who received treatment was 14.25, and the average depression score for those who did not receive treatment was 18.75. These means are shown in Figure 20.1.

The "between" main effect tests if Depression scores (averaged across T_1 and T_2) are different for those who received treatment than those who did not. Obviously, the No Tx group scored higher (18.75) than the Tx group (14.25). Still, we need to test if that difference is statistically significant. To conduct this test, however, we first need to collapse the two Depression scores (T_1 and T_2) into a single Depression score. Once we have a single, combined score, we can define two models (C and A) that predict the combined Depression score: Model C will predict the average combined score for everyone, and Model A will adjust the predicted combined score according to which group (Tx or No Tx) the subject is in. Model C is the null hypothesis that treatment group doesn't matter (i.e., combined Depression scores will

Figure 20.1 Average Depression Scores for Subjects Who Did Not
Receive Treatment (No Tx) and Those Who Did (Tx),
Collapsed Across Times 1 and 2.

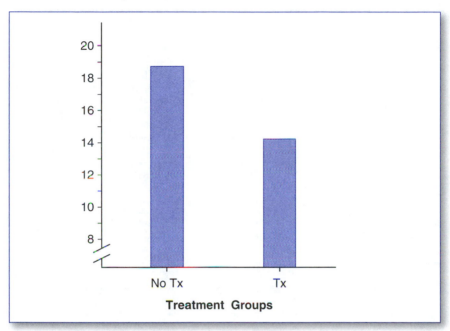

Treatment Groups

be the same for each group). Model A tests the research hypothesis that
Depression scores are different for the groups. We'll compare the error from
the two models to test if adding Treatment Group (Tx) to Model A improved
our prediction of the combined Depression score.

Combining the Depression Scores. For this example, we'll only look at
those subjects who were depressed (It wouldn't make sense to provide treatment to nondepressed subjects, right?). Table 20.1 presents the T_1 and T_2
Depression scores for the subjects from our data set who were depressed
(Subjects 7 through 12 and 19 through 24).

We combine these two scores (T_1 and T_2) just as we did when we were
combining scores to test for differences between them. We assign a weight to
each score, sum the weighted scores, and divide by the square root of the
summed squared weights. This time, however, since we are not interested in
differences between the Depression scores (T_1 and T_2), we assign the same
weight (+1) to both scores. Column 4 in Table 20.1 shows the sum of the two
weighted scores. Next, as we did in Chapter 18, we divide that sum by the square
root of the squared sum of the weights. In this example, we had two weights
(+1 and +1). When we square and sum them we get $1^2 + 1^2 = 1 + 1 = 2$.

Table 20.1 Depression Scores at Time 1 (T_1) and Time 2 (T_2) Are Combined to Create W_0

Subject	Symptom Score (T_1)	Symptom Score (T_2)	$T_1 + T_2$	$W_0 = (T_1 + T_2) \div \sqrt{2}$	Treatment Group
7	19	14	33	23.335	−1
8	15	15	30	21.213	−1
9	16	16	32	22.628	−1
10	16	7	23	16.264	1
11	19	8	27	19.092	1
12	17	9	26	18.385	1
19	24	19	43	30.406	−1
20	24	20	44	31.113	−1
21	22	21	43	30.406	−1
22	23	10	33	23.335	1
23	19	11	30	21.213	1
24	20	12	32	22.628	1
Average	19.5	13.5	33	23.335	
					Tx = +1 No Tx = −1

The square root of 2 is 1.414, so we divide the total combined sum from Column 4 by 1.414 (Column 5). The scores in Column 5 are the combined T_1 and T_2 depression scores, which we'll label W_0.

We now have a W_0 score for each subject. Our next step is to define the two models we want to compare. For the compact Model C, we'll predict the mean W_0 score (23.335) for everyone (see Equation 20.1).

$$\text{Model C: } \hat{W}_0 = \overline{W} = 23.335. \tag{20.1}$$

For the augmented Model A, we create a bivariate regression equation using Treatment Group as an IV to predict W_0. Subjects who received treatment are given a code of $+1$, and subjects who did not receive treatment are coded -1. The regression coefficient ($\beta_1 = -3.182$) describes the relationship between Treatment Group and W_0. The intercept (β_0) is 23.335. Model A is defined as the bivariate regression given in Equation 20.2.

$$\text{Model A: } \hat{W}_0 = \beta_0 + \beta_1 = 23.335 - 3.182(\text{Tx}). \qquad (20.2)$$

With Models A and C defined, we can begin compiling our data in a model comparison box to test the between effect (see Table 20.2).

Table 20.2 Model Comparison Box Testing the Between Effect of the Combined Depression Score (W_0)

Model C:	$\hat{W} = 23.335 + \varepsilon$	PC = 1	$SSE_C =$
Model A:	$\hat{W}_0 = 23.335 - 3.182(\text{Tx}) + \varepsilon$	PA = 2	$SSE_A =$
	Difference = 1		SSR =
	$H_0: \beta_1 = 0$		R^2 (PRE) =

To finish the model Comparison box, we need to find the error from each model. To find the error for Model C (SSE_C), we compute the difference between the predicted and observed W_0 scores (Table 20.3, Column 4). We square and sum those differences to get SSE_C (Table 20.3, Column 5). The resulting SSE_C is 263.

Table 20.3 Computing the Error for Model C

Subject	W_0	$\hat{W}_0$	$W_0 - \hat{W}_0$	$(W_0 - \hat{W}_0)^2$	Treatment Group
7	23.335	23.335	0	0.00	−1
8	21.213	23.335	−2.122	4.50	−1
9	22.628	23.335	−0.707	0.50	−1
10	16.264	23.335	−7.071	50.00	1
11	19.092	23.335	−4.243	18.00	1
12	18.385	23.335	−4.95	24.50	1
19	30.406	23.335	7.071	50.00	−1

(Continued)

Table 20.3 (Continued)

Subject	W_0	$\hat{W}_0$	$W_0 - \hat{W}_0$	$(W_0 - \hat{W}_0)^2$	Treatment Group
20	31.113	23.335	7.778	60.50	−1
21	30.406	23.335	7.071	50.00	−1
22	23.335	23.335	0	0.00	1
23	21.213	23.335	−2.122	4.50	1
24	22.628	23.335	−0.707	0.50	1
			$SSE_C =$	263.00	
					Tx = +1 No Tx = −1

Using the scores in Table 20.4, we'll compute the error of Model A. We use the regression equation for Model A to predict a W_0 score ($\hat{W}_0$) for each subject. We then find the differences between W_0 and $\hat{W}_0$, square those differences, and sum these squared differences to get SSE_A of 141.5.

Table 20.4 Computing the Error for Model A, Testing the Between Effect of Treatment Group

Subject	Treatment Group	W_0	$\hat{W}_0$	$W_0 - \hat{W}_0$	$(W_0 - \hat{W}_0)^2$
7	−1	23.335	26.517	−3.182	10.13
8	−1	21.213	26.517	−5.304	28.13
9	−1	22.628	26.517	−3.889	15.12
10	1	16.264	20.153	−3.889	15.12
11	1	19.092	20.153	−1.061	1.13
12	1	18.385	20.153	−1.768	3.13
19	−1	30.406	26.517	3.889	15.12
20	−1	31.113	26.517	4.596	21.12
21	−1	30.406	26.517	3.889	15.12
22	1	23.335	20.153	3.182	10.13

Subject	Treatment Group	W_0	$\hat{W}_0$	$W_0 - \hat{W}_0$	$(W_0 - \hat{W}_0)^2$
23	1	21.213	20.153	1.06	1.12
24	1	22.628	20.153	2.475	6.13
				$SSE_A =$	141.50
					Tx = +1
					No Tx = −1

We can add the error estimates for Models A and C to complete the model comparison box (see Table 20.5). The difference between SSE_C (263) and SSE_A (141.5) is SSR = 121.5. The proportional reduction in error (PRE or R^2) is SSR $\div$ SSE_C, which is .462. Adding Treatment Group as a predictor variable to Model A explained 46.2% of the variance in combined Depression scores.

Table 20.5   Model Comparison Box Testing the Between Effect of the Combined Depression Score (W_0)

Model C:	$\hat{W}_0 = 23.335 + \varepsilon$	PC = 1	$SSE_C = 263$
Model A:	$\hat{W}_0 = 23.335 - 3.182(\text{Tx}) + \varepsilon$	PA = 2	$SSE_A = 141.5$
	Difference = 1		SSR = 121.5
	$H_0: \beta_1 = 0$	R^2 (PRE) = .462	

To determine if Model A reduced error enough for us to conclude that Treatment Group improved prediction of depression score, we'll transfer the information we've collected from the model comparison box to complete a summary table (Table 20.6), and then use the summary table to finish the ANOVA. In this analysis, our total N was 12 (remember, we only used the depressed subjects), so total df, $N - 1$, is 11. The model comparison used 1 df (PA − PC = 2−1), so residual (error) (11 − 1) is 10. Dividing SSR by 1 df used for the comparison gives us an MS of 121.5; dividing SSE (141.5) by the 10 residual df gives an MSE of 14.15. When we divide MS for the model (121.5) by MSE (14.15) we get $F(1, 10) = 8.587$. The probability of getting an F this large when H_0 is true is .015, which is smaller than the conventional .05.

Table 20.6 Summary Table for the Between Effect Test Repeated Measures ANOVA Comparing Depression Scores Across Times 1, 2, and 3

Source	SS	df	MS	F	p	R^2
W_0 Treatment Group	121.5	1	121.5	8.587	0.015	0.462
Error W_0	141.5	10	14.15			
Total	263	11				

Therefore, we reject H_0 and conclude that Treatment Group is related to the combined depression score (i.e., the Tx group had different combined scores than the No Tx group).

♦ MAIN EFFECT WITHIN GROUPS

We found that depression scores are different for subjects who received treatment and those who did not. Next, we'll test the within main effect. This analysis tests to see if Depression score changed between Time 1 (T_1) and Time 2 (T_2), regardless of whether or not they received treatment. Figure 20.2 shows the average depression scores at T_1 (19.5) and T_2 (13.5) for all 12 depressed subjects (regardless of whether or not they received treatment). The within effects analysis will tell us if the decrease in Depression scores from 19.5 at T_1 to 13.5 at T_2 is a statistically significant decrease.

As we did in Chapter 18, to conduct this test we'll need to compute a weighted Depression score that reflects the differences between T_1 and T_2 Depression scores. Since we have two Depression scores, we only need a single weighted score (W_1). The contrast codes (weights) will be +1 and −1. To get W_1, we'll multiply T_1 Depression by +1 and multiply T_2 Depression by −1. Combining the scores using these weights conceptually describes the difference between scores at T_1 and T_2 (see Equation 20.3).

$$(1 \times T_1) + (-1 \times T_2) = T_1 + (-T_2) = T_1 - T_2. \tag{20.3}$$

After combining these scores, we divide them by the square root of the summed squared weights $\left(\sqrt{(1^2) + (-1^2)}\right)$. Equation 20.4 presents the complete formula to calculate W_1.

$$W_1 = \frac{T_1 - T_2}{\sqrt{(1^2) + (-1^2)}} = \frac{T_1 - T_2}{\sqrt{2}}. \tag{20.4}$$

Figure 20.2   Average Depression Scores at Times 1 and 2, Regardless of Whether or Not Subjects Received Treatment.

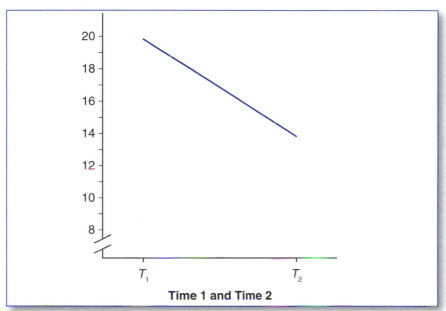

Time 1 and Time 2

Table 20.7 demonstrates how to calculate W_1 for each subject. If there is no change in depression scores, then W_1 should be close to zero (i.e., if $T_1 = T_2$, then $T_1 - T_2 = 0$). Therefore, H_0 for the repeated measure analysis is $\hat{W}_1 = 0$, which is our Model C. As you can see in Table 20.7, $\overline{W}_1 = 4.243$, which certainly is not zero. To determine if 4.243 is different enough from zero for us to reject H_0, we need to compare Model C with a Model A that predicts $\overline{W}_1$ (4.243) for each subject. To make this comparison, we need to know the error for Model C, which predicted zero (SSE_C) and the error for Model A, which predicted $\overline{W}_1$ (SSE_A).

Table 20.7   Calculation of Differences in T_1 and T_2 Depression Scores (W_1)

Subject	Symptom Score (T_1)	Symptom Score (T_2)	$T_1 + (-T_2)$	W_1	Treatment Group
7	19	14	5	3.536	−1
8	15	15	0	0.000	−1
9	16	16	0	0.000	−1

(Continued)

Table 20.7 (Continued)

Subject	Symptom Score (T_1)	Symptom Score (T_2)	$T_1 + (-T_2)$	W_1	Treatment Group
10	16	7	9	6.364	1
11	19	8	11	7.778	1
12	17	9	8	5.657	1
19	24	19	5	3.536	−1
20	24	20	4	2.828	−1
21	22	21	1	0.707	−1
22	23	10	13	9.192	1
23	19	11	8	5.657	1
24	20	12	8	5.657	1
Average	19.5	13.5	6	4.243	
					Tx = +1 No Tx = −1

Table 20.8 provides the information that we need to compute SSE_C. We subtract the Model C predicted score (0 for everyone) from each subject's actual W_1 score (Column 4). Each difference ($W_1 - 0$) is squared (Column 5), and those squared differences are summed. For Model C, $SSE_C = 315$.

Table 20.8 Calculation of Error for Model C That Predicted 0 for Each W_1 Score

Subject	W_1	Model C	$W_1 - 0$	$(W_1 - 0)^2$	Treatment Group
7	3.536	0	3.536	12.50	−1
8	0	0	0	0.00	−1
9	0	0	0	0.00	−1
10	6.364	0	6.364	40.50	1
11	7.778	0	7.778	60.50	1
12	5.657	0	5.657	32.00	1
19	3.536	0	3.536	12.50	−1

Subject	W_1	Model C	$W_1 - 0$	$(W_1 - 0)^2$	Treatment Group
20	2.828	0	2.828	8.00	−1
21	0.707	0	0.707	0.50	−1
22	9.192	0	9.192	84.49	1
23	5.657	0	5.657	32.00	1
24	5.657	0	5.657	32.00	1
			$SSE_C =$	315.00	
					Tx = +1 No Tx = −1

Table 20.9 gives us the information to compute the error for Model A; we subtract the actual score (W_1) from $\overline{W}_1$ (4.243), then square and sum the differences. The SSE_A for Model A = 99.

Table 20.9 Calculation of Error for Model A That Predicted the Average W_1 Score (4.243) for Each Subject

Subject	W_1	Model A	$W_1 - 4.243$	$(W_1 - 4.243)^2$	Treatment Group
7	3.536	4.243	−0.707	0.50	−1
8	0	4.243	−4.243	18.00	−1
9	0	4.243	−4.243	18.00	−1
10	6.364	4.243	2.121	4.50	1
11	7.778	4.243	3.535	12.50	1
12	5.657	4.243	1.414	2.00	1
19	3.536	4.243	−0.707	0.50	−1
20	2.828	4.243	−1.415	2.00	−1
21	0.707	4.243	−3.536	12.50	−1
22	9.192	4.243	4.949	24.49	1

(Continued)

Table 20.9 (Continued)

Subject	W_1	Model A	$W_1 - 4.243$	$(W_1 - 4.243)^2$	Treatment Group
23	5.657	4.243	1.414	2.00	1
24	5.657	4.243	1.414	2.00	1
			$SSE_A =$	99.00	
					Tx = +1 No Tx = −1

We organize the information we've collected in a model comparison box (Table 20.10). We did not calculate any parameters for Model C (it predicted a constant, zero), so PC = 0. We did, however, estimate a single parameter for Model A ($\overline{W}_1$), so PA is 1. The difference between (PA and PC (1) is the *df* used for this analysis. The $SSE_C = 315$, and $SSE_A = 99$; their difference (216) is SSR. The proportional reduction in error (PRE = SSR ÷ SSE_C) is 216 ÷ 315 =.686; thus, the difference in Depression scores between T_1 and T_2 accounted for 68.6% of the variance in depression scores. Put another way, "Time" accounted for 68.6% of the variance in depression score changes.

Table 20.10 Model Comparison Box Testing the Within Effect of Changes in Depression Scores (W_1)

Model C:	$\hat{W}_1 = 0 + \varepsilon$	PC = 0	$SSE_C = 315$
Model A:	$\hat{W}_1 = 4.243 + \varepsilon$	PA = 1	$SSE_A = 99$
	Difference = 1		SSR = 216
	$H_0: \beta_0 = 0$	R^2 (PRE) = .686	

The information organized in the model comparison box can be used to complete the ANOVA summary table (Table 20.11). SSR is 216 and residual SSE is 99. Total *df* is N − PC. Since N = 12 and PC = 0, total *df* is 12. This analysis used 1 *df* (PA − PC), so residual *df* is 12 − 1 = 11. MS Reduced is 216 ÷ 1 = 216, and *MSE* is 99 ÷ 11 = 9. The *F* ratio is MS ÷ MSE (216 ÷ 9), which is 24. $F(1, 11) = 24$ has a probability of occurring less than 1 time out of 1,000 when H_0 is true. Therefore, we reject H_0 and conclude that depression scores really did change from Time 1 to Time 2.

Table 20.11 Summary Table With the Within (Repeated Measure) Results Added

Source	SS	df	MS	F	p	R^2
W_0 Treatment Group	121.5	1	121.5	8.587	0.015	0.462
Error W_0	141.5	10	14.15			
W_1 Depression change	216	1	216	24.00	<.001	0.686
Error W_1	99	11	9			

GROUPS-BY-TREATMENT INTERACTION ◆

We have two significant main effects. We found that depression scores decreased between T_1 and T_2, and we found that subjects who received treatment had lower depression scores than those who did not receive treatment. The interesting question, however, remains—Did scores decrease from T_1 to T_2 more for subjects who received treatment than for those who didn't? This interaction between time and treatment is what we'll test next.

The interaction takes into account all four Depression mean scores that we are comparing: T_1 and T_2 Depression scores for those who received treatment, and T_1 and T_2 Depression scores for those who did not receive treatment. Figure 20.3 graphs the average depression scores at T_1 and T_2 separately for the treated and not treated subjects. The interaction will tell us if the decrease in Depression scores is different for those who received treatment than for those who did not. Eyeballing the graph, it sure looks as though depression scores decreased more for the treated group than for the untreated group. The statistical test of the interaction will tell us if this apparent difference is statistically significant.

The within analysis defined a Model A that predicted the average difference scores (W_1). That model was $\hat{W}_1 = 4.243$. For the interaction, we're still interested in changes in depression scores, so we'll continue to use W_1 as the DV. When we tested the between-groups effect, we used Treatment Group as an IV predictor of W_0 ($\hat{W}_0 = 23.335 - 3.182(\text{Tx})$). Now we want to know if treatment group, as an IV, improves our prediction of the W_1. Our specific question is whether the change in depression score ($\hat{W}_1$) is different for the treatment versus nontreatment groups. Our research hypothesis is that adding Treatment Group to our model improves prediction of W_1 beyond the model that simply predicted $\bar{W}_1$. The previous Model A ($\hat{W}_1 = \bar{W}_1$) is now our

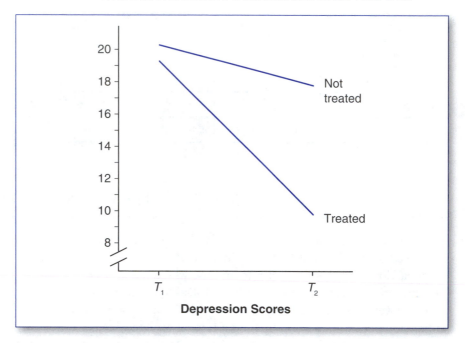

Figure 20.3 Average Depression Scores at Time 1 and Time 2 for Subjects Who Did Not Receive Treatment and Those Who Did.

new Model C (the H_0), and our new Model A ($\hat{W}_1 = \beta_0 + \beta_1 \text{Tx Group}$) is our research hypothesis. If adding Tx Group to the model (new Model A) improved prediction of W_1 beyond when we simply predicted $\bar{W}_1$ (new Model C), then the interaction is significant and we can conclude that depression scores changed differently for those who received treatment than for those who did not.

Equation 20.5 gives our Model C, which predicts $\bar{W}_1$. To get our new Model A, we estimate the regression coefficients (β_0 and β_1) given in Equation 20.6.

$$\text{Model C} \quad \hat{W}_1 = 4.243. \tag{20.5}$$

$$\text{Model A} \quad \hat{W}_1 = 4.243 + 2.47(\text{Tx}). \tag{20.6}$$

To test if treatment group improved the prediction of $\hat{W}_1$, we'll compare the error from new Model A with the error from Model C.

Since the Model C in Equation 20.5 is identical to the old Model A from our within effects analysis, we already know that $SSE_C = 99$ for the interaction.

To calculate the error for the new Model A, we need to predict a W_1 score based on treatment group for each subject. Table 20.12 presents the $\hat{W}_1$ scores predicted by the new Model A for all 12 depressed subjects. Column 5 of Table 20.12 gives the difference in actual and predicted scores ($W_1 - \hat{W}_1$), and Column 6 squares these differences. The sum of these squared differences (SSE_A) is 25.5.

The model comparison box (Table 20.13) compiles the information needed to test the interaction between treatment group and changes in depression scores. The error estimated for Model C, SSE_C, is 99, and the error estimated for Model A, SSE_A, is 25.50. Model C had one calculated parameter (β_0), so PC = 1. Model A estimated two parameters (β_0 and β_1), so PA is 2. The difference (PA − PC = 1) is the *df* used for this analysis. The difference between SSE_C and SSE_A is 73.5 (SSR). The proportional reduction in error (R^2) is 73.5 ÷ 99 = .742. Therefore, adding Treatment Group to the model

Table 20.12 Calculation of the *SSE* for Model A (W_1 = 4.243 + 2.475 Tx)

Subject	W_1	Treatment Group	Model A Prediction	$W_1 - \hat{W}_1$	$\left(W_1 - \hat{W}_1\right)^2$
7	3.536	−1	1.768	1.768	3.126
8	0	−1	1.768	−1.768	3.126
9	0	−1	1.768	−1.768	3.126
10	6.364	1	6.718	−0.354	0.125
11	7.778	1	6.718	1.060	1.124
12	5.657	1	6.718	−1.061	1.126
19	3.536	−1	1.768	1.768	3.126
20	2.828	−1	1.768	1.060	1.124
21	0.707	−1	1.768	−1.061	1.126
22	9.192	1	6.718	2.474	6.121
23	5.657	1	6.718	−1.061	1.126
24	5.657	1	6.718	−1.061	1.126
				SSE_A =	25.50
					Tx = +1 No Tx = −1

Table 20.13 Model Comparison Box Testing the Within Effect of Changes in Depression Scores (W_1)

Model C:	$\hat{W}_1 = 4243 + \varepsilon$	PC = 1	$SSE_C = 99$
Model A:	$\hat{W}_1 = 4.243 + 2.475(Tx) + \varepsilon$	PA = 2	$SSE_A = 25.5$
	Difference = 1		SSR = 73.5
	$H_0: \beta_1 = 0$	R^2 (PRE) = .742	

reduced 74.2% of the error variance when predicting changes in Depression scores from T_1 to T_2.

The information organized in the model comparison box can be used to complete the ANOVA summary table (Table 20.14). The $F(1, 10) = 28.824$ has a probability of less than .001 when H_0 is true. Therefore, we reject H_0 and conclude that changes in depression scores were different for those who received treatment than for those who did not. Specifically, we've found that Depression scores for subjects who received treatment decreased more than Depression scores of those who didn't get treatment. This test is far more interesting and useful than either of the main effects we found earlier in this chapter.

Table 20.14 Final Summary Table That Includes the Main Effect Between Groups (W_0), Main Effect With (W_1), and the Interaction Between Treatment Group and Depression Score Changes

Source	SS	df	MS	F	p	R^2
W_0 Treatment group	121.5	1	121.5	8.587	0.015	0.462
Error W_0	141.5	10	14.15			
W_1 Depression change	216	1	216	24.00	<.001	0.686
Error W_1	99	11	9			
Interaction	73.5	1	73.5	28.824	<.001	0.742
Error interaction	25.5	10	2.55			

SUMMARY ◆

In this chapter, we combined the regular one-way ANOVA, which tested the relationship between a categorical variable (between effect) and a DV, and the repeated measures ANOVA, which tested if scores measured at different times were different (within effect). When we combined these tests into a single analysis, we obtained results for two main effects: (1) the between-group effect and (2) the within (repeated) effect. Perhaps most important, however, is that we also tested the *interaction* of the between-group effect with the repeated measures. This interaction allowed us to determine if change in scores (the within effect) was the same for both groups (treated and not treated) or if the change in score was different for one group than for the other. In the example used in this chapter, we demonstrated that depression scores decreased more for subjects who received treatment than for those who did not. Finding an interaction such as this allows a researcher to conclude that decreases in depression scores depended on whether or not subjects received treatment.

In Chapters 18 and 19, I encouraged you to consider a research question in which you had multiple DV measures of how often a couple argues. We can expand that example into this chapter as well. In Chapter 18, the question was whether members of a couple (say, a wife and husband) were similar or different as to the percentage of time that they argue. It may be that the length of time the couple has been together will influence how much they argue. We would add "Time together" as an IV predicting the couple's ratings of how often they argue.[1] This design would give us two main effects and an interaction. The "between" main effect would test if the IV (time together) is related to judgments of how often a couple fights, and the "within" main effect tests if husbands and wives are similar or different in their ratings. The interaction tests if a difference between wife and husband ratings depends on how long they have been together. What would the different models look like? How would you describe the null hypotheses?

In Chapter 19, we tested models with three DVs. We can design a mixed model that has a DV with three scores. For example, we could use our three depression DV scores and our treatment group IV. We could also test three ratings of couple argument (wife, husband, child) with the length of time together. Consider designs such as this. How many "between" main effects would you test? How many "within" effects (*Hint:* Remember that when we

---

1. "Time together" could be a categorical variable (e.g., fewer than 5 years vs. 5+ years), or a continuous variable (number of years together).

had three DVs we created two combined weighted scores, W_{linear} and $W_{quadratic}$)? How many interactions would we test? Try writing the regression equations needed to test these effects. How many parameters would you estimate?

♦ A FINAL COMMENT

I could go on, perhaps indefinitely, creating and comparing increasingly complex parametric models. Crucial to my development as a research psychologist was the understanding that the general linear model (GLM) underlies most parametric analyses, regardless of how complex it is. I look for Data = Model + Error in all analyses, and when I recognize it, I can understand the analysis. Data = Model + Error, as a foundation to statistics, helped me move beyond the ANOVA models described in this book to multivariate analyses, such as path analysis, factor analysis, confirmatory factor analysis, and structural equation modeling. Had I not understood the GLM foundation, I would have struggled far more to learn these techniques.

Appendices

Remembering the Basics

The greatest strength of the scientific method is its ability to disprove a hypothesis. Science proceeds by endless and ever refining cycles of conjecture and refutation.

—Eric R. Kandel
In Search of Memory: The Emergence of a New Science of Mind

Using this book relies in part on a knowledge of basic statistics and design. The appendices were prepared for students who wish to "brush up" their statistical foundation. These sections are not comprehensive reviews; rather, they are intended to help students retrieve what they may have previously learned.

Appendix A

Research Designs

In the beginning, there was a screwdriver. So humans created the screw to give the screwdriver purpose. And they then inferred that the purpose of the screw was to fasten things together. And they were. . . happy?

No. That can't be right. The tool most definitely did not precede the need.

In the beginning there was the screw, whose purpose was to fasten things, and humans created the screwdriver to make the screw work.

Still a bit far fetched. How about, in the beginning there was a need to fasten things, and humans conceptualized and created the screw and screwdriver, together, as one possible solution to that problem.

Such is the dynamic between statistics and design. In the beginning, there was not statistics, for which people created research designs as something for statistics to do. Possibly there was research design, and statistics were created to make research designs work; however, it is far more realistic to consider that research questions existed, and research design and statistical analysis evolved together to answer those research questions. Statistics and design are forever linked, and it is best not to think of one as isolated from the other.

The context in which data collection occurs informs data analysis and statistical interpretations. Selecting your statistical technique prior to designing a study is like hopping on a plane before you've decided where to go. Research design and data analysis are like yin and yang—each defines the other.

Most natural and social science research is about determining if a relationship exists between two variables. At minimum, your design will include two variables: (1) a predictor or *independent* variable (IV) and (2) an outcome or *dependent* variable (DV). Research designs establish the conditions to collect data, and statistical analyses use the data to test the relationships between the variables. Which statistical test is used depends to a great extent on the conditions under which the data were collected and the types of data (types of variables) collected.

In this brief Appendix, we'll review three basic designs: (1) the experiment, (2) quasi-experiment, and (3) correlational design. For all three designs, the outcome variable (DV) is a continuous variable (either ratio or interval). Two of the designs use a categorical predictor or IV; the third design uses a continuous predictor variable.

♦ EXPERIMENT

The experiment is the gold standard of empirical research designs in the natural and social sciences. It is also one of the more challenging of the basic designs to conduct. An experiment allows us to make a causal conclusion about the relationship between two variables, X and Y. We hypothesize that deliberately changing variable X (IV) in a systematic way will cause corresponding changes in variable Y (DV). We observe those changes and conclude that our manipulation of X (the IV) caused the corresponding changes in Y (the DV).[1] We control variable X by assigning each subject to a certain group, level, or "condition" of X. In an experiment, the groups (or "levels") that make up variable X do not have natural numeric values—they're groups, and therefore, X is a categorical variable (see Appendix B for a review of variable types). In experiments, variable X is called the IV. Each participant should have an equal likelihood of being assigned to a condition or level of X (Alloy, Abramson, Raniere, & Dyller, 1999). Because our research hypothesis is that a person's score on Y will depend on (be influenced by) on the group or condition of X that we assigned the person to, we call variable Y the DV.

Suppose that an experimenter believes that the type of bicycle you ride determines how fast you travel. She hypothesizes that if she manipulates the type of bicycle someone rides, the person's speed will change. To test the relationship between bicycle type (her IV, or X variable) and speed (her DV or Y variable) using an experimental design, the researcher would define an IV called "Bike." She might define the IV "Bike" as consisting of two groups of bicycles. One group is the "Road Bike" condition: Subjects assigned to this group get to ride a 15-speed road bike. The other group is the "Coaster" condition: These participants are assigned to ride an old-fashioned two-speed coaster bike (the kind you peddle backward to brake). All participants ride through a specified course, and the researcher records how long it takes

---

1. Scores on variable Y depend on, or are caused by, what we do to variable X.

each subject to complete the course (Speed). In the Bike variable, each person is assigned to one or the other Bike groups (Road Bike vs. Coaster Bike), and the time to complete the course is the DV.

Once all participants have ridden the course, the experimenter can summarize the data as two distributions of scores: (1) one distribution for the Road Bike group and (2) one distribution for the Coaster group. She computes a mean and standard deviation for each distribution, and uses the means and standard deviations to conduct a statistical test that will help her decide if one group was faster than the other or if both groups were essentially the same. If one group rode faster than the other, the experimenter concludes that it was the type of bike that caused subjects to ride faster.

The two different bike groups, Road Bike and Coaster, constitute two levels of an IV (Bike variable). This research design addressed the first research question (see Chapter 1): Are the two variables (Bike Type and Speed) related? If the two variables are related, then her manipulation of the IV (randomly assigning subjects to Bike group) will systematically affect the DV (Speed); that is, one group rides faster (on average) than the other group.

An experiment has advantages and disadvantages. Experiments allow us to directly observe the effect that manipulating one variable has on another variable. Randomly assigning subjects to a condition (so that each subject has equal probability of being assigned to either group) should spread individual nuisance differences equally across the conditions. "Nuisance conditions"[2] are those extraneous things that can influence individual performance at any given time. Nuisance conditions that might impact bicycle riding could include things such as having a cold on the day of the experiment, having exercise-induced asthma, or being in poor physical shape. These nuisance conditions might impair bicycle riding regardless of which bike someone rode. Random assignment spreads these nuisance conditions across both levels of the Bike IV so that no one group is unduly impaired by them.

The experiment also allowed the experimenter to control other conditions directly that might influence the DV. In this example, she ensured that all participants rode the same route and encountered the same hills and road conditions. With an experiment, we can ensure that identical and standardized instructions and procedures are given to each participant. Controlling nuisance conditions, and using standardized procedures gives us greater confidence to attribute *cause* to the relationship between an IV and DV.

The Bike experiment is pretty simple; real-life questions are often more complex. There are two common ways to expand an experiment to ask more

---

2. "Nuisance conditions" is not a legitimate statistical term or concept (so far as I know). It is just a label I selected to describe these meddling factors.

complex questions. One way is by increasing the number of groups (or levels) that form an IV. The second is to add additional IVs.

In the Bike experiment, the researcher compared two types of bikes: (1) Coaster and (2) Road. If we considered a third type of bike, such as a mountain bike, we'd have a slightly more complex experimental design. The IV (Bike type) would vary across three groups, and the researcher would use a statistical test to compare the means of all three groups.

In the Bike experiment, the researcher was interested in using a type of bike to predict bicycling speed. Other factors, such as toe clips, might also explain bicycling speed. The researcher could conduct an entirely new experiment to test the effects of using toe clips on bicycling speed. She could randomly assign some people to ride without toe clips and others to ride with toe clips, and measure their speed riding the course. It would be more convenient, though, to combine the two experiments (bike type and toe clips) into one experiment. In that experiment, she would have two IVs (type of bike and toe clip). She would randomly assign half of the subjects to ride coasters and half to ride road bikes; then she would randomly assign half of the road bike riders to use toe clips and half of the coaster riders to use toe clips. The rest would ride without toe clips.

For some peculiar reason, IVs are referred to as a "way," and we describe the number of IVs in an experiment as the number of "ways." So when there is one IV (such as the first experiment with "Bike" as the only IV), we'd call it a *one-way* design (one IV = one way). In the example with two IVs (Bike Type and Toe Clips), we'd call it a *two-way* design (two IVs = two way). If we added a third IV (say, type of helmet the rider wears), we would call it a "three-way" design.

To expand things a bit more, we also describe the design according to the number of groups in each IV. The "two-way" design, where we had two bike groups (Road and Coaster) and two toe clip conditions (Clips and No Clips), would be called a 2-by-2 (or 2×2) design. If Bike Type had *three* levels (Road, Coaster, and Mountain), we would call it a 3-by-2 design (3 bike types by 2 toe clip conditions).

When we have two (or more) IVs in a design, the IVs may *interact*. An interaction means that the relationship between the DV and one of the IVs is different depending on the level of the other IV. Consider again our 2×2 bike experiment. We might believe that using toe clips causes speed to improve; we may find, however, that using toe clips improved speed for those in the Road Bike condition but had no effect on those who rode the Coaster bikes (coasters are heavy and clunky regardless of whether you have toe clips or not). Figure A.1 illustrates a hypothetical example of such a relationship. The DV (time to complete the race) is shown along the vertical (Y) axis, and the IV Bike Group (Road or Coaster) is given along the horizontal (X) axis. Two

Figure A.1 Graph of Hypothetical Results of an Experiment That Compares Type of Bike Ridden (Bike Group) and Whether Riders Had Toe Clips.

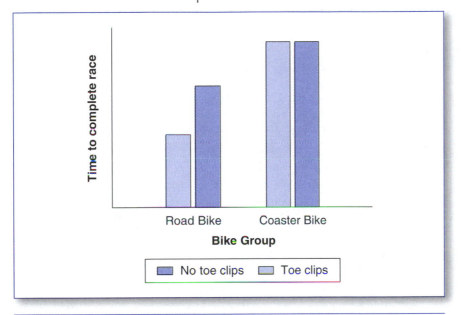

NOTE: The study has two IVs: (1) Bike Group and (2) Toe Clips. The DV is the time it takes to complete the race course.

columns are shown above each bike group: (1) the darker blue columns show the times for riders without toe clips, and (2) the lighter blue columns show times for riders with toe clips. In this example, the effect of toe clips on speed depended on which bike you rode. Therefore, bike type interacted with toe clips to determine your speed.

To summarize, a 2-by-2 design tests three things: (1) the *main* effect of one IV (Bike Type) on the DV, (2) the main effect of the second IV (Toe Clips) on the DV, and (3) the interaction of the two IVs.

Another experimental consideration is a repeated (or multiple) measures design. So far we've only required our subjects to ride the course one time on one type of bike. We randomly assigned subjects to the type of bike to ride so that we could randomly spread out nuisance variables such as physical fitness. Alternatively, we could require each subject to ride the course twice—once on a road bike and once on a coaster. We could then compare the scores *within* each individual. The nuisance variables within each subject are then controlled for by comparing each subject's score on one type of bike with her or his score on the other type of bike. Well, all except one nuisance variable—fatigue. A subject is likely to be more tired the second time through the course and therefore might ride slower. But we can control for fatigue by alternating which bike is ridden first—half of the subjects ride the road bike first, and half ride the coaster first. Analyzing these repeated measures data is described in Chapters 18, 19, and 20.

◆ QUASI-EXPERIMENT

In a moment of pure elucidation, an experimenter gains sudden insight into the process of functional impairment caused by a closed head injury. To test his hypotheses, the experimenter designs an experiment in which he recruits 100 volunteer participants. He measures each subject's memory and then he randomly assigns half to a control condition and half to an experimental condition. Participants assigned to the experimental condition receive a blow of a specific impact velocity, delivered by a blunt instrument, precisely at the level of the nose bridge. After conducting this experimental manipulation (induced head injury vs. no head injury), he then retests the memory of each participant and analyzes whether differences in memory from pretest to posttest depended on the experimental condition (head injury vs. none). His findings are profound. Because he used random assignment, repeated measures, and precisely standardized procedures, he can conclude that the blow to the head with the blunt instrument did, in fact, *cause* a decrease in memory. Surely he'll be nominated for a Nobel Prize in physiology or medicine.

Amidst the fanfare, the camera strobes, the flashing red and blue lights, and the yellow police tape, the experimenter desperately explains to the obtuse detective that he has violated no laws of experimental design. He created, perhaps, the perfect experiment of acquired head injury—one that optimally balanced internal and external validity and permitted conclusion of causal effects. The unimpressed gumshoe listens impassively until the experimenter proudly finishes—QED! Without taking his eyes off the experimenter, the detective wearily rubs his beard-stubbled face, pulls the toothpick from the corner of his mouth and tosses it to the ground, and says to the sergeant at his side, "Book 'im Danno."

The lesson learned from the felonious experimenter's experience is that some of the most interesting human research questions preclude random assignment of research participants (subjects) to experimental conditions. For example, if we want to study neuropsychological functioning following a traumatic brain injury (TBI), we can't randomly assign some people to an experimental group, give that group a TBI, and compare the experimental group with a control group that we hadn't injured. Instead, we rely on nature, and accident, to supply us with our groups of TBI patients and noninjured participants. Since we haven't controlled group assignment (random assignment), we haven't conducted an "experiment." Instead, we have conducted a quasi-experiment.

The quasi-experiment looks a lot like an experiment: the DV is continuous, the IV is a nominal variable, the design can include several IVs, and the IVs can interact. In the quasi-experiment, however, the investigator does not randomly assign participants to groups or levels of the IV. Instead, she uses Nature's assignment to groups.

Because the experimenter does not control each participant's "score" on the IV (i.e., assign subjects to groups), the quasi-experiment is vulnerable to the influences of pre-existing individual differences and "nuisance" variables that might systematically bias a relationship between an IV and a DV. Some people may be more prone than others to suffer a head injury, and those differences may also cause them to score differently on a DV. For example, inattentive people may be more likely to experience a head injury, and they may also be more likely to make inattentive errors that lower their score on a memory test. The conscientious "quasi-experimenter" will attend to and test for potential nuisance factors (confounds) that may disrupt her findings, and if found, she will control for them either by design or statistically.

Consider our TBI example. Substance abuse increases a person's risk for a TBI, and substance abuse is associated with neuropsychological problems. Furthermore, a person who suffers a TBI typically receives medical treatment, perhaps even hospitalization and medication. These experiences (substance abuse and medical treatment) are potential confound variables that may systematically influence scores on the DV yet make it appear that the IV (TBI) determined the person's score on the DV.

Designing a study to manage confound variables may involve matching participants in the two groups based on relevant (i.e., potential confound) variables. For example, the researcher would assess TBI patients for recent alcohol and other drug use, and then strive to identify participants for the control group whose substance use patterns are similar to those in the TBI group. Likewise, the researcher might draw control subjects from among a group of people hospitalized for an orthopedic injury, thus equating the groups (to some degree) on hospital experience.

Another approach to manage confounds is to measure the confounding variable and statistically control for group differences on that variable (a technique called analysis of covariance, Chapter 17). In our TBI example, the researcher first accounts for differences in neuropsychological functioning associated with substance abuse and then tests to see if TBI subsequently accounts for any further neuropsychological differences *above and beyond* the differences associated with substance use.

Demonstrating an association between two variables without using a true experimental design (i.e., no random assignment and no manipulation of the IV) does not demonstrate *cause*. Most statistics students learn the mantra *correlation does not imply causation*. It is good for students to learn and recite this claim.

♦ ASSOCIATIONAL DESIGNS

Both the experiment and quasi-experiment use group variables as the IV and a continuous variable as the DV. It's entirely possible, however, for both variables in a design to be continuous. In this case, neither an experimental nor a quasi-experimental design is applicable because the IV does not have groups. Without groups, we have no group mean scores on the DV to compare. In an associational design, we may call the IV a *predictor variable* and the DV an *outcome variable*, but the concept remains the same—we want to know if the two variables (predictor and outcome) are related to each other.

In general, research designs that use continuous variables for both the IV and DV are called *correlational* designs because a *correlation coefficient* is the statistic that people typically would think of when they want to test for a relationship between two continuous variables.

Association designs can be conducted in a laboratory or in the field. The data can be collected via survey, questionnaire, testing, or observation. The critical issues are that both IV and DV are continuous (the IV is not made up of categories or groups). Participants' scores are not manipulated on the IV because there are no groups to assign subjects to. Without random assignment, the researcher cannot conclude that the IV caused the subjects to get particular scores on the DV.

Although I presented these designs separately, experiments, quasi-experiments, and association (correlation) designs can be combined. Suppose we suspect that the amount of alcohol a person consumes on a weekly basis affects her or his mental performance in our TBI study. That design now has two IVs: (1) a categorical (not randomly assigned) head injury variable and (2) a continuous alcohol consumption variable. This design blends a quasi-experiment with an association (correlational) design.

Likewise, we might suspect that a person's sex influences how quickly she or he rides the trail in our earlier bike experiment. Now we have two categorical IVs: (1) one experimentally manipulated group IV (bike type) and (2) one nonmanipulated IV (we can't assign participants to their "sex"). This design blended an experiment and quasi-experiment.

Finally, imagine that we think age might also play a role in someone's bike riding speed. We'd have a design that blended a manipulated group IV (bike type) with a quasi-experimental IV (sex) and a continuous IV (age).

Appendix B

Variables, Distributions, and Statistical Assumptions

A variable is a measurement or a score that reveals how subjects differ on a characteristic of interest to a behavioral or social scientist. Some variables are categorical (nominal), some are quantitative (continuous), and some reflect ranks (ordinal). Categorical variables cluster certain groups of subjects together based on some common characteristic (e.g., the subject's sex, marital status, or ethnicity). Quantitative variables reflect a certain amount of characteristic a subject has. Ranking variables reveal subjects' characteristic relative to others. The types of variables briefly described here are *nominal*, *continuous*, and *ordinal*.

TYPES OF VARIABLES ♦

Ordinal Variables

An ordinal variable is a rank-ordering of subjects on the variable (e.g., 1st, 2nd, 3rd, etc.). Rather than having a numeric value that conveys an amount (e.g., "how much" of an attribute a subject possesses), an ordinal variable conveys subjects' performance relative to each other, such as from highest to lowest, first to last, most to least. For example, the results of a foot race are ordinal when described as who finished in first, second, and third place. The ordinal score does not reflect how fast each participant ran, nor does it reveal how far the runner who placed 1st finished ahead of the one who placed 2nd. The statistics covered in this book won't deal with ordinal variables.

Nominal Variables

A nominal variable clusters subjects into categories or groups. If we want to compare men and women on some characteristic, then "Sex" would be a nominal variable, and the variable "Sex" would have two *groups* (Men and Women). Groups defined by a nominal variable have no quantitative difference—one group is not quantitatively *more* or *less* than the other group. Men are not "more" nor "less" than women, married subjects are not more nor less than never-married or divorced subjects. The groups are just different. Members of groups may form naturally, as with Sex ("Men" vs. "Women"), or members may be assigned to groups by an experimenter (e.g., members of Group A receive a trial drug; Group B members receive a placebo). In this book, nominal variables are typically used as Independent or Predictor variables. When a nominal variable is the IV, we want to test whether or not the groups that comprise the nominal variable are different on an outcome or DV. For example, we might want to know if subjects assigned to receive a trial drug have different depression scores than those assigned to receive a placebo.

A nominal variable can have any number of groups. A dichotomous variable is a special type of nominal variable that has only two groups or levels. The Sex variable (as described earlier) had only two levels (Men and Women) and therefore is a dichotomous variable. Other nominal variables may have more than two levels. For example, we could define a variable called "Drug Abuse" according to three groups: (1) No Drug Use, (2) Alcohol Use only, and (3) Poly Drug Use.

Continuous Variable

Continuous variables are quantitative scores that convey meaningful information about the amount of a characteristic a subject has. There are two types of continuous variables: (1) *interval variables* and (2) *ratio variables*. The ratio variable is a measure that has a true zero (0) value whereas the interval scale does not. As a result of having a true zero, the ratio scale allows us to describe proportional differences between two scores. The number of drinks consumed is a ratio score—zero is a possible score on the Drinks variable. Therefore, we could conclude that a person who had 5 drinks consumed half as much as a person who downed 10 drinks.

The interval scale has no true zero value; therefore, when looking at two scores, we can only tell that one score is more or less than the other, but we can't infer that one subject scored twice as much as another. For example, zero is not a possible score on an IQ test, so we cannot claim that a person who scored 140 on an IQ test is twice as smart as a person who scored 70.

Figure B.1 Frequency Histogram of Variable X.

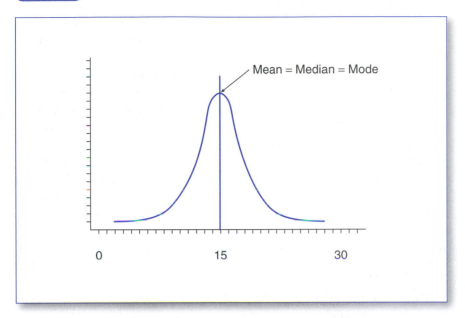

DISTRIBUTIONS OF CONTINUOUS VARIABLES ◆

The scores on a continuous variable can be presented pictorially by graphing the distribution of scores. In Figure B.1, the range of possible scores on the variable is presented along the horizontal axis (0 to 30). The horizontal axis is called the *X*-axis. The vertical axis (called the *Y*-axis) shows the number of times (frequency) that each score on *X* occurred. The graph is called a "frequency histogram," and when it is symmetrical (as in Figure B.1), the shape of the distribution is called "normal."

In addition to the graphic display of the continuous variable, there are descriptive statistics that describe the shape of this histogram. There are four types of descriptive statistics that describe a histogram's shape. The first type describes the typical score or *central tendency* of the distribution (the middle or center of the distribution). Three statistics describe central tendency: (1) mean, (2) median, and (3) mode. The *mean* is the arithmetic average of all of the scores on *X*. We get the mean by summing the scores and dividing by the number of scores (see Equation B.1).

$$\text{Mean} = \frac{\Sigma X}{N}. \qquad (B.1)$$

The *median* is the "middle" score—that score or point along the X-axis where half of the scores are lower values than the median and the other half are higher than the median. The *mode* is the value of X that occurs most often. When a frequency distribution is perfectly symmetrical, the mean, median, and mode are equal (see Figure B.1).

Most scores in a distribution do not equal the typical score. Rather, they are disbursed around the central score. The second type of descriptive statistics describes the dispersion of scores in the histogram. Three statistics describe score dispersion around the central tendency: (1) range, (2) variance, and (3) standard deviation.

The *range* is the difference between the highest and lowest scores. For example, if the lowest score is 2 and the highest is 28, the range is 26 points.

The variance (S^2) is the average squared difference between each score and the mean score. To calculate the variance, we find the difference between each score and the mean $\left(X - \overline{X}\right)$, then square the difference $\left(X - \overline{X}\right)^2$. The result is called the "squared difference." Since we have a squared difference for each subject, we need to add them together to get a sum $\left(\Sigma\left(X - \overline{X}\right)^2\right)$.

This sum of squared differences is called the "Sum of Squares" (SS), a concept that you will be intimately familiar with by the end of this book. Since variance (S^2) is the *average* sum of squared differences, we next divide SS by the number of observations minus 1 ($N - 1$) to get the variance.[1] Equation B.2 gives the formula for variance:

$$S^2 = \frac{\Sigma(X - \overline{X})^2}{N - 1}.$$ (B.2)

Recall that we squared the differences between scores and the mean to compute S^2. As a result, S^2 does not reflect the original scale of the variable. This problem is corrected by simply taking the square root of the variance ($\sqrt{S^2}$). The result is the *standard deviation* (denoted as S). The standard deviation is conceptually (although not precisely) the average difference between observed scores and the mean. Equation B.3 gives the formula for standard deviation:

$$S = \sqrt{\frac{\Sigma(X - \overline{X})^2}{N - 1}}.$$ (B.3)

Two other statistics describe the shape of a distribution of data: (1) *skew* and (2) *kurtosis*. Skew describes how lopsided a distribution is. If the

---

1. Notice that I used $N - 1$ rather than N to estimate the average squared difference. Since we're estimating variance using a sample rather than the entire population, we adjust the estimate by subtracting 1 from the sample size.

distribution has a few values that are larger than and further from the center than most of the other scores, the distribution has a *positive skew* (see Figure B.2, *top panel*). These extreme scores have the effect of pulling the mean away from center. As a result, when a distribution has a positive skew, the mean becomes larger than the median and the mode.

If instead the distribution has some values that are smaller than and further from the mean than most other values, the distribution has a *negative skew* (Figure B.2, *bottom panel*). Once again, these lower outliers pull the mean away from center, causing the mean to be lower than the median and mode.

Figure B.2 Example of Distribution With a Positive Skew (*top*) and Negative Skew (*bottom*).

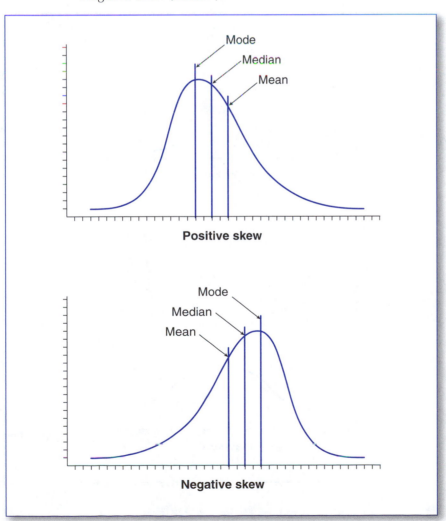

Kurtosis describes how narrow or flat a distribution is. If the distribution has a lot of scores that are close to or equal to the center, then the distribution will look narrow and tall. That distribution is called *leptokurtic* (see Figure B.3, *top*). If instead the distribution has a lot of scores that are spread out from the center, then the distribution appears flat. That distribution is called *platykurtic* (see Figure B.3, *bottom*).

Figure B.3 Examples of Distributions With Leptokurtic (*top*) and Platykurtic (*bottom*) Shapes.

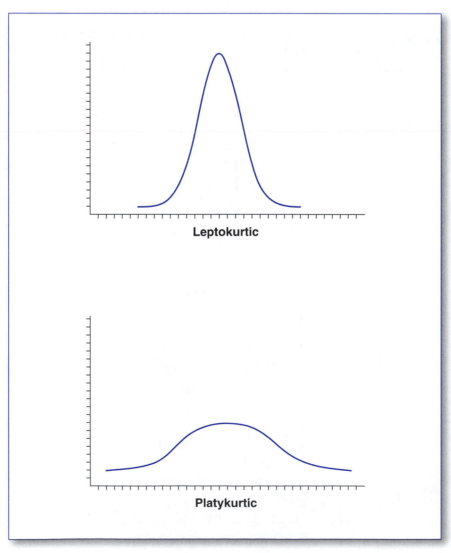

Leptokurtic

Platykurtic

OPERATIONAL DEFINITION ◆

Finally, to understand variables, we also need to know what they measure. Many behavioral constructs are abstract, and to measure an abstract concept requires that we define it precisely. An *operational definition* explicitly describes how the construct was measured for a particular study. For example, one researcher might operationally define "Binge Drinking" as 5 or more drinks consumed within a 2-hour period. Another researcher might conceptualize the "binge drinking" construct differently (e.g., 4+ drinks in a 1 hour period). By reporting the operational definition of a variable used for a given study, other researchers know how it was measured, and (if they desire) they can measure it the same way (consistently and reliably) in subsequent studies. Knowing the operational definitions of a variable can also help researchers understand different findings in studies that purportedly examined similar hypotheses. A clear operational definition, therefore, is critical so that different researchers can replicate or explain differences in each others' findings.

STATISTICAL ASSUMPTIONS ◆

Parametric statistics rely on certain assumptions about the scores on a continuous variable. Refinetti (1996) identified two basic assumptions: (1) normal distribution of the variable and (2) homogeneity of variance.

Normal Distribution

We've already considered a "normal" distribution when we talked about continuous variables. A normal distribution is fairly symmetrical (the mean, median, and mode are close together if not identical), has no outliers (no skew), and is not overly leptokurtic or platykurtic. A variable that is not normally distributed runs the risk of having an artificially larger variance, and larger variance can reduce the statistical power (our ability to detect a true effect).

Homogeneity of Variances

To describe homogeneity of variance, we need to consider two variables (X and Y). A given level of X will have several corresponding Y scores.

Homogeneity of variance requires that the variance of Y scores at one level of X is the same at all other levels of X.

To understand homogeneity of variance, let's graph X and Y using a scatterplot. Look at Figure B.4 (*top*) where scores on X are represented along the horizontal axis, and scores on Y are given along the vertical axis. Each subject has a score on X and a score on Y; the scatterplot places a dot for each subject

Figure B.4 Frequency Histogram of Variable X.

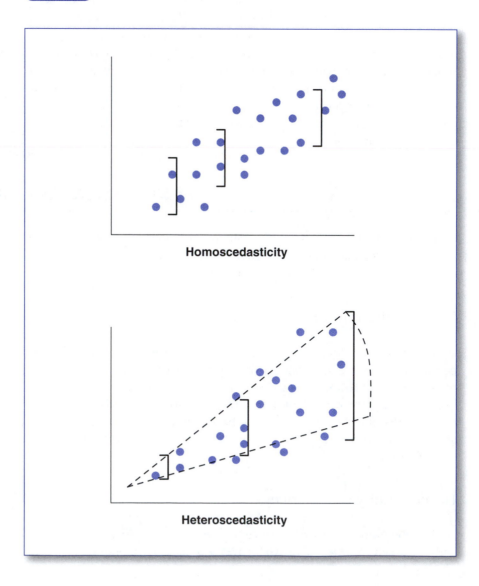

Homoscedasticity

Heteroscedasticity

at the place where that subject's score on X intersects with her or his score on Y. Notice that the dispersion of scores on Y is fairly similar at various levels of X (the brackets look the same size). We can feel fairly comfortable concluding that the top panel reflects data that are "homoscedastic" (variance is similar at all levels of X).

Now look at the bottom panel of Figure B.4 and notice that as X gets larger, the dispersion of Y scores appears to increase (the brackets increase in size as we move along the X-axis. In fact, the dots seem to spread out as X gets bigger (it looks rather like a bugle). At small values of X (furthest to the left), there is not much dispersion of Y scores, but at large values of X (*far right*) there is a lot of Y score dispersion. Looking at these data, we would not feel confident that variance was the same—in fact, it looks quite different, so we would describe the scatter in the lower panel as "heteroscedastic." In that case, the variable violates the assumption of homogeneity of variance.

Appendix C

Sampling and Sample Sizes

Since it is usually unreasonable to measure every subject in a population, a research study relies on a sample of observations drawn from the population. A sample of scores is used to estimate the true score of a population. An important consideration when drawing a sample is the number of observations or scores included in the sample. A small number of scores is vulnerable to random outliers that can distort the estimate. Therefore, larger sample sizes are preferred over smaller—smaller samples are more likely than larger to generate an estimate of the mean that is far from the population's true mean.

To demonstrate the importance of sample size, imagine that we have a population of scores. We'll draw a sample of 10 scores from that population and calculate the mean of those 10 scores. If we repeat this process a bunch of times (say 60), we end up with 60 means (each computed from 10 scores). Once we have all 60 means, we can treat them as a "sample of means," and we can compute the average and standard deviation of this sample of means.[1]

It is important to note that any randomly drawn sample of scores, when summed and averaged, is unlikely to equal exactly the true average score. Table C.1 lists these 60 means (each based on samples of 10 scores). This collection of 60 means ranged from a low of 24 to a high of 124. The average of these mean scores is 52.35, and the standard deviation (average distance from the mean) is 19.69.

---

[1]. These "scores" are in fact my "winnings" on a computer solitaire game. According to the scoring rules, each card game costs $52, and the player receives $5 for each card placed. To make money on this game, a player needs to place 11 or more cards, on average (earning $55 per game, on average). Possible earnings in a game range from zero to $260.

Table C.1 60 Sample Means Based on 10 Scores per Mean

Sample	Mean	Sample	Mean	Sample	Mean
1	25.5	21	26.5	41	24.0
2	27.0	22	32.0	42	24.5
3	29.0	23	39.0	43	25.5
4	31.0	24	40.0	44	30.5
5	31.5	25	41.0	45	35.5
6	37.5	26	42.5	46	38.0
7	41.0	27	48.5	47	40.0
8	41.5	28	50.0	48	43.5
9	42.0	29	52.0	49	47.0
10	43.0	30	53.0	50	48.5
11	52.5	31	53.0	51	50.0
12	54.5	32	54.5	52	51.0
13	58.5	33	55.5	53	53.0
14	62.5	34	55.5	54	58.0
15	69.0	35	56.0	55	64.5
16	72.5	36	57.0	56	68.0
17	76.0	37	63.0	57	70.5
18	79.5	38	63.5	58	73.0
19	84.5	39	64.5	59	75.0
20	98.5	40	93.0	60	124.0
		Mean of means = 52.35			
		SD of means = 19.69			

Now I'll repeat this process, but this time I'll calculate each Mean using 20 scores instead of 10. The results are given in Table C.2. Notice that the average of these mean scores is 54.82 (which isn't all that different from 52.35), but the standard deviation (14.59) is about 5 points lower than the standard deviation was when we used 10 scores to calculate the means. A smaller standard deviation indicates that the means based on 20 scores were closer to the central tendency (54.82) than when we used 10 scores for each mean. Using more scores to calculate the means (20 instead of 10) has brought our estimates of the true mean closer together.

Table C.2 60 Sample Means Based on 20 Scores per Mean

Sample	Mean	Sample	Mean	Sample	Mean
1	59.0	21	42.0	41	47.0
2	44.5	22	34.0	42	52.0
3	50.5	23	61.0	43	17.0
4	64.0	24	48.0	44	65.0
5	54.5	25	48.0	45	54.0
6	45.0	26	42.5	46	83.0
7	65.0	27	60.5	47	48.5
8	50.0	28	50.0	48	73.5
9	88.5	29	72.5	49	79.0
10	41.0	30	74.5	50	55.5
11	23.0	31	58.0	51	51.0
12	48.0	32	70.0	52	46.0
13	64.5	33	40.5	53	65.0
14	73.0	34	52.0	54	43.0
15	54.0	35	29.5	55	42.5
16	61.0	36	72.0	56	71.0
17	51.5	37	77.0	57	36.0
18	46.0	38	59.0	58	67.5
19	55.5	39	44.0	59	63.0
20	54.5	40	31.0	60	70.5

Mean of means = 54.82

SD of means = 14.59

So, if more scores lowered the variation in our means, let's see what happens when we use 50 scores to calculate each mean. These mean scores are given in Table C.3. The average of these 60 means (based on 50 scores each) is again similar to the previous means (52.45).

Table C.3 60 Sample Means Based on 50 Scores per Mean

Sample	Mean	Sample	Mean	Sample	Mean
1	49.9	21	45.1	41	74.8
2	45.7	22	44.1	42	64.6
3	56.3	23	52.9	43	49.1
4	51.8	24	52.5	44	55.7
5	40.0	25	55.4	45	28.1
6	50.3	26	52.6	46	56.7
7	60.3	27	69.2	47	52.1
8	39.7	28	57.5	48	68.4
9	72.0	29	55.4	49	47.6
10	52.7	30	44.4	50	50.6
11	53.0	31	54.9	51	45.5
12	61.3	32	32.2	52	71.8
13	36.7	33	48.7	53	53.5
14	61.7	34	46.7	54	36.1
15	62.3	35	48.8	55	56.7
16	58.3	36	43.0	56	51.6
17	58.4	37	55.6	57	58.8
18	58.1	38	51.0	58	50.5
19	63.1	39	47.0	59	47.7
20	49.3	40	48.5	60	40.6
		Mean of means = 52.45			
		SD of means = 9.37			

Evidently, the central tendency of a collection of mean scores doesn't change a whole lot as the number of scores used to compute the mean increases. What's important, however, is that the standard deviation *does* change—the dispersion of means gets narrower as the number of scores used to calculate the means increases. In other words, we obtain fewer means that are extremely different than the central tendency when our samples are based on more scores (i.e., the means cluster closer to the central tendency when the number of scores is large vs. when it's small). Table C.4 presents the means and variation scores of these three demonstrations. Just consider the range of means in each of these three demonstrations. There was a 100-point range in means when each was computed using 10 scores. The range dropped 71.5 points when 20 scores were used to compute the means, and it was 46.7 points when means were computed with 50 scores. The key point is that a researcher is less likely to obtain an unusually small or an unusually large mean when she uses a larger number of scores to calculate the mean. In other words, I can have greater confidence that the estimated mean is close to the true population mean when it is based on many scores.

Table C.4 Descriptive Statistics for Three Samples of Means (Mean, Standard Deviation, and Range)

Scores per Mean	Mean of Means	Standard Deviation	Lowest Mean	Highest Mean	Range
10	52.35	19.69	24.0	124.0	100.0
20	54.82	14.59	17.0	88.5	71.5
50	52.45	9.37	28.1	74.8	46.7

Figure C.1 gives a pictorial impression of the different distributions created for these three distributions of means. The dotted line (distribution of means based on 10 scores each) is wider and shorter than the solid line, which reflects the means based on 50 scores each. The dashed line falls in between and is the distribution of means based on 20 scores each.

Figure C.1 Frequency Histograms Demonstrating How Distributions of Mean Scores Become Narrower as the Number of Scores Used to Calculate the Means Increases From 10 to 20 to 50.

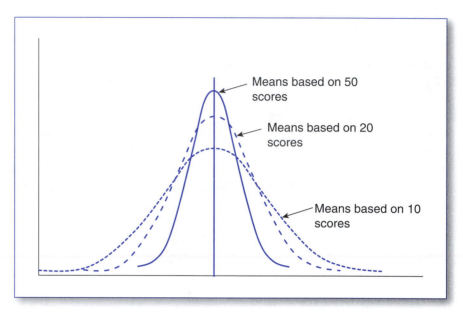

Appendix D

Null Hypothesis, Statistical Decision Making, and Statistical Power

NULL HYPOTHESIS ◆

We usually begin a study with a *working hypothesis* of what we hope to find. Typically, we suspect that two variables are related, and we want to demonstrate their association. For example, we might hypothesize that grade point average (GPA) is related to scores on the Scholastic Aptitude Test (SAT). We then propose a *null hypothesis* (abbreviated H_0), which states that *there is no relationship* between these two variables. In the example above, we believe that GPA and SAT are related, so our H_0 is that GPA and SAT are *not* related.

Our research goal is to *reject* the H_0. If we can reject the H_0, we can infer that there is *not NO-relationship* between SAT and GPA. Bad grammar aside, if we decide that there is not NO-relationship, then we can infer that there IS a relationship between SAT and GPA. If SAT and GPA are *not un*-related, then they must be related. In other words, if it is *false* that there is *no relationship* (H_0), then it must be *true* that there *is a relationship* between the two variables.

STATISTICAL DECISION ◆

The analysis of the data yields a statistic that describes the relationship between the variables.[1] We use the result of the statistical analysis to decide

---

1. As this book reveals, there are several statistics that describe the relationship between two variables (e.g., correlation, *t* test, ANOVA). The good news (a central focus of this book) is that they are functionally the same.

whether or not we think the H_0 is true (which we typically don't want) or false (which typically is our hope). If the analysis leads us to decide that H_0 is false, then we *reject* the H_0. If the statistical analysis leads us to decide that H_0 may be true, then we *fail to reject* the H_0.[2] Our decision boils down to one of two choices: reject H_0 or fail to reject H_0. The statistic obtained helps us decide if we can reject H_0 and infer that a relationship exists between the two variables.

Hypothesis testing presumes that, in reality, H_0 is either "true" or it is "false." The concept of statistical decision-making contrasts the true *reality* about H_0 (it is either "true" or "false") with the *decision* we make about the H_0 based on our statistical test (we either reject or fail to reject H_0). When we decide to "reject" or "fail to reject" H_0, that *decision* is either "correct" or "incorrect" in relationship to reality. There are two ways to be correct: (1) reject a false H_0 or (2) fail to reject a true H_0. Likewise, there are two ways to be incorrect or to make errors: (3) reject a true H_0, which is called a Type I error, or (4) fail to reject a false H_0, which is called a Type II error.

Table D.1 contrasts our decision about H_0 (reject/fail to reject) with the two possible realities about H_0 (true/false). In the left decision column, we decided to reject H_0. If in reality H_0 is false (bottom square of Column 1), then we made a correct decision about H_0. If in reality H_0 is true, then by rejecting a true H_0 we made an incorrect decision. We label that mistake a Type I error (we rejected a true H_0).

Now move to the second decision column, where we failed to reject H_0. If we fail to reject H_0 and it is really true (top square of Column 2), we made a correct decision. If, however, H_0 is really false and we failed to reject it (bottom square of Column 2), then we've made another incorrect decision—one we'll label a Type II error.

Even though there are two ways to be correct, the desired way to be correct is to *reject a false H_0* (lower left cell of Table D.1). This scenario is so good, that it has also been called *power*. Power is our ability to detect a real relationship between two variables.

It's good to be correct, even when the conclusion isn't what you hoped to find. That's (hopefully) the case when the statistical analysis leads a researcher to "fail to reject" the H_0,[3] and in reality, H_0 is true.

---

2. We never "prove" or accept the H_0 as true. This is because we can never prove that there is no relationship between variables. There are far too many design and statistical influences that can lead us to find no relationship between two variables.

3. The temptation, when the statistic does not lead us to reject H_0, is to "accept" or "retain" H_0; technically, however, such a statement is incorrect. You haven't proven H_0 is true; you've only failed to show H_0 is false. Proper terminology, therefore, is to "fail to reject" H_0.

| Table D.1 | Decision Matrix That Compares a Decision to Reject or Fail to Reject the Null Hypothesis With the Reality That the Null Hypothesis Is Either True or False |

	Decision	
	Reject H_0	Fail to reject H_0
H_0 is true	Incorrect decision Type I (α) error	Correct decision
REALITY		
H_0 is false	Correct decision "Power"	Incorrect decision Type II (β) error

Table D.1 shows two ways that a decision about H_0 can be incorrect. The first is when H_0 is true, but the statistical result leads us to reject H_0. In this case, the two variables really are not related, but by fluke chance, the statistic we calculated leads us to reject H_0 and incorrectly infer the variables are related. This type of error is called a Type I error.

We are so concerned about making a Type I error that when we reject H_0, we report the probability that we might have made a Type I error. The probability we report (called the p value) is the probability of getting the obtained statistic (which led us to reject H_0) if H_0 is really true.

On occasion, two variables really are related (H_0 is false), but the statistical analysis doesn't compel us to reject H_0. In this case, we incorrectly "failed to reject" this fiendishly false H_0 and sadly conclude that two (truly) related constructs aren't related. We've failed to find what we thought we'd find, even though our hypothesis was correct all along. We call this a Type II error. We hate this kind of error. It's one thing to be wrong about your hypothesis that two variables are related; it's another thing to be right yet fail to show the world that you're right. To avoid these despicable Type II errors, we try to maximize our statistical power.

Statistical decision making receives a lot of criticism (which is beyond the focus of this book), yet the approach endures. Bausell and Li (2002) offer their insight as to the enduring popularity of statistical decision making:

There is, in fact, something rather comforting to many scientists about the definitiveness of a decision-making process in which "truth" is always obtained at the end of a study and questions can always be answered with a simple "yes" or "no" and not prefaced with such qualifiers as "perhaps" or "maybe." (p. 2)

◆ STATISTICAL POWER

In the course of describing statistical decision making, I labeled one type of correct decision as "power" (correctly rejecting a false H_0). *Statistical power* is the ability to detect (find) a relationship that truly exists between two variables. A Type II error is like kryptonite to Superman's power. If we could decrease the probability of making a Type II error, we would increase our power. As I mentioned above, we really don't like it when we fail to find the relationship we expected when it truly exists (Type II error).

We can increase statistical power by attending to design issues *before conducting the study* that might improve the precision of our results. In contrast to statistical significance testing, which occurs after data collection is complete, a statistical power analysis informs us *before* the study begins how likely it is we'll be able to reject a false H_0 (Bausell & Li, 2002). There are design considerations that can reduce the probability of a Type II error (and therefore increase statistical power). Obtaining enough study participants, adjusting the acceptable probability for a Type I error, and accurately measuring the variables (i.e., reducing measurement error) to maximize effect sizes reduces the probability of making a Type II error and increases the likelihood that we'll find an association between two variables.

Appendix C demonstrated the importance of using a sufficiently large sample size. Recall that as sample sizes increased, the likelihood of obtaining a widely discrepant sample mean decreased. In short, sample statistics (e.g., mean and variance) are more likely to reflect the true population characteristics when the sample is based on a larger versus smaller sample size. Accurate estimates of population parameters (central tendency, score dispersion) will improve the ability to detect relationships between variables if they truly exist.

We define the conventionally accepted probability of making a Type I error as fewer than or equal to 5 out of 100 (if we conducted the same study 100 times, we'd only make a Type I error 5 times). Adopting a conservative restriction on the probability of a Type I error ($p \leq .05$) in turn increases the likelihood of failing to reject a false H_0 (Type II error). It's simple—making it harder to reject a true H_0 makes it easier to fail-to-reject a false H_0. The easier it is to fail-to-reject H_0, the more likely it is we could make a Type II error, and statistical power therefore decreases. The solution is simple—adopt a less conservative probability of making a Type I error (e.g., use $p \leq .1$ instead of $p \leq .05$).

Finally, increasing the relationship (called "effect size") between two variables can improve power. Of course, the true relationship between two variables cannot be changed, but we can take steps to ensure that we accurately measure the effect size. Perhaps the most effective way to accurately assess effect size is to reduce error in our measurements of variables (hence the importance of a precise operational definition and use of psychometrically sound measures). Additional methods to enhance estimates of effect size (i.e., reduce error of measurement) include employing covariates to reduce measurement error, using fewer groups in group comparison designs, not hypothesizing interactions, and adopting variables that have a proximal (direct) rather than distal (indirect) relationship to the other variables (Bausell & Li, 2002).

References

Alloy, L. B., Abramson, L. Y., Raniere, D., & Dyller, I. M. (1999). Research methods in adult psychopathology. In P. C. Kendall, J. N. Butcher, & G. N. Holmbeck (Eds.), *Handbook of research methods in clinical psychology* (2nd ed., pp. 466–498). Hoboken, NJ: Wiley.

American heritage dictionary of the English language (4th ed.). (2000). Boston, MA: Houghton Mifflin.

Bausell, R. B., & Li, Y. (2002). *Power analysis for experimental research: A practical guide for the biological, medical and social sciences*. Cambridge, MA: Cambridge University Press.

Cohen, J., Cohen, P., West, S. G., & Aiken, L. S. (2003). *Applied multiple regression/correlation analysis for the behavioral sciences* (3rd ed.). Mahwah, NJ: Lawrence Erlbaum.

Judd, C. M., & McClelland, G. H. (1989). *Data analysis: A model comparison approach*. New York, NY: Harcourt Brace Jovanovich.

Judd, C. M., McClelland, G. H., & Ryan, C. S. (2009). *Data analysis: A model comparison approach*. New York, NY: Routledge.

Kahane, L. H. (2001). *Regression basics*. Thousand Oaks, CA: Sage.

Kenny, D. A. (1987). *Statistics for the social and behavioral sciences*. Boston, MA: Little, Brown & Company.

Keppel, G., & Zedeck, S. (2002). *Data analysis for research designs: Analysis of variance and multiple regression/correlation approaches*. New York: W. H. Freeman.

Lomax, R. G. (2001). *Statistical concepts: A second course for education and the behavioral sciences* (2nd ed.). Mahwah, NJ: Lawrence Erlbaum.

Refinetti, R. (1996). Demonstrating the consequences of violations of assumptions in between-subjects analysis of variance. *Teaching of Psychology, 23*(1), 51–54.

Steinberg, W. J. (2011). *Statistics alive!* (2nd ed.). Thousand Oaks, CA: Sage.

Warner, R. M. (2008). *Applied statistics: From bivariate through multivariate techniques*. Thousand Oaks, CA: Sage.

Index

Note: Page numbers followed by n, f, or t indicate notes, figures, or tables, respectively.

SAGE researchmethods

The essential online tool for researchers from the world's leading methods publisher

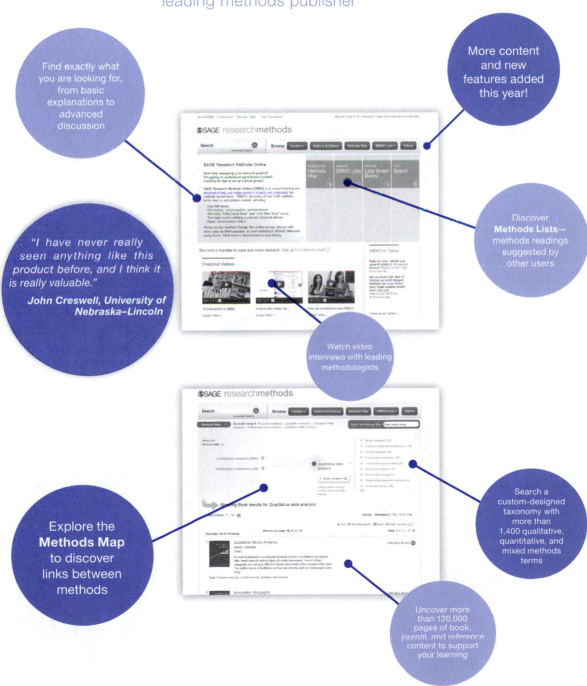

Find exactly what you are looking for, from basic explanations to advanced discussion

More content and new features added this year!

Discover **Methods Lists—** methods readings suggested by other users

"I have never really seen anything like this product before, and I think it is really valuable."

John Creswell, University of Nebraska–Lincoln

Watch video interviews with leading methodologists

Explore the **Methods Map** to discover links between methods

Search a custom-designed taxonomy with more than 1,400 qualitative, quantitative, and mixed methods terms

Uncover more than 120,000 pages of book, journal, and reference content to support your learning

Find out more at
www.sageresearchmethods.com